SCREEN

WORLD

by

JOHN WILLIS

1967

Volume 18

CROWN PUBLISHERS, INC.

New York

TO

GRETA GARBO

Page Left pictures of Greta Garbo in: Top Row: (left to right): "Mata Hari" (1931), "Camille" (1936) with Robert Taylor, "Susan Lenox, Her Rise and Fall" (1931) with Clark Gable; Second Row: "Queen Christina" (1933), portrait, "Conquest" (1937) with Charles Boyer; Third Row: "The Single Standard" (1929) with Nils Asther, "Inspiration" (1931) with Robert Montgomery, "Ninotchka" (1939) with Melvyn Douglas; Bottom Row: "Anna Christie" (1930) with Marie Dressler, "Anna Karenina" (1932) with Fredric March, "Two-Faced Woman" (1941) with Constance Bennett, Melvyn Douglas, and Robert Sterling.

Elizabeth Taylor, Richard Burton
in
"WHO'S AFRAID OF VIRGINIA WOOLF?"

CONTENTS

Assistant Editor: Harold Stephens

Staff: Jane Monroe, Charlotte Rahaim, Eugenio Moya,
Stanley Reeves, Evan Romero

Michael Caine

Shirley MacLaine

David Niven

Natalie Wood

Suzanne Pleshette

Jean-Paul Belmondo

Angela Lansbury

Stephen Boyd

Gregory Peck

Joanne Woodward

Sean Connery

Rosalind Russel

Claudia Cardinale

Sammy Davis, Jr.

Audrey Hepburn

Henry Fonda

Jack Hawkins

Eva Marie Saint

David McCallum

Melina Mercouri

Virna Lisi

Frank Sinatra

Elke Sommer

Omar Sharif

1966 RELEASES

Eleanor Parker

Peter O'Toole

Flora Robson

Eli Wallach

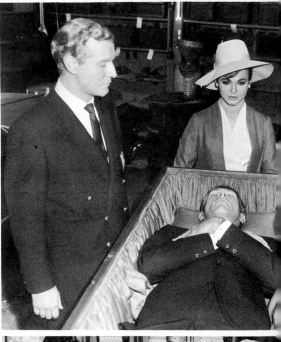

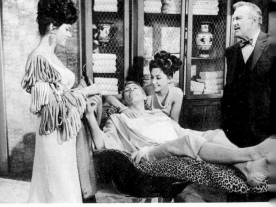

James Coburn, Gila Golan. Top: James Coburn, Michael St. Clair

James Coburn, Lee J. Cobb. Above: Edward Mulha Gila Golan, James Coburn. Top (L): James Coburn

OUR MAN FLINT

(20th CENTURY-FOX) Producer, Saul David; Director, Daniel Mann; Screenplay, Hal Fimberg; Story, Hal Fimberg; Music, Jerry Goldsmith; Costumes, Ray Aghayan; Director of Photography, Daniel L. Fapp; Assistant Director, David Silver; In Cinemascope and DeLuxe Color. January release.

CAST

Flint	James Coburn
Cramden	Lee J. Cobb
Gila	Gila Golan
Malcolm Rodney	Edward Mulhare
Dr. Schneider	Benson Fong
Gina	Gianna Serra
Anna	Sigrid Valdis
Leslie	Shelby Grant
Sakito	Helen Funai
Gruber	Michael St. Clair
Dr. Krupov	Rhys Williams
American General	Russ Conway
WAC	Ena Hartman
American Diplomat	William Walker
Dr. Wu	Peter Brocco

...mes Coburn, Gila Golan. Above: James Coburn

James Coburn with Sigrid Valdis, Helen Funai, Gianna Serra, Shelby Grant. Above and Top: James Coburn, Lee J. Cobb

APACHE UPRISING

(PARAMOUNT) Producer, A. C. Lyles; Director, R. G. "Bud" Springsteen; Director of Photography, W. Wallace Kelley; Screenplay, Harry Sanford, Max Lamb; Assistant Directors, Dale Coleman, Bob Templeton; Music, Jimmie Haskell; In Technicolor and Techniscope. January release.

CAST

Jim Walker	Rory Calhoun
Janice MacKenzie	Corinne Calvet
Vance Buckner	John Russell
Charlie Russell	Lon Chaney
Jess Cooney	Gene Evans
Captain Gannon	Richard Arlen
Hoyt Taylor	Robert H. Harris
Bill Gibson	Arthur Hunnicutt
Toby Jack Saunders	DeForest Kelley
Jace Asher	George Chandler
Sheriff Ben Hall	Johnny Mack Brown
Mrs. Hawkes	Jean Parker
Young Apache Chief	Abel Fernandez
Henry Belden	Don Barry
Old Antone	Paul Daniel

Lon Chaney, Robert H. Harris, Corinne Calvet, Richard Arlen, Rory Calhoun, John Russell, DeForest Kelley, Gene Evans

MADE IN PARIS

(MGM) Producer, Jose Pasternak; Director, Boris Sagal; Screenplay, Stanley Roberts; Director of Photography, Milton Krasner; Music, George Stoll; Choreography, David Winters; Songs, Burt Bacharach, Hal David, Sammy Fain, Paul Francis Webster, Quincy Jones, Red Skelton; Title Song sung by Trini Lopez; Gowns, Helen Rose; Assistant Director, Donald C. Klune; A Euterpe Production in Panavision and Metrocolor; Music played by Count Basie and His Octet, and Mongo Santamaria and His Band. February release.

CAST

Maggie Scott	Ann-Margret
Marc Fontaine	Louis Jourdan
Herb Stone	Richard Crenna
Irene Chase	Edie Adams
Ted Barclay	Chad Everett
Roger Barclay	John McGiver
Georges	Marcel Dalio
Cecile	Matilda Calnan
Denise Marton	Jacqueline Beer
Attendant	Marcel Hillaire
Elise	Michele Montau
American Bar Singer	Reta Shaw

Edie Adams, Ann-Margret, Chad Everett, John McGiver. Above: Louis Jourdan, Ann-Margret, Richard Crenna (C) Left: Ann-Margret, Louis Jourdan

Robert Vaughn, David McCallum

TO TRAP A SPY

(MGM) Executive Producer, Norman Felton; Director, Don Medford; Screenplay, Sam Rolfe; Director of Photography, Joseph Biroc; Music, Jerry Goldsmith; Assistant Director, Maurice Vaccarino; An Arena Production in Metrocolor. February release.

CAST

Napoleon Solo	Robert Vaughn
Angela	Luciana Paluzzi
Elaine May Donaldson	Patricia Crowley
Vulcan	Fritz Weaver
Mr. Allison	Will Kuluva
Ashumen	William Marshall
Soumarin	Ivan Dixon
Illya	David McCallum
Gracie Ladovan	Victoria Shaw
Lancer	Miguel Landa
Alfred Ghist	Eric Berry
Del Floria	Mario Siletti
Nobuk	Rupert Crosse

Maureen O'Hara, James Stewart

THE RARE BREED

(UNIVERSAL) Producer, William Alland; Director, Andrew V. McLaglen; Director of Photography, William Clothier; Assistant Directors, Terry Morse, Jr., Tom Schmidt; In Technicolor and Panavision. February release.

CAST

Sam Burnett	James Stewart
Martha Evans	Maureen O'Hara
Alexander Bowen	Brian Keith
Hilary Price	Juliet Mills
Jamie Bowen	Don Galloway
Charles Ellsworth	David Brian
Deke Simons	Jack Elam
Jeff Harter	Ben Johnson
Ed Mabry	Hugh Carey, Jr.
Juan	Perry Lopez

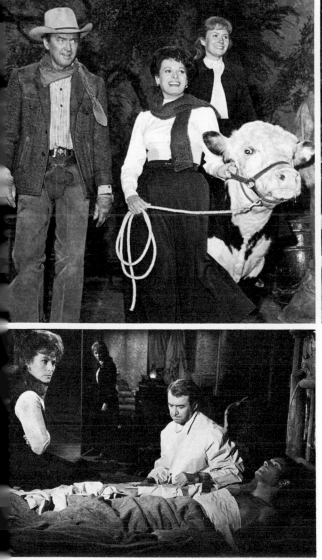

Maureen O'Hara, Juliet Mills, James Stewart, Don Galloway.
Above: James Stewart, Maureen O'Hara, Juliet Mills,
Vindicator

Broderick Crawford, Julio Pena, Don Murray, Janet Leigh

KID RODELO

(PARAMOUNT) Executive Producer, Ellis Sard; Producers, Jack O. Lamont, James J. Storrow, Jr.; Director, Richard Carlson; Associate Producers, Eduardo Manzanos, Arturo Marcos; Screenplay, Jack Natteford; Story, Louis L'Amour; Director of Photography, Manuel Mering; Music, Johnny Douglas; Song, Tom Glazer; A Trident Films and Fenix Film Production. February release.

CAST

Kid Rodelo .... Don Murray
Nora .... Janet Leigh
Joe Harbin .... Broderick Crawford
Link .... Richard Carlson
Thomas Reese .... Joseph Nieto
Balsas .... Julio Pena
Chavas .... Miguel Del Castillo
Cavalry Hat .... Jose Villa Sante
Gopher .... Alfonso San Felix
Warden .... Emilio Rodriguez
Perryman .... Fernando Hilbeck
Doctor .... Roberto Rubenstein
Guard .... Billy Christmas

LORD LOVE A DUCK

(UNITED ARTISTS) Producer-Director, George Axelrod; Screenplay, Larry H. Johnson, George Axelrod; Based on novel by Al Hine; Director of Photography, Daniel L. Fapp; Music, Neal Hefti; Assistant Director, Herman Webber; Costumes, Paula Giokaris; Title Song, Ernie Sheldon; Sung by The Wild Ones; A Charleston Enterprises Production. February release.

CAST

Alan "Mollymauk" Musgrave ....Roddy McDowall
Barbara Ann Greene .... Tuesday Weld
Marie Greene .... Lola Albright
Bob Barnard .... Martin West
Stella Barnard .... Ruth Gordon
Weldon Emmett .... Harvey Korman
Miss Schwartz .... Sarah Marshall
Sally Grace .... Lynn Carey
Howard Greene .... Max Showalter
Phil Neuhauser .... Donald Murphy
Mrs. Butch Neuhauser .... Judith Loomis
Dr. Lippman .... Joseph Mell
Used Car Salesman .... Don Frazer
Inez .... Martine Bartlett
Kitten .... Jo Collins
Harry Belmont .... Martin Gabel

Tuesday Weld, Max Showalter. Above: Lola Albrig
Tuesday Weld. Left: Tuesday Weld, Roddy McDow

AGENT FOR H.A.R.M.

(UNIVERSAL) Producer, Joseph F. Robertson; Director, Gerd Oswald; Associate Producers, Edward F. Abrams, Jack Bartlett; Screenplay, Blair Robertson; Director of Photography, James Crab; Assistant Director, David Marks; Music, Gene Kauer, Douglas Lackey; A Dimension IV Production in Color. February release.

CAST

Adam Chance	Mark Richman
Jim Graff	Wendell Corey
Prof. Janos Steffanic	Carl Esmond
Ava Vestok	Barbara Bouchet
Malko	Martin Kosleck
Luis	Rafael Campos
Mid-Eastern Contact	Alizia Gur
Marian	Donna Michelle
Borg	Robert Quarry
Morgue Attendant	Robert Donner
Billy	Steve Stevens
Conrad	Marc Snegoff
Helgar	Horst Ebersberg
Schloss	Chris Anders
Manson	Ray Dannis
Police Lieutenant	Ronald Von
Police Officer	Robert Christopher

Mark Richman, Alizia Gur

Charlie Ruggles, Suzanne Pleshette

Suzanne Pleshette, Dean Jones, also above with
Kelly Thordsen

THE UGLY DACHSHUND

(BUENA VISTA) Producer, Walt Disney; Co-Producer, Winston Hibler; Director, Norman Tokar; Screenplay, Albert Aley; Based on book by G. B. Stern; Music, George Bruns; Director of Photography, Edward Colman; Costumes, Chuck Keehne, Gertrude Casey; Assistant Director, Tom Leetch; In Technicolor. February release.

CAST

Mark Garrison	Dean Jones
Fran Garrison	Suzanne Pleshette
Dr. Pruitt	Charlie Ruggles
Officer Carmody	Kelly Thordsen
Mel Chadwick	Parley Baer
Mr. Toyama	Robert Kino
Kenji	Mako
Judge	Charles Lane

THE CHASE

(COLUMBIA) Producer, Sam Spiegel; Director, Arthur Penn; Screenplay, Lillian Hellman; Based on novel and play by Horton Foote; Director of Photography, Joseph LaShelle; Assistant Director, Russell Saunders; Costumes, Donfeld; Music, John Barry; In Panavision and Technicolor. February release.

CAST

Calder	Marlon Brando
Anna	Jane Fonda
Bubber	Robert Redford
Val Rogers	E. G. Marshall
Ruby Calder	Angie Dickinson
Emily Stewart	Janice Rule
Mrs. Reeves	Miriam Hopkins
Mary Fuller	Martha Hyer
Damon Fuller	Richard Bradford
Edwin Stewart	Robart Duvall
Jason "Jake" Rogers	James Fox
Elizabeth Rogers	Diana Hyland
Briggs	Henry Hull
Mrs. Briggs	Jocelyn Brando
Verna Dee	Katherine Walsh
Cutie	Lori Martin
Paul	Marc Seaton
Seymour	Paul Williams
Lem	Clifton James
Mr. Reeves	Malcolm Atterbury
Mrs. Henderson	Nydia Westman
Lester Johnson	Joel Fluellen
Archie	Steve Ihnat
Moore	Maurice Manson
Sol	Bruce Cabot
Slim	Steve Whittaker
Mrs. Sifftifieus	Pamela Curran
Sam	Ken Renard

Marlon Brando, Angie Dickinson

Robert Redford, Marlon Brando.
Above: Miriam Hopkins, Marlon Brando

Janice Rule, Martha Hyer, Clifton James, Robert Duvall
Above: E. G. Marshall, James Fox, Jane Fonda

THE SPY WITH MY FACE

(MGM) Executive Producer, Norman Felton; Director, John Newland; Screenplay, Clyde Ware, Joseph Calvelli; Story, Clyde Ware; Producer, Sam Rolfe; Director of Photography, Fred Koenekamp; Music, Morton Stevens; Assistant Director, E. Darrell Hallenbeck; An Arena Production in Metrocolor. February release.

CAST

Napoleon Solo	Robert Vaughn
Serena	Senta Berger
Illya Kuryakin	David McCallum
Alexander Waverly	Leo G. Carroll
Darius Two	Michael Evans
Sandy Wister	Sharon Farrell
Arsene Coria	Fabrizio Mioni
Kitt Kittridge	Donald Harron
Namana	Bill Gunn
Taffy	Jennifer Billingsley
Director	Paula Raymond
Nina	Donna Michelle
Doctor	Harold Gould
Wanda	Nancy Hsueh
Maggie	Michele Carey
Clerk	Paul Siemion
Waiter	Jan Arvan

ght: David McCallum, Robert Vaughn, Leo G. Carroll

nor Blackman, Sean Garrison. Above: Sean Garrison, Jean Seberg, and right with Arthur Hill

MOMENT TO MOMENT

(UNIVERSAL) Producer-Director, Mervyn LeRoy; Screenplay, John Lee Mahin; Based on Story by Alec Coppel; Director of Photography, Harry Stradling; Gowns, Yves St. Laurent; Assistant Director, Phil Bowles; In Technicolor. February release.

CAST

Kay Stanton	Jean Seberg
Daphne Fields	Honor Blackman
Mark Dominic	Sean Garrison
Neil Stanton	Arthur Hill
Timmy	Peter Robbins
Edward DeFargo	Gregoire Aslan

15

Julie Harris, Paul Newman

Paul Newman, Shelley Winters

HARPER

(WARNER BROS.) Producers, Jerry Gershwin, Elliott Kastner; Director, Jack Smight; Screenplay, William Goldman; Based on novel "The Moving Target" by Ross Macdonald; Director of Photography, Conrad Hall; Music, Johnny Mandel; Song "Livin' Alone" by Dory and Andre Previn; Assistant Director, James H. Brown; In Technicolor and Panavision. March release.

CAST

Harper	Paul Newman
Mrs. Sampson	Lauren Bacall
Betty Fraley	Julie Harris
Albert Graves	Arthur Hill
Susan Harper	Janet Leigh
Miranda Sampson	Pamela Tiffin
Alan Traggert	Robert Wagner
Dwight Troy	Robert Webber
Fay Estabrook	Shelley Winters
Sheriff Spanner	Harold Gould
Claude	Strother Martin
Puddler	Roy Jensen
Deputy	Martin West
Mrs. Kronberg	Jacqueline de Wit
Felix	Eugene Iglesias
Fred Platt	Richard Carlyle

Paul Newman, Julie Harris, Strother Martin, Shelley Winters, Robert Webber. Above: Janet Leigh, Paul Newman. Left: Pamela Tiffin, Robert Wagner

Virginia Grey, Ricardo Montalban, Constance Bennett, Lana Turner, John Forsythe

Constance Bennett, Lana Turner, John Forsythe

MADAME X

(UNIVERSAL) Producer, Ross Hunter; Director, David Lowell Rich; Director of Photography, Russell Metty; Assistant Directors, Doug Green, Charles Scott, Jr.; In Technicolor. March release.

CAST

Holly Anderson	Lana Turner
Clay Anderson	John Forsythe
Phil Benton	Ricardo Montalban
Clay, Jr. as a boy	Teddy Quinn
Clay, Jr. grown up	Keir Dullea
Estelle	Constance Bennett
Christian Torbin	John Van Dreelen
Scott Lewis	Neil Hamilton

Lana Turner, John Van Dreelen. Above: Ricardo Montalban, Lana Turner. Left: John Forsythe, Lana Turner, Teddy Quinn

17

GUNPOINT

(UNIVERSAL) Producer, Gordon Kay; Director, Earl Bellamy; Director of Photography, Bill Margulies; Assistant Directors, Phil Bowles, William Gilmore; In Technicolor. March release.

CAST

Chad Lucas	Audie Murphy
Uvalde	Joan Staley
Nate Harlan	Warren Stevens
Bull	Edgar Buchanan
Cap Hold	Denver Pyle
Mitch Mitchell	Robert Pine
Drago	Morgan Woodward
Mark Emerson	David Macklin
Mac	Nick Dennis
Hoag	William Bramley
Ab	Kelly Thorsden
Ode	Royal Dano

Right: Morgan Woodward, Joan Staley, Audie Murphy

FINNEGANS WAKE

(BRANDON) Producer-Director, Mary Ellen Bute; Based on play by Mary Manning and novel by James Joyce; Associate Producer and Director of Photography, Ted Nemeth; Shooting Script, M. E. Bute, T. J. Nemeth, Jr., Romana Javitz; Music, Elliot Kaplan; An Expanding Cinema Presentation. March release.

CAST

Finnegan (H. C. Earwicker)	Martin J. Kelly
Anna Livia Plurabelle (ALP)	Jane Reilly
Shem	Peter Haskell
Shaun	Page Johnson
Commentator	John V. Kelleher
Young Shem	Ray Flanagan
Young Iseult	Maura Pryor
Young Shaun	Jo Jo Slavin
Accordion Player	Luke J. O'Malley
Celebrants	Joseph Alderham, Ray Allen, Virginia Blue, Sean Brancato, Joan Campbell, Paddy Croft, Leonard Frey, Eileen Koch, Joe Maher, Janis Markhouse, Kevin O'Leary, Herbert Prah, Jan Thompson, Virginia J. Wallace, Carmen P. Zavick

Jo Jo Slavin, Maura Pryor, Martin J. Kelly, Jane Reilly, Ray Flanagan. Above: Ray Allen, Peter Haskell, Page Johnson, Paddy Croft. Left: Janis Markhouse, Jane Reilly, Peter Haskell

PROMISE HER ANYTHING

(PARAMOUNT) Producer, Stanley Rubin; Director, Arthur Hiller; Director of Photography, Douglas Slocombe; Screenplay, William Peter Blatty; Story, Arne Sultan, Marvin Worth; Costumes, Beatrice Dawson; Assistant Director, Ted Sturgis; Music, Lynn Murray; Title Song, Hal David and Burt Bacharach; A Ray Stark-Seven Arts Presentation in Technicolor. March release.

CAST

Harley Rummel	Warren Beatty
Michele O'Brien	Leslie Caron
Dr. Peter Brock	Bob Cummings
Mrs. Luce	Hermione Gingold
Sam	Lionel Stander
Rusty	Asa Maynor
Ange	Keenan Wynn
Dr. Brock's mother	Cathleen Nesbitt
John Thomas	Michael Bradley
Woman in pet shop	Bessie Love
Glue Sniffer	Riggs O'Hara
First Moving Man	Hal Galili
Middle-aged Woman	Mavis Villiers
Panelist	Warren Mitchell
Fettucini	Ferdy Mayne
First Panelist	Sydney Tafler
Stripper	Margaret Nolan
Third Stripper	Vivienne Ventura
Baby Sitter	Anita Sharp Bolster
Dancer	George Moon
Dancer's Wife	Charlotte Holland
Grocery Clerk	Chuck Julian
Beatnik	Michael Chaplin

Keenan Wynn, Warren Beatty. Above: Cathleen Nesbitt, Bob Cummings

Hermione Gingold, Warren Beatty. Above: Michael Bradley, Bob Cummings, Leslie Caron, Warren Beatty. Top: Leslie Caron, Michael Bradley, Warren Beatty

19

Clockwise: Candice Bergen, Shirley Knight, Joanna Pettet, Jessica Walter, Kathleen Widdoes, Mary-Robin Redd, Elizabeth Hartman, Joan Hackett

THE GROUP

(UNITED ARTISTS) Producer, Sidney Buchman; Director, Sidney Lumet; Screenplay, Sidney Buchman; Based on novel by Mary McCarthy; Music, Charles Gross; Director of Photography, Boris Kaufman; Costumes, Anna Hill Johnstone; Assistant Directors, Dan Eriksen, Tony Belletier; Presented by Charles K. Feldman; A FamArtists and Famous Artists Production in DeLuxe Color. March release.

CAST

Lakey	Candice Bergen
Dottie	Joan Hackett
Priss	Elizabeth Hartman
Polly	Shirley Knight
Kay	Joanna Pettet
Pokey	Mary-Robin Redd
Libby	Jessica Walter
Helena	Kathleen Widdoes
Dr. Ridgeley	James Broderick
Sloan	James Congdon
Harald	Larry Hagman
Gus LeRoy	Hal Holbrook
Dick Brown	Richard Mulligan
Mr. Andrews	Robert Emhardt
Norine	Carrie Nye
Mrs. Hartshorn	Philippa Bevans
Mrs. Prothero	Leta Bonynge
Mrs. Davison	Sarah Burton
Mrs. MacAusland	Flora Campbell
Nils	Bruno di Cosmi
Mrs. Renfrew	Leora Dana
Bill	Bill Fletcher
Brook Latham	George Gaynes
Mrs. Bergler	Martha Greenhouse
Mr. Davison	Russell Hardie
Mr. Eastlake	Vince Harding
Nurse Swenson	Doreen Lang
Mr. Schneider	Baruch Lumet
Putnam Blake	John O'Leary
Nurse Catherine	Hildy Parks
The Baroness	Lidia Prochnicka
Mrs. Andrews	Polly Rowles
Mr. Prothero	Douglas Rutherford
Mr. Bergler	Turman Smith
Mrs. Eastlake	Loretta White
Radio Man	Chet London
His Wife	Marion Brash

Joan Hackett, Richard Mulligan. Above: James Congdon, Elizabeth Hartman, Mary-Robin Redd, Philippa Bevans

...athleen Widdoes, Larry Hagman, Carrie Nye. Above: Hal Holbrook, Shirley Knight

Joanna Pettet, Elizabeth Hartman, Shirley Knight, Kathleen Widdoes, Joan Hackett, Jessica Walter. Above: Hal Holbrook, Jessica Walter

THE OSCAR

(EMBASSY) Executive Producer, Joseph E. Levine; Producer, Clarence Greene; Director, Russell Rouse; Screenplay, Harlan Ellison, Russell Rouse, Clarence Greene; Based on novel by Richard Sale; Music, Percy Faith; Director of Photography, Joseph Ruttenberg; Gowns, Edith Head; Songs, Leo Robin and Ralph Rainger, Sammy Cahn and James Van Heusen; Assistant Director, Dick Moder; Choreography, Steven Peck; A Green-Rouse Production in Pathecolor. March release.

CAST

Frank Fane	Stephen Boyd
Kay Bergdahl	Elke Sommer
Kappy Kapstetter	Milton Berle
Sophie Cantaro	Eleanor Parker
Kenneth H. Regan	Joseph Cotten
Laurel Scott	Jill St. John
Hymie Kelly	Tony Bennett
Trina Yale	Edie Adams
Barney Yale	Ernest Borgnine
Grobard	Ed Begley
Orrin C. Quentin	Walter Brennan
Sheriff	Broderick Crawford
Network Executive	James Dunn
Edith Head	Edith Head
Hedda Hopper	Hedda Hopper
Steve Marks	Peter Lawford
Merle Oberon	Merle Oberon
Nancy Sinatra	Nancy Sinatra
Sam	Jack Soo
Cheryl Barker	Jean Hale

Left: Stephen Boyd, Tony Bennett, Milton Berle

Walter Brennan, Jean Bartell, Milton Berle, James Dunn.
Above: Milton Berle, Eleanor Parker

Broderick Crawford, Stephen Boyd, Tony Benne
Above: Edie Adams, Ernest Borgnine,
Stephen Boyd, Elke Sommer

22

Tony Bennett, Stephen Boyd, Elke Sommer.
Above: Joseph Cotten, Stephen Boyd. Top: Tony Bennett, Jill St. John

Eleanor Parker, Stephen Boyd. Top: Stephen Boyd, Elke Sommer

THE SILENCERS

(COLUMBIA) Producer, Irving Allen; Director, Phil Karlson; Screenplay, Oscar Saul; Based on "The Silencers" and "Death Of A Citizen" by Donald Hamilton; Music, Elmer Bernstein; Songs, Elmer Bernstein, Mack David; Sung by Dean Martin and Vikki Carr; Choreography, Robert Sidney; Director of Photography, Burnett Guffey; Associate Producer, Jim Schmerer; Costumes, Moss Mabry; Assistant Director, Clark Paylow; A Meadway-Claude Production in Pathe Color. March release.

CAST

Matt Helm	Dean Martin
Gail	Stella Stevens
Tina	Daliah Lavi
Tung-Tze	Victor Buono
Wigman	Arthur O'Connell
Sam Gunther	Robert Webber
MacDonald	James Gregory
Barbara	Nancy Kovack
Andreyev	Roger C. Carmel
Sarita	Cyd Charisse
Lovey Kravezit	Beverly Adams
Domino	Richard Devon
Dr. Naldi	David Bond
Traynor	John Reach
Armed Man	Robert Phillips
M. C.	John Willis
Frazer	Frank Gerstle
Radio Man	Grant Woods
Hotel Clerk	Patrick Waltz

James Gregory, Dean Martin

Dean Martin, Beverly Adams.
Above: Arthur O'Connell

Dean Martin, Daliah Lavi. Above: Victor Buono,
Stella Stevens, Dean Martin

Agnes Moorehead, Greer Garson, Debbie Reynolds

THE SINGING NUN

(MGM) Producer, John Beck; Director, Henry Koster; Screenplay, Sally Benson, John Furia, Jr.; Co-Producer, Hayes Goetz; Story, John Furia, Jr.; Music, Harry Sukman; Songs, Soeur Sourire, Randy Sparks; Director of Photography, Milton Krasner; Assistant Director, Kevin Donnelly; Associate Producer, Hank Moonjean; In Panavision and Metrocolor. April release.

CAST

Sister Ann	Debbie Reynolds
Father Clementi	Ricardo Montalban
Mother Prioress	Greer Garson
Sister Cluny	Agnes Moorehead
Robert Gerarde	Chad Everett
Nicole Arlien	Katharine Ross
Himself	Ed Sullivan
Sister Mary	Juanita Moore
Dominic Arlien	Ricky Cordell
Mr. Arlien	Michael Pate
Fitzpatrick	Tom Drake
Mr. Duvries	Larry D. Mann
Marauder	Charles Robinson
Sister Michele	Monique Montaigne
Sister Elise	Joyce Vanderveen
Sister Brigitte	Anne Wakefield
Sister Gertrude	Pam Peterson
Sister Marthe	Marina Koshetz
Sister Therese	Nancy Walters
Sister Elizabeth	Violet Rensing
Sister Consuella	Inez Pedroza

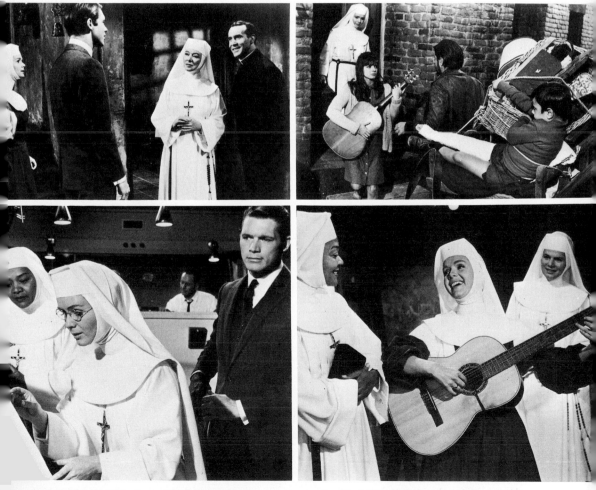

Juanita Moore, Debbie Reynolds, Chad Everett. Above: Debbie Reynolds, Chad Everett, Greer Garson, Ricardo Montalban

Juanita Moore, Debbie Reynolds, Monique Montaigne. Above: Debbie Reynolds, Katharine Ross, Michael Pate, Rickey Cordell

GHOST IN THE INVISIBLE BIKINI

(AMERICAN INTERNATIONAL) Producers, James H. Nicholson, Samuel Z. Arkoff; Director, Don Weis; Screenplay, Louis M. Heyward, Elwood Ullman; Story, Louis M. Heyward; Co-Producer, Anthony Carras; Director of Photography, Stanley Cortez; Music, Les Baxter; Songs, Guy Hemric, Jerry Styner; Choreography, Jack Baker; Costumes, Richard Bruno; Assistant Director, Clark Paylow; In Panavision and Pathecolor. April release.

CAST

Chuck Phillips	Tommy Kirk
Lili Morton	Deborah Walley
Bobby	Aron Kincaid
Sinistra	Quinn O'Hara
J. Sinister Hulk	Jesse White
Eric Von Zipper	Harvey Lembeck
Vicki	Nancy Sinatra
Reginald Ripper	Basil Rathbone
Myrtle Forbush	Patsy Kelly
The Corpse	Boris Karloff
The Ghost	Susan Hart
Lulu	Claudia Martin
Malcolm	Francis X. Bushman
Chicken Feather	Benny Rubin
Princess Yolanda	Bobbi Shaw
Monstro	George Barrows
Piccola	Piccola Pupa

and Luree Holmes, Ed Garner, Mary Hughes, Patti Chandler, Frank Alesia, Salli Sachse, Sue Hamilton, Alberta Nelson, Andy Romano, Myrna Ross, Jerry Brutsche, Bob Harvey, John Macchia, Alan Fife, The Bobby Fuller Four

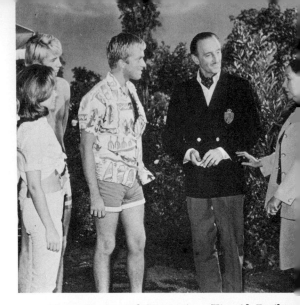

Nancy Sinatra, Ed Garner, Aron Kincaid, Basil Rathbone, Patsy Kelly. Below: Nancy Sinatra, Aron Kincaid, Basil Rathbone, Deborah Walley, Patsy Kelly, Tommy Kirk

JOHNNY TIGER

(UNIVERSAL) Producer, John Jugh; Director, Paul Wendkos; Screenplay, Paul Crabtree, Thomas Blackburn; Director of Photography, R. John Hugh; Assistant Director, Max Stein. April release.

CAST

Dean	Robert Taylor
Doc	Geraldine Brooks
Barbara	Brenda Scott
Johnny	Chad Everett
Billie	Marc Lawrence
Wendy	Carol Seflinger
Randy	Steven Wheeler
Shalonee	Pamela Melendez

Chad Everett, Brenda Scott, Robert Taylor, Geraldine Brooks. Above: Chad Everett, Brenda Scott, Robert Taylor

A MAN COULD GET KILLED

(UNIVERSAL) Producer, Robert Arthur; Director, Ronald Neame; Director of Photography, Gabor Pogany; Assistant Director, Doug Green; In Technicolor. April release.

CAST

William Beddoes	James Garner
Aurora Celeste da Costa	Melina Mercouri
Amy Franklin	Sandra Dee
Steve-Antonio	Tony Franciosa
Hatton-Jones	Robert Coote
Dr. Mathieson	Roland Culver
Mrs. Mathieson	Brenda De Banzie
Sir Huntley Frazier	Cecil Parker
Lady Frazier	Nora Swineburne
Linda Frazier	Jennifer Agutter
Miss Bannister	Isabel Dean
Miss Nolan	Ann Firbank
Captain of "Mary Boodwill"	Niall MacGinnis
Ludmar	John Bartha
Carmo	Pasquale Fasciano
Florian	Gregoire Aslan
Abdul	Nello Pazzafini
Osman	Daniel Vargas
Politanu	Martin Benson
Milo	Arnold Diamond
Zarek	Peter Illing
Max	Eric Demain

Right: Melina Mercouri, Sandra Dee, James Garner, Cecil Parker, Tony Franciosa. Below: James Garner, Melina Mercouri

...is Presley, Donna Douglas, Anthony Eisley, Nancy Kovack. Above: Elvis Presley, Donna Douglas, Harry Morgan, Audrey Christie

FRANKIE AND JOHNNY

(UNITED ARTISTS) Executive Producer, Edward Small; Director, Frederick de Cordova; Associate Producer, Alex Gottlieb; Screenplay, Alex Gottlieb; Story, Nat Perrin; Director of Photography, Jacques Marquette; Dance Director, Earl Barton; Music, Fred Karger; In Technicolor. April release.

CAST

Johnny	Elvis Presley
Frankie	Donna Douglas
Cully	Harry Morgan
Mitzi	Sue Ane Langdon
Nellie Bly	Nancy Kovack
Peg	Audrey Christie
Blackie	Robert Strauss
Braden	Anthony Eisley
Wilbur	Jerome Cowan
Earl Barton Dancers	Wilda Taylor
Larri Thomas, Dee Jay Mattis, Judy Chapman	

CAST A GIANT SHADOW

(UNITED ARTISTS) Producer-Director, Melville Shavelson; Co-Producer, Michael Wayne; Screenplay, Melville Shavelson; Based on book by Ted Berkman; Music, Elmer Bernstein; Director of Photography, Aldo Tonti; Costumes, Margaret Furse; Assistant Directors, Jack Reddish, Charles Scott, Jr., Tim Zinnemann; A Mirisch-Llenroc-Batjac Production in Panavision and DeLuxe Color. April release.

CAST

Col. David "Mickey" Marcus	Kirk Douglas
Magda Simon	Senta Berger
Emma Marcus	Angie Dickinson
Safir	James Donald
Ram Oren	Stathis Giallelis
Jacob Zion	Luther Adler
Pentagon Chief of Staff	Gary Merrill
Abou Ibn Kader	Haym Topol
Vince	Frank Sinatra
Asher Gonen	Yul Brynner
Gen. Mike Randolph	John Wayne
Mrs. Chaison	Ruth White
James McAfee	Gordon Jackson
British Ambassador	Michael Hordern
British Immigration Officer	Allan Cuthbertson
Senior British Officer	Jeremy Kemp
Junior British Officer	Sean Barrett
Andre	Michael Shillo
Rona	Rina Ganor
Bert Harrison	Roland Barthrop
Mrs. Martinson	Vera Dolen
General Walsh	Robert Gardett
Sentries	Michael Balston, Claude Aliotti
Belly Dancer	Samra Dedes
Truck Driver	Michael Shagrir
U.N. Officers	Frank Lattimore, Ken Buckle
Aide to General Randolph	Rodd Dana
Aide to Chief of Staff	Robert Ross
Pentagon Officer	Arthur Hansell
Parachute Jump Sergeant	Don Sturkie
Yaakov	Hillel Rave
Yussuff	Shlomo Hermon

Yul Brynner, Stathis Giallelis. Above: Allan Cuthbertson, James Donald, Kirk Douglas, Senta Berger

28

Frank Sinatra. Top Left: Kirk Douglas Angie Dickinson

k Douglas, Stathis Giallelis. Above: Senta Berger,
k Douglas. Top Right: John Wayne, Kirk Douglas

Stathis Giallelis, Yul Brynner, Kirk Douglas, James
Donald. Above: Senta Berger, Yul Brynner,
Stathis Giallelis, Kirk Douglas

THE TROUBLE WITH ANGELS

(COLUMBIA) Producer, William Frye; Director, Ida Lupino; Screenplay, Blanche Hanalis; Based on novel by Jane Trahey; Music, Jerry Goldsmith; Director of Photography, Lionel Lindon; Assistant Director, Terry Nelson; In Pathe Color. April release.

CAST

Mother Superior	Rosalind Russell
Sister Celestine	Binnie Barnes
Sister Constance	Camilla Sparv
Sister Clarissa	Mary Wickes
Sister Liguori	Marge Redmond
Sister Rose Marie	Dolores Sutton
Sister Barbara	Margalo Gillmore
Sister Elizabeth	Portia Nelson
Sister Ursula	Marjorie Eaton
Sister Margaret	Barbara Bell Wright
Sister Prudence	Judith Lowry
Mary Clancy	Hayley Mills
Rachel Devery	June Harding
Marvel-Ann	Barbara Hunter
Valerie	Bernadette Withers
Charlotte	Vicky Albright
Sheila	Patsy Gerrity
Kate	Vicki Draves
Sandy	Wendy Winkelman
Ginnie-Lou	Jewel Jaffe
Priscilla	Gail Liddle
Ruth	Michael-Marie
Gladys	Betty Jane Royale
Helen	Ronne Troup
Brigette	Catherine Wyles
Mrs. Phipps	Gypsy Rose Lee
Mr. Gottschalk	Jim Boles
Uncle George	Kent Smith
Mr. Devery	Pat McCaffrie
Mr. Grissom	Harry Harvey, Sr.
Mrs. Eldridge	Mary Young

Hayley Mills, June Harding (also above), Gypsy Rose Lee

June Harding, Hayley Mills. Above (C): Rosalind Russell, and top with Hayley Mills

RIDE BEYOND VENGEANCE

(COLUMBIA) Producer, Andrew J. Fenady; Director, Bernard McEveety; Screenplay, Andrew J. Fenady; From novel "The Night Of The Tiger" by Al Dewlen; Music, Richard Markowitz; Song, Richard Markowitz, Andrew J. Fenady; Sung by Glenn Yarbrough; Director of Photography, Lester Shorr; Assistant Director, Lee H. Katzin; A Mark Goodson-Bill Todman, Sentinel, Fenady Associates Production in Pathe Color. April release.

CAST

Jonas Trapp	Chuck Connors
Brooks Durham	Michael Rennie
Jessie	Kathryn Hays
Mrs. Lavender	Joan Blondell
Bonnie Shelley	Gloria Grahame
Dub Stokes	Gary Merrill
Johnsy Boy Hood	Bill Bixby
Elwood Coates	Claude Akins
Hanley	Paul Fix
Maria	Marrisa Mathes
Vogan	Harry Harvey, Sr.
Bartender	William Bryant
Pete	Jamie Farr
Mexican Boy	Larrie Domasin
Drunk	William Catching
Census Taker	James MacArthur
Narrator	Arthur O'Connell
Aunt Gussie	Ruth Warrick
Mr. Katz	Buddy Baer
Tom Wisdom	Frank Gorshin
Hotel Clerk	Robert Q. Lewis

Left: Chuck Connors, Kathryn Hays, Joan Blondell, Gary Merrill. Below: Arthur O'Connell, James MacArthur

THE LAST OF THE SECRET AGENTS?

(PARAMOUNT) Producer-Director, Norman Abbott; Associate Producer, Mel Tolkin; Screenplay, Mel Tolkin; Story, Norman Abbott, Mel Tolkin; Director of Photography, Harold Stine; Assistant Director, Francisco Day; Costumes, Edith Head; Music, Pete King; Song "You Are", Neal Hefti; Choreography, Andre Tayir; Title Song by Lee Hazlewood; Sung by Nancy Sinatra. May release.

CAST

Marty Johnson	Marty Allen
Steve Donovan	Steve Rossi
J. Frederick Duval	John Williams
Micheline	Nancy Sinatra
Papa Leo	Lou Jacobi
Baby May Zoftig	Carmen
Zoltan Schubach	Theo Marcuse
Florence	Connie Sawyer
Harry	Ben Lessy
Them one	Remo Pisani
Them two	Larry Duran
GGI one	Wilhelm Von Homburg
Belly dancer	Aida Fries
German Colonel	Harvey Korman

arty Allen, John Williams, Nancy Sinatra, Steve Rossi
Above: Steve Rossi, Marty Allen, John Williams, Sig Ruman

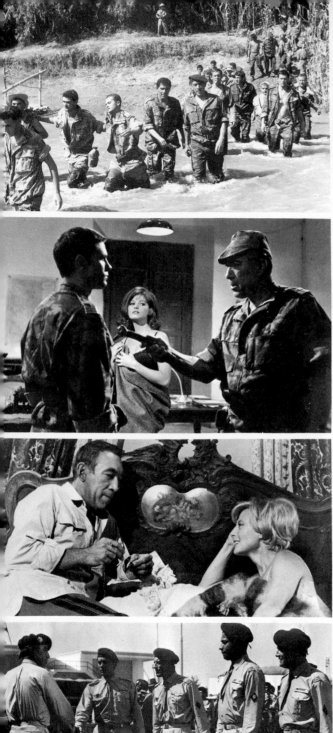

Anthony Quinn, Maurice Sarfati, Burt Kwouk,
George Segal, Alain Delon. Left: Alain Delon
Claudia Cardinale, Anthony Quinn. Top: Georg
Segal, Anthony Quinn, Maurice Ronet, Alain De

LOST COMMAND

(COLUMBIA) Producer-Director, Mark Robson; Associate Producer, John R. Sloan; Screenplay, Nelson Gidding; Based on novel "The Centurions" by Jean Larteguy; Music, Franz Waxman; Director of Photography, Robert Surtees; Assistant Director, Joe Ochoa; Filmed by Red Lion Productions in Pathe Color. May release.

CAST

Lt. Col. Raspeguy	Anthony Quinn
Esclavier	Alain Delon
Mahidi	George Segal
Countess de Clairefons	Michele Morgan
Boisfeuras	Maurice Ronet
Aicha	Claudia Cardinale
Ben Saad	Gregoire Aslan
General Melies	Jean Servais
Merle	Maurice Sarfati
Orsini	Jean-Claude Bercq
Verte	Syl Lamont
Mayor	Jacques Marin
DeGuyot	Jean Paul Moulinot
Ahmed	Andres Monreal
Dia	Gordon Heath
Sapinsky	Simono
Fernand	Rene Havard
Administration Officer	Armand Mestral
Viet Officer	Burt Kwouk
Mugnier	Al Mulock
Mother Raspeguy	Marie Burke
Ibrahim	Aldo Sanbrell
Priest	Jorge Rigaud
Manuel	Roberto Robles
Father Mahidi	Emilio Carrer
Mother Mahidi	Carmen Tarrazo
Pilot	Howard Hagan
Geoffrin	Mario De Barros
Major M.P.	Walter Kelly
Yusseff	Robert Sutton
Arab Customer	Simon Benzakein
Bakhti	Hector Quiroga
Aged Speaker	Felix De Pomes

Anthony Quinn, Alain Delon, Jean-Claude Bercq, Gordon
Heath, Maurice Ronet. Above: Anthony Quinn,
Michele Morgan

DUEL AT DIABLO

(UNITED ARTISTS) Producers, Fred Engel, Ralph Nelson; Director, Ralph Nelson; Screenplay, Marvin Albert, Michel Grilikhes; Based on novel "Apache Rising" by Marvin Albert; Director of Photography, Charles F. Wheeler; Assistant Directors, Emmett Emerson, Philip N. Cook; Music, Neal Hefti; Costumes, Yvonne Wood; In DeLuxe Color. May release.

CAST

Jess Remsberg	James Garner
Toller	Sidney Poitier
Ellen Grange	Bibi Andersson
Willard Grange	Dennis Weaver
Lt. Scotty McAllister	Bill Travers
Sgt. Ferguson	William Redfield
Chata	John Hoyt
Clay Dean	John Crawford
Major Novak	John Hubbard
Norton	Kevin Coughlin
Tech	Jay Ripley
Casey	Jeff Cooper
Nyles	Ralph Bahnsen
Swenson	Bobby Crawford
Forbes	Richard Lapp
Ramirez	Armand Alzamora
Colonel Foster	Alf Elson
Chata's Wife	Dawn Little Sky
Alchise	Eddie Little Sky
Miner	Al Wyatt
Cpl. Harrington	Bill Hart
Crowley	J. R. Randall

and John Daheim, Phil Schumacher, Richard Farnsworth, Joe Finnegan

Right: James Garner, Sidney Poitier, Bill Travers
Above: Bill Travers, Sidney Poitier, Dennis Weaver

Dennis Weaver, Bibi Andersson

James Garner, Bibi Andersson

THE RUSSIANS ARE COMING

(UNITED ARTISTS) Producer-Director, Norman Jewison; Screenplay, William Rose; Based on novel "The Off-Islanders" by Nathaniel Benchley; Director of Photography, Joseph Biroc; Music, Johnny Mandel; Assistant Director, Kurt Neuman, Jr.; A Mirisch Corporation presentation of a Norman Jewison Production in Panavision and DeLuxe Color. May release.

CAST

Walt Whittaker	Carl Reiner
Elspeth	Eva Marie Saint
Rozanov	Alan Arkin
Link Mattocks	Brian Keith
Norman Jonas	Jonathan Winters
The Captain	Theodore Bikel
Fendall Hawkins	Paul Ford
Alice Foss	Tessie O'Shea
Kolchin	John Phillip Law
Alison	Andrea Dromm
Luther Grilk	Ben Blue
Pete Whittaker	Sheldon Golomb
Annie Whittaker	Cindy Putnam
Lester Tilly	Guy Raymond
Charlie Hinkson	Cliff Norton
Oscar Maxwell	Dick Schaal
Mr. Porter	Philip Coolidge
Irving Christiansen	Don Keefer
Mr. Everett	Parker Fennelly
Muriel Everett	Doro Merande
Mr. Bell	Vaughn Taylor
Jerry Maxwell	Johnnie Whitaker
Russians	Danny Klega, Ray Baxter, Paul Verdier, Nikita Knatz, Constantine Baksheef, Alex Hassilev, Milos Milos, Gino Gottarelli

Carl Reiner, Sheldon Golomb, Eva Marie
Saint, John Phillip Law, Alan Arkin
Top: Theodore Bikel, Alan Arkin

Jonathan Winters, Guy Raymond, Brian Keith
Carl Reiner, Alan Arkin

Paul Ford (C) Above with Dick Schaal, Brian Keith, Guy Raymond. Top: Andrea Dromm, John Phillip Law

Doro Merande, Parker Fennelly. Above: Jonathan Winters. Top: Carl Reiner, Tessie O'Shea

Colleen Dewhurst, Patrick O'Neal, John Lormer, Clive Revill, Sean Connery. Left: Sean Connery, John Fiedler, Charles Welsh

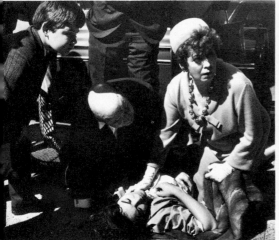

A FINE MADNESS

(WARNER BROS.) Producer, Jerome Hellman; Director, Irvin Kershner; Screenplay, Elliott Baker; Based on his novel; Director of Photography, Ted McCord; Music, John Addison; Costumes, Ann Roth; Assistant Director, Russell Llewellyn; A Pan Arts Production in Technicolor. June release.

CAST

Samson	Sean Connery
Rhoda	Joanne Woodward
Lydia	Jean Seberg
Dr. Oliver West	Patrick O'Neal
Dr. Vera Kropotkin	Colleen Dewhurst
Dr. Menken	Clive Revill
Dr. Vorbeck	Werner Peters
Daniel K. Papp	John Fiedler
Mrs. Fish	Kay Medford
Mr. Fitzgerald	Jackie Coogan
Mrs. Tupperman	Zohra Lampert
Leonard Tupperman	Sorrell Booke
Miss Walnicki	Sue Ane Langdon
Mrs. Fitzgerald	Bibi Osterwald
Chairwoman	Mabel Albertson
Chester Quirk	Gerald S. O'Loughlin
Rollie Butter	James Millhollin
Dr. Huddleson	Jon Lormer

Jean Seberg, Joanne Woodward, Sean Connery. Above: Joanne Woodward, Bibi Osterwald, Jackie Coogan Left: Sean Keeping, Sorrell Booke, Kay Medford, Zohra Lampert

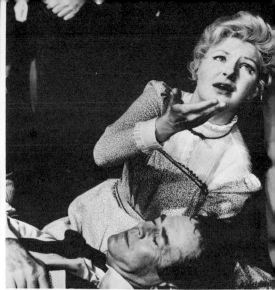

Charles Bickford, John Qualen, Robert Middleton,
Kevin McCarthy, Jason Robards, Joanne Woodward
Right: Henry Fonda, Joanne Woodward

...son Robards, Joanne Woodward. Above: Henry Fonda,
Joanne Woodward, Burgess Meredith. Right: Joanne
Woodward, Gerald Michenaud

A BIG HAND FOR THE LITTLE LADY

(WARNER BROS.) Producer-Director, Fielder Cook; Screenplay, Sidney Carroll; Director of Photography, Lee Garmes; Associate Producer, Joel Freeman; Music, David Raksin; An Eden Production in Technicolor. June release.

CAST

Meredith	Henry Fonda
Mary	Joanne Woodward
Henry Drummond	Jason Robards
Ballinger	Paul Ford
Benson Tropp	Charles Bickford
Doc Scully	Burgess Meredith
Otto Habershaw	Kevin McCarthy
Dennis Wilcox	Robert Middleton
Jesse Buford	John Qualen
Sam Rhine	James Kenny
Toby	Allen Collins
Pete	Jim Boles
Jackie	Gerald Michenaud
Mrs. Drummond	Virginia Gregg
Man in Saloon	Chester Conklin
Mrs. Craig	Mae Clarke
Owney Price	Ned Glass
Mr. Stribling	James Griffith
Sparrow	Noah Keen

OUT OF SIGHT

(UNIVERSAL) Producer, Bart Patton; Director, Lennie Weinrib; Director of Photography, Jack Russell; Assistant Director, Tom Schmidt; In Technicolor. June release.

CAST

Homer	Jonathan Daly
Sandra	Karen Jensen
Greg	Robert Pine
Scuba	Wendy Wagner
Big Daddy	John Lawrence
Marvin	Carol Shelyne
R. F.	Jimmy Murphy
Huh	Norman Grabowski
Wipe Out	Maggie Thrett
Tuff Bod	Deanna Lund
F.L.U.S.H.	Rena Harton
Janet	Vicki Fee
Tom	Coby Denton
Madge	Pamela Rogers
Mike	Deon Douglas
Stamp	John Lodge
Mr. Carter	Forrest Lewis

and Gary Lewis and The Playboys, Freddie and The Dreamers, The Turtles, Dobie Grey, The Astronauts, The Knickerbockers

Deanna Lund, Jimmy Murphy, Jonathan Daly, Norman Grabowski, John Lawrence

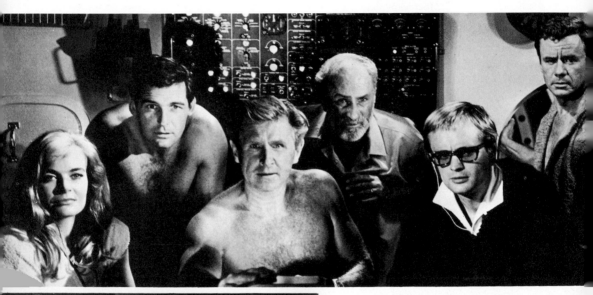

AROUND THE WORLD UNDER THE SEA

(MGM) Producer-Director, Andrew Marton; Screenplay, Arthur Weiss, Art Arthur; Music, Harry Sukman; Director of Photography, Clifford Poland; Underwater Photography, Lamar Boren; Diving Sequences, Ricou Browning; Associate Producer, Ben Chapman; Assistant Director, James Gorden McLean; An Ivan Tors Production in Panavision and Metrocolor. June release.

CAST

Dr. Doug Standish	Lloyd Bridges
Dr. Maggie Hanford	Shirley Eaton
Dr. Craig Mosby	Brian Kelly
Dr. Phil Volker	David McCallum
Hank Stahl	Keenan Wynn
Dr. Orin Hillyard	Marshall Thompson
Dr. August Boren	Gary Merrill
Brinkman	Ron Hayes
Prof. Hamuru	George Shibata
Capt. of Diligence	Frank Logan
Sonar Man	Don Wells
Vice President	Donald Linton
Lt. of Coast Guard	George DeVries
Officer	Tony Gulliver
Technician	Joey Carter
Secretary	Celeste Yarnall
Pilot	Paul Gray

Brian Kelly, David McCallum, Lloyd Bridges also above with Shirley Eaton, Keenan Wynn, Marshall Thompson

AND NOW MIGUEL

(**UNIVERSAL**) Producer, Robert B. Radnitz; Director, James B. Clark; Based on novel by Joseph Krumgold; Director of Photography, Clifford Stine; Assistant Directors, Phil Bowles, James Welch; In Technicolor. June release.

CAST

Miguel	Pat Cardi
George Perez	Guy Stockwell
Juan Marquez	Clu Gulager
Blas Chavez	Michael Ansara
Padre De Chavez	Joe DeSantis
Tomasita Chavez	Pilar Del Rey
Gabriel Chavez	Buck Taylor
Pedro Chavez	Peter Robbins
Eli Chavez	Edmund Hashim
Faustina Chavez	Emma Tyson
Bonifacio Chavez	Richard Brehm
Indian Chief	Ted Butterfield

Right: Joe DeSantis, Pat Cardi, Buck Taylor

Peter Robbins, Pat Cardi, also above with
Emma Tyson, Michael Ansara, Pilar Del Rey

Pat Cardi

39

BLINDFOLD

(UNIVERSAL) Executive Producer, Robert Arthur; Producer, Marvin Schwartz; Director, Philip Dunne; Screenplay, Philip Dunne, W. H. Menger; Based on novel by Lucille Fletcher; Director of Photography, Joseph MacDonald; Gowns, Jean Louis; Assistant Directors, Terry Nelson, Bill Gilmore; A Universal-Seven Picture in Technicolor. June release.

CAST

Dr. Bartholomew Snow	Rock Hudson
Vicky Vincenti	Claudia Cardinale
Fitzpatrick	Guy Stockwell
General Pratt	Jack Warden
Harrigan	Brad Dexter
Smitty	Anne Seymour
Arthur Vincenti	Alejandro Rey
Captain Davis	Hari Rhodes
Mario	John Megna
Barker	Paul Comi

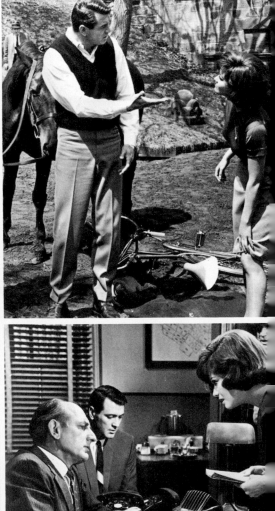

Jack Warden, Rock Hudson, Hari Rhodes. Above: Rock Hudson, Guy Stockwell. Top: Anne Seymour, Rock Hudson, Brad Dexter

Robert F. Simon, Rock Hudson, Claudia Cardin Above: Rock Hudson, Claudia Cardinale

Claudia Cardinale, Rock Hudson, Vito Scotti
bove: Jack Warden, Hari Rhodes, Alejandro Rey,
Claudia Cardinale, Rock Hudson

Rock Hudson, Claudia Cardinale,
also above, and top (L&R)

41

Cesare Danova, Elke Sommer. Left: Bob Hope, Phyllis Diller

BOY, DID I GET A WRONG NUMBER!

(UNITED ARTISTS) Producer, Edward Small; Director, George Marshall; Associate Producer, George Beck; Screenplay, Burt Styler, Albert E. Lewin, George Kennett; Original Story, George Beck; Director of Photography, Lionel Lindon; Music, Richard LaSalle, By Dunham; Assistant Director, Herbert S. Greene; Fashion Designer, Marjorie Corso; In DeLuxe Color. June release.

CAST

Tom Meade	Bob Hope
Didi	Elke Sommer
Lily	Phyllis Diller
Pepe	Cesare Danova
Martha Meade	Marjorie Lord
Schwartz	Kelly Thordsen
Regan	Benny Baker
Doris Meade	Terry Burnham
Telephone Operator	Joyce Jameson
Newscaster	Harry Von Zell
Larry Meade	Kevin Burchett
Plympton	Keith Taylor
Newsboy	John Todd Roberts

42

Bob Hope, Elke Sommer, Phyllis Diller. Above: Bob Hope, Terry Burnham, Marjorie Lord

FIREBALL 500

(AMERICAN INTERNATIONAL) Producers, James H. Nicholson, Samuel Z. Arkoff; Co-Producer, Burt Topper; Director, William Asher; Screenplay, William Asher, Leo Townsend; Director of Photography, Floyd Crosby; Music, Les Baxter; Songs, Guy Hemric and Jerry Styner; Choreography, Ronnie Riordan; Costumes, Richard Bruno; Associate Producer, Gene McCabe; Assistant Director, Dale Hutchinson; In Panavision and Pathecolor. June release.

CAST

Dave	Frankie Avalon
Jane	Annette Funicello
Leander	Fabian
Big Jaw	Chill Wills
Charlie Bigg	Harvey Lembeck
Martha	Julie Parrish
Hastings	Doug Henderson
Bronson	Baynes Barron
Joey	Mike Nader
Herman	Ed Garner
Announcer	Vince Scully
Farmer's Daughter	Sue Hamilton
Herman's Wife	Rene Riano
Man in Garage	Len Lesser
Jobber	Billy Beck
Herman's Friend	Tex Armstrong
Leander Fans	Mary Hughes, Patti Chandler,

Karla Conway, Hedy Scott, Sallie Sachse, Jo Collins, Maria McBane, Linda Bent and The Don Randi Trio Plus One, The Carole Lombard Singers

Right: Fabian, Frankie Avalon, Salli Sachse, Mary Hughes

vey Lembeck, Chill Wills, Frankie Avalon, Annette icello. Above: Frankie Avalon, Annette Funicello

Julie Parrish, Frankie Avalon. Above: Annette Funicello, Fabian, Frankie Avalon

43

KHARTOUM

(UNITED ARTISTS) Producer, Julian Blaustein; Director, Basil Dearden; Screenplay, Robert Ardrey; Music, Frank Cordell; Director of Photography, Edward Scaife; Assistant Directors, John Peverall, Bluey Hill; In Cinerama, Ultra-Panavision, and Technicolor. June release.

CAST

Gen. Charles Gordon	Charlton Heston
The Mahdi	Laurence Olivier
Col. J. D. H. Stewart	Richard Johnson
Mr. Gladstone	Ralph Richardson
Sir Evelyn Baring	Alexander Knox
Khaleel	Johnny Sekka
Lord Granville	Michael Hordern
Zobeir Pasha	Zia Mohyeddin
Sheikh Osman	Marne Maitland
General Wolseley	Nigel Green
Lord Hartington	Hugh Williams
The Khalifa Abdullah	Douglas Wilmer
Colonel Hicks	Edward Underdown
Bordeini Bey	Alec Mango
Giriagis Bey	George Pastell
Major Kitchener	Peter Arne
Awaan	Alan Tilvern
Herbin	Michael Anthony
Frank Power	Jerome Willis
The Dancer	Leila
Lord Northbrook	Ronald Leigh Hunt
Sir Charles Dilke	Ralph Michael

Charlton Heston, Laurence Olivier, Richard Johnson. Top: Ralph Richardson, Charlton Heston

Charlton Heston (also top), Laurence Olivier
Above: Richard Johnson, Charlton Heston,
Alexander Knox, Leila

Alec Mango, Richard Johnson (both at top), Charlton
Heston. Above (C): Richard Johnson

AN EYE FOR AN EYE

(EMBASSY) Producer, Carroll Case; Director, Michael Moore; Screenplay, Bing Russell, Sumner Williams; Associate Producer, Frank Beetson; Music, Raoul Kraushaar; Director of Photography, Lucien Ballard; Assistant Director, Jim Rosenberger; A Circle Production in Pathecolor. June release.

CAST

Talion	Robert Lansing
Benny	Pat Wayne
Ike Slant	Slim Pickens
Bri Quince	Gloria Talbot
Quince	Paul Fix
Trumbull	Strother Martin
Charles	Henry Wills
Jonas	Jerry Gatling
Harry	Rance Howard
Jo-Hi	Clint Howard

Right: Robert Lansing, Pat Wayne

THE DAYDREAMER

(EMBASSY) Produced and Written by Arthur Rankin, Jr.; Director, Jules Bass; Based on Stories and Characters created by Hans Christian Andersen; Music, Maury Laws; Lyrics, Jules Bass; Theme Song sung by Robert Goulet; Associate Producer, Larry Roemer; Presented by Joseph E. Levine; A Videocraft International Production in Animagic and Eastman Color. June release.

CAST

The Sandman	Cyril Ritchard
Chris (Hans Christian Andersen)	Paul O'Keefe
Papa Anderson	Jack Gilford
The Pieman	Ray Bolger
Mrs. Klopplebobbler	Margaret Hamilton
The Little Mermaid	Hayley Mills
Father Neptune	Burl Ives
The Sea Witch	Tallulah Bankhead
First Tailor: Brigidier	Terry-Thomas
Second Tailor: Zebro	Victor Borge
The Emperor	Ed Wynn
Big Claus	Robert Harter
Thumbelina	Patty Duke
The Rat	Boris Karloff
The Mole	Sessue Hayakawa

Margaret Hamilton, Jack Gilford, Paul O'Keefe
Above: Paul O'Keefe. Right: A dream

PARADISE, HAWAIIAN STYLE

(PARAMOUNT) Producer, Hal Wallis; Associate Producer, Paul Nathan; Director, Michael Moore; Screenplay, Allan Weiss, Anthony Lawrence; Story, Allan Weiss; Director of Photography, W. Wallace Kelley; Music, Joseph J. Lilley; Choreography, Jack Regas; Costumes, Edith Head; Assistant Director, James Rosenberger; In Technicolor. June release.

CAST

Rick Richards	Elvis Presley
Judy Hudson (Friday)	Suzanna Leigh
Danny Kohana	James Shigeta
Lani	Marianna Hill
Jan Kohana	Donna Butterworth
Pua	Irene Tsu
Lehua	Linda Wong
Joanna	Julie Parrish
Betty Kohana	Jan Shepard
Donald Belden	John Doucette
Moke	Philip Ahn
Mr. Cubberson	Grady Sutton
Andy Lowell	Dan Collier
Mrs. Barrington	Doris Packer
Mrs. Belden	Mary Treen
Peggy	Gi Gi Verone

...is Presley, James Shigeta, Grady Sutton. Above: Elvis Presley with (clockwise) Irene Tsu, Julie Parrish, Suzanna Leigh, Marianna Hill, Linda Wong

Elvis Presley, Donna Butterworth
Above: Elvis Presley, Suzanna Leigh

47

ASSAULT ON A QUEEN

(PARAMOUNT) Producer, William Goetz; Associate Producer and Director of Photography, William H. Daniels; Director, Jack Donohue; Assistant Director, Richard Lang; Costumes, Edith Head; Music, Duke Ellington; Screenplay, Rod Serling; From novel by Jack Finney; A Seven Arts-Sinatra Enterprises Production in Panavision and Technicolor. June release.

CAST

Mark Brittain	Frank Sinatra
Rosa Lucchesi	Virna Lisi
Vic Rossiter	Tony Franciosa
Tony Moreno	Richard Conte
Eric Lauffnauer	Alf Kjellin
Linc Langley	Errol John
Captain	Murray Matheson
Master-at-Arms	Reginald Denny
Bank Manager	John Warburton
Doctor	Lester Matthews
Trench	Val Avery
Junior Officer	Laurence Conroy
Officers	Gilchrist Stuart, Ronald Long, Leslie Bradley, Arthur E. Gould-Porter

Alf Kjellin, Frank Sinatra, Virna Lisi. Above: Richard Conte, Errol John, Virna Lisi. Top: Frank Sinatra, Alf Kjellin, Tony Franciosa

Frank Sinatra, Virna Lisi. Above with Errol John, Tony Franciosa, Alf Kjellin

THREE ON A COUCH

(COLUMBIA) Producer-Director, Jerry Lewis; Associate Producer, Joe E. Stabile; Screenplay, Bob Ross, Samuel A. Taylor; Based on story by Arne Sultan, Marvin Worth; Music, Louis Brown; "A Now And A Later Love" sung by Danny Costello; Costumes, Moss Mabry; Assistant Director, Rusty Meek; Director of Photography, W. Wallace Kelley; A Jerry Lewis Production in Pathe Color. June release.

CAST

Christopher Pride, Warren, Ringo, Rutherford, Heather	Jerry Lewis
Attache	Fritz Feld
Ambassador	Renzo Cesana
Drunk	Buddy Lester
Murphy	Kathleen Freeman
Mary Lou Mauve	Leslie Parrish
Anna Jacque	Gila Golan
Susan Manning	Mary Ann Mobley
Dr. Ben Mizer	James Best
Dr. Elizabeth Acord	Janet Leigh

Janet Leigh, Jerry Lewis. Above: Mary Ann Mobley, Jerry Lewis

Gila Golan, Jerry Lewis. Above: Jerry Lewis, Leslie Parrish. Top: James Best, Jerry Lewis, Janet Leigh 49

STAGECOACH

(20th CENTURY-FOX) Producer, Martin Rackin; Associate Producer, Alvin G. Manuel; Director, Gordon Douglas; Screenplay, Joseph Landon; Based on screenplay by Dudley Nichols; From story by Ernest Haycox; Music, Jerry Goldsmith; Song "Stagecoach To Cheyenne" by Lee Pockriss, Paul Vance; Sung by Wayne Newton; Director of Photography, William H. Clothier; Assistant Director, Joseph E. Rickards; In Cinemascope and DeLuxe Color. June release.

CAST

Dallas	Ann-Margret
Mr. Peacock	Red Buttons
Hatfield	Michael Connors
Ringo	Alex Cord
Doc Boone	Bing Crosby
Mr. Gatewood	Bob Cummings
Curly	Van Heflin
Buck	Slim Pickens
Mrs. Lucy Mallory	Stefanie Powers
Luke Plummer	Keenan Wynn
Matt Plummer	Brad Weston
Lt. Blanchard	Joseph Hoover
Capt. Mallory	John Gabriel
Mr. Haines	Oliver McGowan
Billy Picket	David Humphreys Miller
Trooper	Bruce Mars
Sergeant	Brett Pearson
Woman	Muriel Davidson
Ike Plummer	Ned Wynn
Townsman	Norman Rockwell
Sergeant Major	Edwin Mills
Bartender	Hal Lynch

Below: Bing Crosby, Red Buttons, Ann-Margret, Keenan Wynn, Bob Cummings, Stefanie Powers, Michael Connors Atop Stage: Slim Pickens, Van Heflin, Alex Cord. Above Stefanie Powers, Bing Crosby, Ann-Margret. Left: Alex Cord, Ann-Margret. Top: Van Heflin, Alex Cord, Ann-Margret, Michael Connors, Red Buttons, Bob Cummings

BEAU GESTE

(UNIVERSAL) Producer, Walter Seltzer; Director, Douglas Heyes; Director of Photography, Bud Thackery; Assistant Director, Terry Morse, Jr.; In Technicolor. July release.

CAST

Beau	Guy Stockwell
John	Doug McClure
De Ruse	Leslie Nielsen
Boldini	David Mauro
Fouchet	Robert Wolders
Dagineau	Telly Savalas
Krauss	Leo Gordon
Rostov	Michael Constantine
Kerjacki	Malachai Throne
Beaujolais	Joe De Santis
Vallejo	X Brands
Sergeant	Michael Carr
Surgeon	Patrick Whyte
Captain	Ted Jacques
Platoon Sergeant	George Keymas
Dancer	Ava Zamora
Legionnaires	Duane Grey, Hal Hopper, David Gross, Jeff Nelson, Chuck Wood

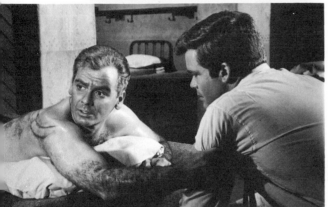

Guy Stockwell, Telly Savalas. Above: Guy Stockwell, Doug McClure. Top: Telly Savalas

Robert Wolders, Doug McClure
Above: Doug McClure, Guy Stockwell

LT. ROBIN CRUSOE, U.S.N.

(BUENA VISTA) Producer, Walt Disney; Co[
Producers, Bill Walsh, Ron Miller; Director[
Byron Paul; Screenplay, Bill Walsh, Don Da[
Gradi; Based on Story by Retlaw Yensic[
Music, Bob Brunner; Director of Photography[
William Snyder; Costumes, Bill Thomas; Assis[
tant Director, Tom Leetch; In Technicolor. Jul[
release.

CAST

Lt. Robin Crusoe _____ Dick Van Dyk[
Wednesday _____ Nancy Kwa[
Tanamashu _____ Akim Tamiro[
Umbrella Man _____ Arthur Male[
Captain _____ Tyler McVe[
Pilot _____ P. L. Renoude[
Co-Pilot _____ Peter Durye[
Crew Chief _____ John Denni[
Native Girls _____ Nancy Hsueh, Victoria Young[
     Yvonne Ribuca, Bebe Louie, Lucia Valer[

Dick Van Dyke. Above: Dick Van Dyke, Nancy Kwan

Nancy Kwan, Akim Tamiroff
Above: Akim Tamiroff

Dick Martin, John McGiver, Edward Andrews,
Paul Lynde, Rod Taylor

Doris Day, Alice Pearce

THE GLASS BOTTOM BOAT

(MGM) Producers, Martin Melcher, Everett Freeman; Director, Frank Tashlin; Screenplay, Everett Freeman; Director of Photography, Leon Shamroy; Music, De Vol; Songs, Joe Lubin, Jerome Howard; Costumes, Ray Aghayan; Assistant Director, Al Jennings; An Arwin-Reame Picture, Melcher-Freeman Production in Panavision and Metrocolor. July release.

CAST

Jennifer Nelson	Doris Day
Bruce Templeton	Rod Taylor
Axel Nordstrom	Arthur Godfrey
Ralph Goodwin	John McGiver
Homer Cripps	Paul Lynde
Gen. Wallace Bleecker	Edward Andrews
Edgar Hill	Eric Fleming
Julius Pritter	Dom De Luise
Zack Molloy	Dick Martin
Nina Bailey	Elisabeth Fraser
Mr. Fenimore	George Tobias
Mrs. Fenimore	Alice Pearce
Anna Miller	Ellen Corby
Donna	Dee J. Thompson

Doris Day, Eric Fleming, Dom De Luise
Above: Arthur Godfrey, Elisabeth Fraser
Left: Doris Day, Paul Lynde

53

ARABESQUE

(UNIVERSAL) Producer, Stanley Donen; Associate Producer, Denis Holt; Director, Stanley Donen; Based on novel by Gordon Cotler; Director of Photography, Chris Challis; Assistant Director, Eric Rattray; In Technicolor. July release.

CAST

David Pollock	Gregory Peck
Yasmin Azir	Sophia Loren
Nejim Beshraavi	Alan Badel
Yussef	Kieron Moore
Sloane	John Merivale
Webster	Duncan Lamont
Professor Ragheeb	George Coulouris
Hassan Jena	Carl Duering
Mohammed Lufti	Harold Kasket
Fanshaw	Gordon Griffin

Alan Badel, Sophia Loren. Above: Gregory Peck (R). Left: Alan Badel and Gregory Peck Top: Gregory Peck, Sophia Loren

Gregory Peck, Sophia Loren, Carl Duering. Top: Kieron Moore, Sophia Loren, Gregory Peck

WHAT DID YOU DO IN THE WAR, DADDY?

(UNITED ARTISTS) Executive Producer, Owen Crump; Producer-Director, Blake Edwards; Screenplay, William Peter Blatty; Story, Blake Edwards, Maurice Richlin; Music, Henry Mancini; Associate Producer, Dick Crockett; Director of Photography, Philip Lathrop; Costumes, Jack Bear; Choreography, Carey Leverett; Assistant Directors, Mickey McCardle, Tim Zinnemann, Charles Scott, Jr.; A Mirisch-Geoffrey Production in Panavision and DeLuxe Color. July release.

CAST

Lieutenant Christian	James Coburn
Captain Cash	Dick Shawn
Captain Oppo	Sergio Fantoni
Gina Romano	Giovanna Ralli
Sergeant Rizzo	Aldo Ray
Major Pott	Henry Morgan
General Bolt	Carroll O'Connor
Kastorp	Leon Askin
Benedetto	Henry Rico Cattani
Romano	Jay Novello
Federico	Vito Scotti
Vittorio	Johnny Seven
Pfc. Needleman	Art Lewis
Cpl. Minow	William Bryant
German Captain	Kurt Kreuger
Cook	Robert Carricart
Waiter	Ralph Manza
Bus Boy	Danny Francis
Lumpe	Herb Ellis
Blair	Ken Wales
Hitler	Carl Ekberg

and Rex Morhan, Richard Nile, Karla Most, Ivana Kislinger, Mina Darno, Giovanna Coppola, Louise DeCarlo, Sondra Farrell, Emily LaRue, Jeanne Ranier, Eric Anderson, Ken Del Conte, Tom Hunter, Kelly Johnson, Herb Andreas, Horst Graf, Vince Barbie, Joe LaPresti, Benito Prezia, Cosimo Renna, Neil Rosso, Mario Cimino, Phil Garris, James Lanphier, Jerry Martin, Joe Polina

Dick Shawn, Sergio Fantoni, Aldo Ray Above: James Coburn, Sergio Fantoni

Dick Shawn, James Coburn. Also at top Left

NEVADA SMITH

(PARAMOUNT) Executive Producer, Joseph E. Levine; Producer-Director, Henry Hathaway; Story and Screenplay, John Michael Hayes; Based on character in "The Carpetbaggers" by Harold Robbins; Music, Alfred Newman; Director of Photography, Lucien Ballard; Assistant Directors, Daniel J. McCauley, Joseph Lenzi; A Solar Production in Panavision and Color. July release.

CAST

Nevada Smith	Steve McQueen
Tom Fitch	Karl Malden
Jonas Cord	Brian Keith
Bill Bowdre	Arthur Kennedy
Pilar	Suzanne Pleshette
Father Zaccardi	Raf Vallone
Neesa	Janet Margolin
Big Foot	Pat Hingle
Warden	Howard Da Silva
Jesse Coe	Martin Landau
Sheriff Bonnell	Paul Fix
Sam Sand	Gene Evans
Mrs. Elvira McCanles	Josephine Hutchinson
Uncle Ben McCanles	John Doucette
Buck Mason	Val Avery
Sheriff	Sheldon Allman
Jack Rudabaugh	Lyle Bettger
Quince	Bert Freed
Romero	David McLean
Buckshot	Steve Mitchell
Cipriano	Ric Roman
Hogg	John Lawrence
Doctor	John Litel
Hudson	Ted de Corsia
Storekeeper	Stanley Adams
Paymaster	George Mitchell

Right: Steve McQueen, Janet Margolin
Above: Steve McQueen, Raf Vallone

Brian Keith, Steve McQueen

Arthur Kennedy, Suzanne Pleshette, Steve McQueen

Jim Hutton, Cary Grant

Samantha Eggar, Jim Hutton

WALK, DON'T RUN!

(COLUMBIA) Producer, Sol C. Siegel; Director, Charles Walters; Screenplay, Sol Saks; Based on story by Robert Russell, Frank Ross; Music, Quincy Jones; Director of Photography, Harry Stradling; Assistant Director, Jim Myers; Costumes, Morton Haack; In Panavision and Technicolor; A Granley Company presentation. July release.

CAST

William Rutland	Cary Grant
Christine Easton	Samantha Eggar
Steve Davis	Jim Hutton
Julius P. Haversack	John Standing
Aiko Kurawa	Miiko Taka
Yuri Andreyovitch	Ted Hartley
Dimitri	Ben Astar
Police Captain	George Takei
Mr. Kurawa	Teru Shimada
Mrs. Kurawa	Lois Kiuchi

Samantha Eggar, Miiko Taka, Ben Astar, Ted Hartley, Cary Grant, Jim Hutton. Seated: John Standing, George Takei. Left: Samantha Eggar, Cary Grant

Peter Lawford, Michael Lipton, Sammy Davis, Jr.

Sammy Davis Jr., Frank Sinatra, Jr.,
Cicely Tyson, Ossie Davis, Louis Armstrong

A MAN CALLED ADAM

(EMBASSY) Producers, Ike Jones, James
Waters; Executive Producer, Joseph E. Levine;
Director, Leo Penn; Screenplay, Les Pine,
Tina Rome; Music, Benny Carter; Director
of Photography, Jack Priestly; A Trace-Mark
Production. July release.

CAST

Adam Johnson	Sammy Davis, Jr.
Willie "Sweet Daddy" Ferguson	Louis Armstrong
Nelson Davis	Ossie Davis
Claudia Ferguson	Cicely Tyson
Vincent	Frank Sinatra, Jr.
Manny	Peter Lawford
Mel Torme	Mel Torme
Theo	Lola Falana
Martha	Jeanette DuBois
Les	Johnny Brown
Leroy	George Rhodes
George	Michael Silva
Bobby Gales	Michael Lipton

Sammy Davis, Jr., Lola Falana. Above: Cicely Tyson,
Louis Armstrong, Sammy Davis, Jr. Right: Cicely
Tyson, Sammy Davis, Jr.

THE WILD ANGELS

(AMERICAN INTERNATIONAL) Producer-Director, Roger Corman; Associate Producer, Laurence Cruikshank; Screenplay, Charles B. Griffith; Assistant Director, Paul Rapp; Director of Photography, Richard Moore; In Panavision and Pathecolor. July release.

CAST

Heavenly Blues	Peter Fonda
Mike	Nancy Sinatra
Loser	Bruce Dern
Joint	Lou Procopio
Bull Puckey	Coby Denton
Frankenstein	Marc Cavell
Dear John	Buck Taylor
Medic	Norm Alden
Pigmy	Michael J. Pollard
Gaysh	Diane Ladd
Mama Monahan	Joan Shawlee
Suzie	Gayle Hunnicutt
Thomas	Art Baker
Preacher	Frank Maxwell
Hospital Policeman	Frank Gertsel
Nurse	Kim Hamilton

Left: Nancy Sinatra, Diane Ladd, Peter Fonda

Burt Ward, Adam West, Neil Hamilton
Above: Burgess Meredith, Cesar Romero,
Burt Ward, Adam West, Frank Gorshin,
Lee Meriwether

BATMAN

(20th CENTURY-FOX) Producer, William Dozier; Associate Producer, Charles B. Fitz-Simons; Director, Leslie H. Martinson; Screenplay, Lorenzo Semple, Jr.; Based on characters appearing in comic strip by Bob Kane; Music, Nelson Riddle; Director of Photography, Howard Schwartz; Assistant Director, William Derwin; Batman Theme, Neil Hefti; In De-Luxe Color. August release.

CAST

Batman (Bruce Wayne)	Adam West
Robin (Dick Grayson)	Burt Ward
Catwoman (Kitka)	Lee Meriwether
The Joker	Cesar Romero
The Penguin	Burgess Meredith
The Riddler	Frank Gorshin
Alfred	Alan Napier
Commissioner Gordon	Neil Hamilton
Chief O'Hara	Stafford Repp
Aunt Harriet Cooper	Madge Blake
Commodore Schmidlapp	Reginald Denny
Vice Admiral Fangschliester	Milton Frome
Bluebeard	Gil Perkins
Morgan	Dick Crockett
Quetch	George Sawaya

HOW TO STEAL A MILLION

(20th CENTURY-FOX) Producer, Fred Kohlmar; Director, William Wyler; Screenplay, Harry Kurnitz; Based on Story by George Bradshaw; Music, Johnny Williams; Director of Photography, Charles Lang; Assistant Director, Paul Feyder; Gowns, Givenchy; A William Wyler Production in Panavision and DeLuxe Color. August release.

CAST

Nicole	Audrey Hepburn
Simon Dermott	Peter O'Toole
David Leland	Eli Wallach
Bonnet	Hugh Griffith
DeSolnay	Charles Boyer
Grammont	Fernand Gravet
Senor Faravideo	Marcel Dalio
Chief Guard	Jacques Marin
Guard	Moustache
Auctioneer	Roger Treville
Insurance Clerk	Eddie Malin
Marcel	Bert Bertram

Left: Audrey Hepburn, Peter O'Toole

arles Boyer, Hugh Griffith. Above: Hugh Griffith, Audrey Hepburn

Eli Wallach, Audrey Hepburn. Above: Fernand Gravet, Peter O'Toole, Audrey Hepburn

WHO'S AFRAID OF VIRGINIA WOOLF?

(WARNER BROS.) Director, Mike Nichols; Screenplay, Ernest Lehman; Based on play by Edward Albee; Director of Photography, Haskell Wexler; Assistant Director, Bud Grace; Music, Alex North; Costumes, Irene Sharaff. August release.

CAST

Martha	Elizabeth Taylor
George	Richard Burton
Nick	George Segal
Honey	Sandy Dennis

Left: Elizabeth Taylor, Richard Burton also below left and right

Elizabeth Taylor, Sandy Dennis, George Segal, Richard Burton

Elizabeth Taylor, George Segal. Above: George
Segal, Richard Burton, Sandy Dennis,
Elizabeth Taylor

Elizabeth Taylor, Richard Burton, and above
with George Segal, Sandy Dennis

Julie Andrews, Paul Newman

Julie Andrews, Paul Newman, Gunter Strack

TORN CURTAIN

(UNIVERSAL) Producer-Director, Alfred Hitchcock; Screenplay, Brian Moore; Director of Photography, John F. Warren; Costumes, Edith Head; Music, John Addison; Assistant Director, Donald Baer; In Technicolor. August release.

CAST

Prof. Michael Armstrong	Paul Newman
Sarah Sherman	Julie Andrews
Countess Kuchinska	Lila Kedrova
Heinrich Gerhard	Hansjoerg Felmy
Ballerina	Tamara Toumanova
Hermann Gromek	Wolfgang Kieling
Prof. Karl Manfred	Gunter Strack
Prof. Gustav Lindt	Ludwig Donath
Mr. Jacobi	David Opatoshu
Dr. Koska	Gisela Fischer
Farmer	Mort Mills
Farmer's Wife	Carolyn Conwell
Freddy	Arthur Gould-Porter
Fraulein Mann	Gloria Gorvin
Hotel Travel Clerk	Erik Holland
Airlines Official	Hedley Mattingly
Gutman	Norbert Schiller
Olaf Hengstrom	Peter Bourne
Jacobi	Charles Radilack
Taxi Driver	Peter Lorr
Factory Manager	Frank Aberschal

Ludwig Donath, Paul Newman. Above:
David Opatoshu, Julie Andrews, Paul Newman
Right: Carolyn Conwell, Paul Newman

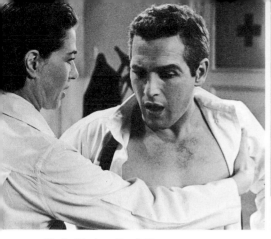

Gisela Fischer, Paul Newman   Lila Kedrova, Julie Andrews, Paul Newman

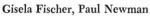

Julie Andrews, Paul Newman (Also above)   Paul Newman, Julie Andrews

THIS PROPERTY IS CONDEMNED

(PARAMOUNT) Producer, John Houseman; Director, Sydney Pollack; Screenplay, Francis Ford Coppola, Fred Coe, Edith Sommer; Suggested by Tennessee Williams' one-act play; Director of Photography, James Wong Howe; Music, Kenyon Hopkins; Songs, Jay Livingston, Ray Evans, Sam Coslow, W. Franke Harling, Arthur Johnston, Mildred J. and Patty S. Hill; Costumes, Edith Head, Ann Landers; Assistant Director, Eddie Saeta; Presented by Seven Arts and Ray Stark; In Technicolor. August release.

CAST

Alva Starr	Natalie Wood
Owen Legate	Robert Redford
J. J. Nichols	Charles Bronson
Hazel Starr	Kate Reid
Willie Starr	Mary Badham
Knopke	Alan Baxter
Sidney	Robert Blake
Johnson	John Harding
Salesman	Dabney Coleman
Jimmy Bell	Ray Hemphill
Charlie Steinkamp	Brett Pearson
Tom	Jon Provost
Hank	Quentin Sondergaard
Max	Michael Steen
Lindsay Tate	Bruce Watson
Tiny	Bob Random

Mary Badham, Jon Provost

Robert Redford, Natalie Wood. Above: Kate Reid, Natalie Wood

Mary Badham, Natalie Wood. Above: Natalie Wood, Charles Bronson

66

AN AMERICAN DREAM

(WARNER BROS.) Executive Producer, William Conrad; Director, Robert Gist; Screenplay, Mann Rubin; Based on novel by Norman Mailer; Director of Photography, Sam Leavitt; Assistant Director, Sherry Shourds; Music, Johnny Mandel; Song "A Time For Love" by Johnny Mandel, Paul Francis Webster; Costumes, Howard Shoup; In Technicolor. September release.

CAST

Stephen Rojack	Stuart Whitman
Cherry McMahon	Janet Leigh
Deborah	Eleanor Parker
Roberts	Barry Sullivan
Barney Kelly	Lloyd Nolan
Arthur Kabot	Murray Hamilton
Lt. Leznicki	J. D. Cannon
Ruta	Susan Denberg
Nicky	Les Crane
Johnny Dell	Warren Stevens
Eddie Ganucci	Joe DeSantis
Detective O'Brien	Stacy Harris
Shago Martin	Paul Mantee
Ganucci's Lawyer	Harold Gould
Ord Long	George Takei
Freya	Kelly Jean Peters

Barry Sullivan, Warren Stevens, Joe DeSantis, Les Crane, Stuart Whitman

PICTURE MOMMY DEAD

(EMBASSY) Producer-Director, Bert I. Gordon; Screenplay, Robert Sherman; Assistant Director, Dennis Donnelly; Director of Photography, Ellsworth Fredricks; Costumes, Leah Rhodes; In Pathecolor. September release.

CAST

Edward Shelley	Don Ameche
Francene Shelley	Martha Hyer
Jessica	Zsa Zsa Gabor
Susan Shelley	Susan Gordon
Anthony	Maxwell Reed
Clayborn	Wendell Corey
Sister Rene	Signe Hasso
Elsie Kornwald	Anna Lee
First Woman	Paule Clark
Second Woman	Marlene Tracy
Third Woman	Steffi Henderson
Father	Robert Sherman
Boy	Kelly Corcoran

Don Ameche, Susan Gordon, Martha Hyer

CHAMBER OF HORRORS

(WARNER BROS.) Producer-Director, Hy Averback; Screenplay, Stephen Kandel; Director of Photography, Richard Kline; Story, Ray Russell, Stephen Kandel; Associate Producer, Jim Barnett; Music, William Lava; Assistant Director, Sam Schneider; In Technicolor. September release.

CAST

Anthony Draco	Cesare Danova
Harold Blount	Wilfrid Hyde-White
Marie Champlain	Laura Devon
Vivian	Patrice Wymore
Barbara Dixon	Suzy Parker
Senor Pepe de Reyes	Tun Tun
Inspector Strudwick	Philip Bourneuf
Mrs. Ewing Perryman	Jeanette Nolan
Madame Corona	Marie Windsor
Sgt. Albertson	Wayne Rogers
Jason Cravette	Patrick O'Neal
Judge Randolph	Vinton Hayworth
Dr. Cobb	Richard O'Brien
Cloria	Inger Stratton
Chun Sing	Berry Kroeger
Dr. Hopewell	Charles Seel
Barmaid	Ayllene Gibbons

Wilfrid Hyde-White, Tun Tun (L), Cesare Danova (R)

AMBUSH BAY

(UNITED ARTISTS) Executive Producer, Aubrey Schenck; Producer, Hal Klein; Director, Ron Winston; Screenplay, Marve Feinberg, Ib Melchior; Director of Photography, Emmanuel Rojas; Music, Richard LaSalle; Assistant Director, E. Read Killgore; A Schenck-Zabel Production in DeLuxe Color. September release.

CAST

First Sgt. Steve Corey _____ Hugh O'Brian
Sgt. Ernest Wartell _____ Mickey Rooney
Pfc. James Grenier _____ James Mitchum
Sgt. William Maccone _____ Pete Masterson
Cpl. Alvin Ross _____ Harry Lauter
Cpl. Stanley Parrish _____ Greg Amsterdam
Pvt. Henry Reynolds _____ Jim Anauo
Pvt. George George _____ Tony Smith
Capt. Alonzo Davis _____ Clem Stadler
Amado _____ Amado Abello
Midori _____ Juris Sulit
Max _____ Max Quismundo
Ramon _____ Bruno Punzalan
Miyazaki _____ Tisa Chang
Lt. Tokuzo _____ Buff Fernandez
Capt. Kayamatsu _____ Joaquin Farjado
Man _____ Limbo Lagdameo
Soldier _____ Nonong Arceo

Mickey Rooney, Hugh O'Brian, James Mitchum

WHAT'S UP, TIGER LILY?

(AMERICAN INTERNATIONAL) Executive Producer, Henry G. Saperstein; Associate Producer, Woody Allen; Screenplay, Woody Allen; Title Song and Score written and performed by The Lovin' Spoonful; A Henry G. Saperstein Reuben Bercovitch Production; Presented by James H. Nicholson and Samuel Z. Arkoff. September release.

CAST

Mie Hama
Akiko Wakabayashi

Woody Allen
The Lovin' Spoonful

Right: Woody Allen, China Lee

WACO

(PARAMOUNT) Producer, A. C. Lyles; Director, R. G. Springsteen; Screenplay, Steve Fisher; Based on novel "Emporia" by Harry Sanford, Max Lamb; Director of Photography, Robert Pittack; Costumes, Edith Head; Music, Jimmie Haskell; Title Song by Hal Blair, Jimmie Haskell; Sung by Lorne Greene; Assistant Director, James Rosenberger; In Technicolor and Techniscope. September release.

CAST

Waco _____ Howard Keel
Jill Stone _____ Jane Russell
Ace Ross _____ Brian Donlevy
Preacher Sam Stone _____ Wendell Corey
Dolly _____ Terry Moore
Joe Gore _____ John Smith
George Gates _____ John Agar
Deputy Sheriff O'Neill _____ Gene Evans
Sheriff Billy Kelly _____ Richard Arlen
Scotty Moore _____ Ben Cooper
Patricia West _____ Tracy Olsen
Bill Rile _____ DeForest Kelley
Ma Jenner _____ Anne Seymour
Mayor Ned West _____ Robert Lowery
Pete Jenner _____ Willard Parker
Kallen _____ Jeff Richards
Ike Jenner _____ Reg Parton
Telegraph Operator _____ Fuzzy Knight

Howard Keel (L), Anne Seymour

THE PAD . . .
(AND HOW TO USE IT)

(UNIVERSAL) Producer, Ross Hunter; Director, Brian Hutton; Screenplay based on play "The Private Ear" by Peter Shaffer; Director of Photography, Ellsworth Fredericks; Assistant Directors, Phil Bowles, Joe Boston; In Technicolor and Techniscope. September release.

CAST

Bob Handman	Brian Bedford
Ted Veasey	James Farentino
Doreen	Julie Sommars
Lavinia	Edy Williams

Right: Brian Bedford, Julie Sommars, James Farentino

Edy Williams, James Farentino, also above
with Nick Navarro (R)

Julie Sommars, Brian Bedford. Above: James
Farentino, Brian Bedford

69

JOHN F. KENNEDY: YEARS OF LIGHTNING, DAY OF DRUMS

(EMBASSY) Producer, George Stevens, Jr.; Directed, Written and Music Composed by Bruce Herschensohn; Commentary by Gregory Peck; A U.S.I.A. Production in Pathe Color; Presented by the John F. Kennedy Center For The Performing Arts, Washington, D.C. through the distribution facilities of Joseph E. Levine.

Full-length documentary story of the two years and ten months of John F. Kennedy's suddenly-terminated service as President of The United States. All profits go to the Kennedy Center in Washington.

The funeral cortege for President John F. Kennedy
Above: His inauguration

NAMU, THE KILLER WHALE

(UNITED ARTISTS) Executive Producer, Ivan Tors; Producer-Director, Laslo Benedek; Screenplay, Arthur Weiss; Associate Producer and Director of Photography, Lamar Boren; Music, Samuel Matlovsky; Assistant Director, Jack R. Berne; In DeLuxe Color. September release.

CAST

Hank Donner	Robert Lansing
Joe Clausen	John Anderson
Kate Rand	Lee Meriwether
Deke	Richard Erdman
Lisa Rand	Robin Mattson
Burt	Joe Higgins
Nick	Michael Shea
Carrie	Clara Tarte
Charlie	Edwin Rochelle

Right: Namu, Lee Meriwether

Namu

Robert Lansing, Robin Mattson

FANTASTIC VOYAGE

(20th CENTURY-FOX) Producer, Saul David; Director, Richard Fleischer; Screenplay, Harry Kleiner; Adaptation, David Duncan; Based on story by Otto Klement, Jay Lewis Bixby; Music, Leonard Rosenman; Director of Photography, Ernest Laszlo; Assistant Director, Ad Schaumer; In Cinemascope and DeLuxe Color. October release.

CAST

Grant	Stephen Boyd
Cora Peterson	Raquel Welch
General Carter	Edmond O'Brien
Doctor Michaels	Donald Pleasence
Col. Donald Reid	Arthur O'Connell
Capt. Bill Owens	William Redfield
Doctor Duval	Arthur Kennedy
Jan Benes	Jean Del Val
Communications Aide	Barry Coe
Secret Service Man	Ken Scott
Nurse	Shelby Grant
Technician	James Brolin
Wireless Operator	Brendan Fitzgerald

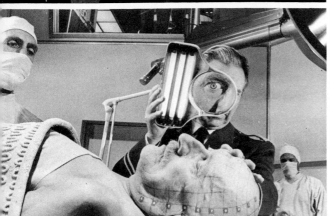

Arthur O'Connell, Edmond O'Brien, Arthur Kennedy, William Redfield, Raquel Welch, Stephen Boyd, Donald Pleasence, and above with Jean Del Val
Top: Jean Del Val (C)

Arthur Kennedy, Raquel Welch, Donald Pleasence, William Redfield, Stephen Boyd

Raquel Welch, Stephen Boyd

Barry Coe, Edmond O'Brien, Arthur O'Connell

MISTER BUDDWING

(MGM) Producers, Douglas Laurence, Delbert Mann; Director, Delbert Mann; Screenplay, Dale Wasserman; Based on novel "Buddwing" by Evan Hunter; Music, Kenyon Hopkins; Director of Photography, Ellsworth Fredricks; Gowns, Helen Rose; Assistant Director, Erich von Stroheim, Jr.; A DDD-Cherokee Production. October release.

CAST

Mister Buddwing	James Garner
The Blonde	Jean Simmons
Fiddle	Suzanne Pleshette
Janet	Katharine Ross
Gloria	Angela Lansbury
Shabby Old Man	George Voskovec
Mr. Schwartz	Jack Gilford
First Cab Driver	Joe Mantell
Hank	Raymond St. Jacques
Dan	Ken Lynch
Policeman	Beeson Carroll
Second Cab Driver	Billy Halop
Counterman	Michael Hadge
Printer	Charles Seel
Tony	John Tracy
Chauffeur	Bart Conrad

Dice Players .... Wesley Addy, Romo Vincent, Nichelle Nichols, John Dennis, Kam Tong, James O'Rear, Rafael Campos, Pat Li, Rikki Stevens

Nichelle Nichols, Jean Simmons, James Garner, Raymond St. Jacques, Rafael Campos, Rikki Stevens

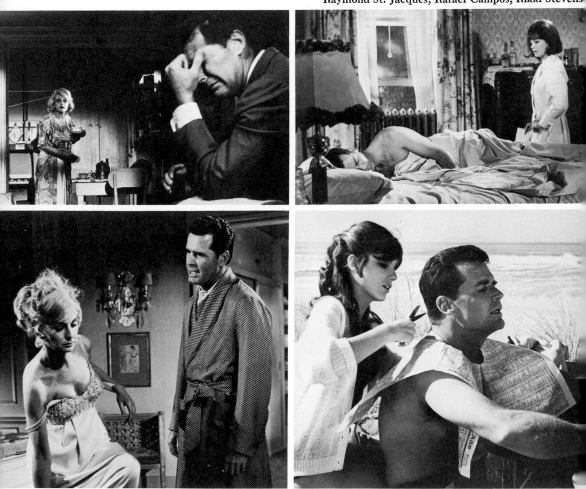

Jean Simmons, James Garner. Above: Angela Lansbury, James Garner

Katharine Ross, James Garner. Above: James Garner, Suzanne Pleshette

SPINOUT

(MGM) Producer, Joe Pasternak; Director, Norman Taurog; Screenplay, Theodore J. Flicker, George Kirgo; Director of Photography, Daniel L. Fapp; Music, George Stoll; Associate, Robert Van Eps; Musical Numbers Staged by Jack Baker; Vocal backgrounds, The Jordanaires; Assistant Director, Claude Binyon, Jr.; Associate Producer, Hank Moonjean; A Euterpe Picture in Panavision and Metrocolor. October release.

CAST

Mike McCoy	Elvis Presley
Cynthia Foxhugh	Shelley Fabares
Diana St. Clair	Diane McBain
Les	Deborah Walley
Susan	Dodie Marshall
Curly	Jack Mullaney
Lt. Tracy Richards	Will Hutchins
Philip Short	Warren Berlinger
Larry	Jimmy Hawkins
Howard Foxhugh	Carl Betz
Bernard Ranley	Cecil Kellaway
Violet Ranley	Una Merkel
Blodgett	Frederic Worlock
Harry	Dave Barry

Right Top: Warren Berlinger, Jack Mullaney, Carl Betz, Jimmy Hawkins, Elvis Presley, Una Merkel, Deborah Walley, Cecil Kellaway, Diane McBain, Shelley Fabares

LET'S KILL UNCLE

(UNIVERSAL) Producer-Director, William Castle; Screenplay, Mark Rodgers; Based on novel by Rohan O'Grady; Associate Producer, Dona Holloway; Director of Photography, Harold Lipstein; Assistant Director, Carl Beringer; In Technicolor. October release.

CAST

Harrison	Nigel Green
Chrissie	Mary Badham
Barnaby	Pat Cardi
Travis	Robert Pickering
Justine	Linda Lawson
Ketch-man	Reff Sanchez

Right: Pat Cardi, Nigel Green, Mary Badham

RETURN OF THE SEVEN

(UNITED ARTISTS) Producer, Ted Richmond; Director, Burt Kennedy; Associate Producer, Robert Goodstein; Screenplay, Larry Cohen; Music, Elmer Bernstein; Director of Photography, Paul Vogel; Assistant Director, Jose Lopez Rodero; In Panavision and DeLuxe Color; A Mirisch Productions presentation. October release.

CAST

Chris	Yul Brynner
Vin	Robert Fuller
Chico	Julian Mateos
Colbee	Warren Oates
Manuel	Jordan Christopher
Frank	Claude Akins
Luis	Virgilio Texeira
Lorca	Emilio Fernandez
Lopez	Rudy Acosta
Petra	Elisa Montes
Priest	Fernando Rey

Jordan Christopher, Warren Oates, Robert Fuller, Yul Brynner, Julian Mateos, Virgilio Texeira, Claude Akins

Jack Lemmon, Walter Matthau

THE FORTUNE COOKIE

(UNITED ARTISTS) Producer-Director, Billy Wilder; Associate Producers, I.A.L. Diamond, Doane Harrison; Screenplay, Billy Wilder, I.A.L. Diamond; Music, Andre Previn; Director of Photography, Joseph LaShelle; Assistant Director, Jack Reddish; In Panavision; A Phalanx-Jalem Production; A Mirisch Corporation presentation. October release.

CAST

Harry Hinkle	Jack Lemmon
Willie Gingrich	Walter Matthau
Luther "Boom Boom" Jackson	Ron Rich
Mr. Purkey	Cliff Osmond
Sandy	Judi West
Mother Hinkle	Lurene Tuttle
O'Brien	Harry Holcombe
Thompson	Les Tremayne
Charlotte Gingrich	Marge Redmond
Max	Noam Pitlik
Dr. Krugman	Harry Davis
Sister Veronica	Ann Shoemaker
Nurse	Maryesther Denver
Kincaid	Lauren Gilbert
Doc Schindler	Ned Glass
Prof. Winterhalter	Sig Ruman
Mr. Jackson	Archie Moore
Nun	Dodie Heath
Maury	Herbie Faye

and Howard McNear, Bill Christopher, Bartlett Robinson, Robert P. Lieb, Martin Blaine, Ben Wright, Billy Beck, Judy Pace, Helen Kleeb, Lisa Jill, John Todd Roberts, Keith Jackson, Herb Ellis, Don Reed, Louise Vienna, Bob Doqui

Jack Lemmon, and top right with Judi West

Maryesther Denver, Jack Lemmon, Walter Matthau
Above: Walter Matthau, Jack Lemmon, Ned Glass

THE APPALOOSA

(UNIVERSAL) Producer, Alan Miller; Director, Sidney J. Furie; Screenplay, James Bridges, Roland Kibbee; Based on novel by Robert Mac-Leod; Director of Photography, Russell Metty; Music, Frank Skinner; Assistant Director, Douglas Green; Costumes, Rosemary Odell, Helen Colvig; In Technicolor. October release.

CAST

Matt	Marlon Brando
Trini	Anjanette Comer
Chuy	John Saxon
Lazaro	Emilio Fernandez
Squint-Eye	Alex Montoya
Ana	Miriam Colon
Paco	Rafael Campos
Ramos	Frank Silvera
Priest	Larry D. Mann
Yaqui Woman	Argentina Brunetti

Anjanette Comer, Marlon Brando

John Saxon, Marlon Brando. Above: Rafael Campos, Marlon Brando

Marlon Brando, Anjanette Comer. Above: Anjanette Comer, Alex Montoya, John Saxon

Khigh Dhiegh, Rock Hudson   Murray Hamilton, Rock Hudson

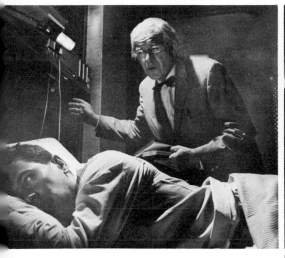

SECONDS

(PARAMOUNT) Producer, Edward Lewis; Director, John Frankenheimer; Screenplay, Lewis John Carlino; Based on novel by David Ely; Director of Photography, James Wong Howe; Music, Jerry Goldsmith; Songs, Johnny Mercer and Harold Arlen, Leo Robin and Lewis E. Gensler; Assistant Directors, Francisco Day, Michael Glick; A Douglas & Lewis Productions Presentation. October release.

CAST

Antiochus Wilson	Rock Hudson
Nora Marcus	Salome Jens
Arthur Hamilton	John Randolph
Old Man	Will Geer
Mr. Ruby	Jeff Corey
Dr. Innes	Richard Anderson
Charlie	Murray Hamilton
Dr. Morris	Karl Swenson
Davalo	Khigh Dhiegh
Emily Hamilton	Frances Reid
John	Wesley Addy
Texan	John Lawrence
Plump Blonde	Elisabeth Fraser
Sue Bushman	Dody Heath
Mayberry	Robert Brubaker
Mrs. Filter	Dorothy Morris
Secretary	Barbara Werle
Man in station	Frank Campanella
Taylor shop presser	Edgar Stehli
Meat Man	Aaron Magidow
Nurse	De De Young
Girl in boudoir	Francoise Ruggieri
Dayroom attendant	Thom Conroy
Henry Bushman	Ned Young
Mr. Filter	Kirk Duncan
Doctor in operating room	William Richard Wintersole

Rock Hudson, Frances Reid. Above: Salome Jens, Rock Hudson, Elisabeth Fraser Left: Rock Hudson, Will Geer   79

(UNITED ARTISTS) Producer, Walter Mirisch; Director, George Roy Hill; Associate Producer, Lewis J. Rachmil; Screenplay, Dalton Trumbo, Daniel Taradash; Based on novel by James A. Michener; Director of Photography, Russell Harlan; Music, Elmer Bernstein; Song "My Wishing Doll" by Mack David, Elmer Bernstein; Costumes, Dorothy Jeakins; Assistant Director, Ray Gosnell; Choreographer, Miriam Nelson; In Panavision and DeLuxe Color; A Mirisch Corporation Presentation. October release.

CAST

Jerusha Bromley	Julie Andrews
Abner Hale	Max Von Sydow
Rafer Hoxworth	Richard Harris
Charles	Carroll O'Connor
Abigail	Elizabeth Cole
Charity	Diane Sherry
Mercy	Heather Menzies
Rev. Thorn	Torin Thatcher
John Whipple	Gene Hackman
Immanuel Quigley	John Cullum
Abraham Hewlett	Lou Antonio
Queen Malama	Jocelyne LaGarde
Keoki	Manu Tupou
Kelolo	Ted Nobriga
Noelani	Elizabeth Logue
Iliki	Lokelani S. Chicarell
Gideon	Malcolm Atterbury
Hepzibah	Dorothy Jeakins
Captain Janders	George Rose
Mason	Michael Constantine
Collins	John Harding
Cridland	Robert Crawford
Micah at 4	Robert Oakley
Micah at 7	Henrik Von Sydow
Micah at 12	Clas S. Von Sydow
Micah at 18	Bertil Werjefelt

Julie Andrews, Max Von Sydow, also above with George Rose

Elizabeth Logue, Manu Topou

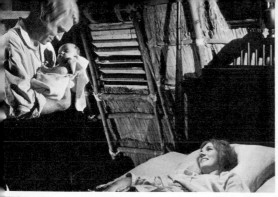

Max Von Sydow, Henrik Von Sydow. Above: Jocelyne LaGarde, Julie Andrews, Max n Sydow. Top: Max Von Sydow, Julie Andrews

Julie Andrews, Clas Von Sydow. Above: Julie Andrews, Max Von Sydow. Top: Richard Harris, Julie Andrews

Donald Barry, Richard Widmark, Duke Hobbie

Richard Rust, Richard Widmark, William Holden

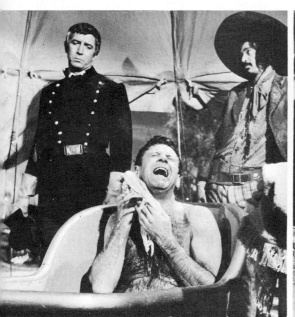

ALVAREZ KELLY

(COLUMBIA) Producer, Sol C. Siegel; Director, Edward Dmytryk; Screenplay, Franklin Coen, Elliott Arnold; Director of Photography, Joseph MacDonald; Music, John Green; Song, John Green, Johnny Mercer; Sung by The Brothers Four; Assistant Director, Frank Baur; In Panavision and Pathe Color. October release.

CAST

Alvarez Kelly	William Holden
Col. Tom Rossiter	Richard Widmark
Liz Pickering	Janice Rule
Maj. Albert Stedman	Patrick O'Neal
Charity Warwick	Victoria Shaw
Capt. Angus Ferguson	Roger C. Carmel
Sergeant Hatcher	Richard Rust
Captain Towers	Arthur Franz
Lt. Farrow	Donald Barry
John Beaurider	Duke Hobbie
Cpl. Peterson	Harry Carey, Jr.
McIntyre	Howard Caine
Ely Harrison	Mauritz Hugo
Gen. Kautz	G. B. Atwater
Capt. Williams	Robert Morgan
Capt. Webster	Paul Lukather
Mary Ann	Stephanie Hill
Melinda	Indus Arthur
Union Lieutenant	Clint Ritchie

Duke Hobbie, Richard Widmark, Victor Shaw
Above: William Holden, Janice Rule, Richard Widma
Left: Patrick O'Neal, William Holden, Robert Contre

George C. Scott, Donna Danton, Tony Curtis

NOT WITH MY WIFE, YOU DON'T!

(WARNER BROS.) Producer-Director, Norman Panama; Screenplay, Norman Panama, Larry Gelbart, Peter Barnes; Story, Norman Panama, Melvin Frank; Director of Photography, Charles Lang; Associate Producer, Joel Freeman; Music, Johnny Williams; Songs, Johnny Williams, Johnny Mercer; Choreography, Shela Hackett; Costumes, Edith Head; Assistant Director, Jack Aldworth; In Technicolor. November release.

CAST

Tom Ferris	Tony Curtis
Julie Ferris	Virna Lisi
"Tank" Martin	George C. Scott
General Parker	Carroll O'Connor
General Walters	Richard Eastham
Sgt. Gilroy	Eddie Ryder
Sgt. Dogerty	George Tyne
Doris Parker	Ann Doran
Nurse Sally Ann	Donna Danton
Lillian Walters	Natalie Core

Tony Curtis, Virna Lisi, George C. Scott, also above

Virna Lisi, George C. Scott. Above: Virna Lisi, Tony Curtis

83

SEVEN WOMEN

(MGM) Producer, Bernard Smith; Director, John Ford; Screenplay, Janet Green, John McCormick; Based on Short Story "Chinese Finale" by Norah Lofts; Music, Elmer Bernstein; Director of Photography, Joseph LaShelle; Assistant Director, Wingate Smith; Costumes, Walter Plunkett; In Panavision and Metrocolor. November release.

CAST

Dr. D. R. Cartwright	Anne Bancroft
Emma Clark	Sue Lyon
Agatha Andrews	Margaret Leighton
Miss Binns	Flora Robson
Jane Argent	Mildred Dunnock
Florrie Pether	Betty Field
Mrs. Russell	Anna Lee
Charles Pether	Eddie Albert
Tunga Khan	Mike Mazurki
Lean Worrior	Woody Strode
Miss Ling	Jane Chang
Kim	Hans William Lee
Coolie	H. W. Gim
Chinese Girl	Irene Tsu

Anne Bancroft, Sue Lyon, Mildred Dunnock, Margaret Leighton, Eddie Albert, Betty Field

Anna Lee, Jane Chang, Flora Robson, Anne Bancroft
Above: Sue Lyon, Flora Robson, Anne Bancroft

84

Flora Robson, Margaret Leighton, Sue Lyon, Betty Field, Anne Bancroft, Woody Strode
Above: Anne Bancroft, Mildred Dunnock

FOLLOW ME, BOYS!

(BUENA VISTA) Producer, Walt Disney; Co-Producer, Winston Hibler; Director, Norman Tokar; Screenplay, Louis Pelletier; Based on book "God and My Country" by MacKinlay Kantor; Music, George Bruns; Director of Photography, Clifford Stine; Assistant Director, Terry Morse, Jr.; Costumes, Bill Thomas; Title Song by Robert B. and Richard M. Sherman; In Technicolor. November release.

CAST

Lemuel Siddons	Fred MacMurray
Vida Downey	Vera Miles
Hetty Seibert	Lillian Gish
Ralph Hastings	Elliott Reid
Whitey	Kurt Russell
Nora White	Luana Patten
Melody Murphy	Ken Murray
Edward White, Jr.	Donald May

and Sean McClory, Steve Franken, Parley Baer, William Reynolds, Lem's Boys, Craig Hill, Tol Avery, Willis Bouchey, John Zaremba, Madge Blake, Carl Reindel, Hank Brandt, Richard Bakalyan, Tim McIntire, Willie Soo Hoo, Tony Regan, Robert B. Williams, Jimmy Murphy, Adam Williams

Lillian Gish, Fred MacMurray, Elliott Reid

d MacMurray, Vera Miles, Lillian Gish, Elliott Reid. Above: Fred MacMurray, Ken Murray

Fred MacMurray, Luana Patten, Donald May, Vera Miles
Above: Fred MacMurray, Kurt Russell, Vera Miles

Peter Falk, Bill Gunn, Natalie Wood

Lou Jacobi, Natalie Wood, Lila Kedrova

PENELOPE

(MGM) Producer, Arthur Loew, Jr.; Director, Arthur Hiller; Executive Producer, Joe Pasternak; Screenplay, George Wells; From novel by E. V. Cunningham; Director of Photography, Harry Stradling; Music, Johnny Williams; Songs, Johnny Williams, Gale Garnett; Sung by Natalie Wood; Assistant Director, Terence Nelson; Costumes, Ann Landers, Edith Head; A Euterpe Production in Panavision and Metrocolor. November release.

CAST

Penelope	Natalie Wood
James B. Elcott	Ian Bannen
Dr. Gregory Mannix	Dick Shawn
Lt. Bixbee	Peter Falk
Professor Klobb	Jonathan Winters
Sadaba	Lila Kedrova
Ducky	Lou Jacobi
Mildred	Norma Crane
Major Higgins	Arthur Malet
Bank Manager	Jerome Cowan
Miss Serena	Amzie Strickland
Honeysuckle Rose	Arlene Golonka
Miss Serena	Amzie Strickland
Sgt. Rothschild	Bill Gunn
Boom Boom	Carl Ballentine
Store Owner	Iggie Wolfington

Natalie Wood, Ian Bannen, Norma Crane. Above: Di[c]k Shawn, Natalie Wood. Left: Jonathan Winters, Natalie Wood

Joey Bishop, Dean Martin, Alain Delon

TEXAS ACROSS THE RIVER

(UNIVERSAL) Producer, Harrly Keller; Director, Michael Gordon; Director of Photography, Russell Metty; Costumes, Vince Dee; Assistant Directors, Terry Morse, Jr., John Anderson; In Technicolor. Novemmber release.

CAST

Hollis	Dean Martin
Andrea	Alain Delon
Kronk	Joey Bishop
Phoebe Ann Naylor	Rosemary Forsyth
Lonetta	Tina Marquand
Stimpson	Peter Graves
Sibley	Andrew Prine
Cottle	Stuart Anderson
Iron Jacket	Michael Ansara
Floyd Willet	George Wallace
Cy Morton	Roy Barcroft
Gabe Hutchins	John Harmon
Medicine Man	Dick Farnsworth
Yellow Knife	Linden Chiles

Tina Marquand, Joey Bishop, Alain Delon, Dean Martin, Rosemary Forsyth. Above: Tina Marquand, Alain Delon

Alain Delon, Rosemary Forsyth, Dean Martin. Above: Dean Martin, Joey Bishop, Peter Graves

87

A FUNNY THING HAPPENED ON THE WAY TO THE FORUM

(UNITED ARTISTS) Producer, Melvin Fran; Director, Richard Lester; Screenplay, Melvin Frank, Michel Pertwee; Based on Musical Comedy by Burt Shevelove, Larry Gelbart, Stephen Sondheim; Director of Photography, Nicolas Roeg; Costumes, Tony Walton; Songs, Stephen Sondheim; Assistant Director, Jose Lopez Rodero; Choreography, Ethel and George Martin; Incidental Music, Ken Thorne; In De-Luxe Color. November release.

CAST

Pseudolus	Zero Mostel
Lycus	Phil Silvers
Erronius	Buster Keaton
Hysterium	Jack Gilford
Hero	Michael Crawford
Philia	Annette Andre
Domina	Patricia Jessel
Senex	Michael Hordern
Miles	Leon Greene
Gymnasia	Inga Neilsen
Vibrata	Myrna White
Panacea	Lucienne Bridou
Tintinabula	Helen Funai
Geminae	Susan and Jennifer Baker
Fertilla	Janet Webb

Zero Mostel, Phil Silvers. Top: Zero Mostel

Zero Mostel, Inga Neilsen

Zero Mostel, Jack Gilford. Above: Annette Andre, Michael Crawford

Milton Frome, Ann-Margret, Mary LaRoche

Michael Quinn, Ann-Margret, Tony Franciosa

Ann-Margret, Horace McMahon. Above: Ann-
90 Margret, Robert Coote, Tony Franciosa
Right: Ann-Margret, Tony Franciosa

THE SWINGER

(PARAMOUNT) Producer-Director, George
Sidney; Screenplay, Lawrence Roman; Director
of Photography, Joseph Biroc; Music, Marty
Paich; Costumes, Edith Head; Choreography,
David Winters; Title Song, Andre and Dory
Previn; Assistant Director, Daniel J. Mc-
Cauley; In Technicolor. November release.

CAST

Kelly Olsson	Ann-Margret
Ric Colby	Tony Franciosa
Sir Hubert Charles	Robert Coote
Karen Charles	Yvonne Romain
Detective Sgt. Hooker	Horace McMahon
Aunt Cora	Nydia Westman
Sammy Jenkins	Craig Hill
Mr. Olsson	Milton Frome
Mrs. Olsson	Mary LaRoche
Clete Roberts	Clete Roberts
Sally	Myrna Ross
Sir Hubert's Secretary	Corinne Cole
Police Captain	Bert Freed
Jack Happy	Romo Vincent
Man with fish	Steven Geray
John Mallory	Larry D. Mann
Warren	Lance Le Gault
Svengali	Diki Lerner
Blossom LaTour	Barbara Nichols

Jerry Lewis, Connie Stevens, Robert Morley

Jerry Lewis, Dick Shawn, Anita Ekberg,
Connie Stevens

WAY . . . WAY OUT!

(20th CENTURY-FOX) Producer, Malcolm Stuart; Director, Gordon Douglas; Screenplay, William Bowers, Laslo Vadnay; Music, Lalo Schifrin; Title Song, Hal Winn, Lalo Schifrin; Sung by Gary Lewis and The Playboys; Costumes, Moss Mabry; Director of Photography, William H. Clothier; Assistant Director, Joseph E. Rickards; Narrator, Colonel John "Shorty" Powers; A Coldwater-Jerry Lewis Production in Cinemascope and DeLuxe Color. November release.

CAST

Peter	Jerry Lewis
Eileen	Connie Stevens
Quonset	Robert Morley
Hoffman	Dennis Weaver
Schmidlap	Howard Morris
General Hallenby	Brian Keith
Igor	Dick Shawn
Anna	Anita Ekberg
Ponsonby	William O'Connell
Esther Davenport	Bobo Lewis
Russian Delegate	Milton Frome
Deuce	Alex D'Arcy
Peggy	Linda Harrison
Ted	James Brolin

Anita Ekberg, Jerry Lewis, Connie Stevens: Above:
William O'Connell, Robert Morley, Jerry Lewis
Left: Dennis Weaver, Jerry Lewis, Howard Morris

DEAD HEAT ON A MERRY-GO-ROUND

(COLUMBIA) Producer, Carter DeHaven; Direction and Screenplay, Bernard Girard; Director of Photography, Lionel Lindon; Music, Stu Phillips; Assistant Director, William Kissel; In Pathe Color. November release.

CAST

Eli Kotch	James Coburn
Inger Knudson	Camilla Sparv
Eddie Hart	Aldo Ray
Frieda Schmid	Nina Wayne
Milo Stewart	Robert Webber
Margaret Kirby	Rose-Marie
Alfred Morgan	Todd Armstrong
Dr. Marion Hague	Marian Moses
Paul Feng	Michael Strong
Miles Fisher	Severn Darden
Jack Balter	James Westerfield
George Logan	Phillip E. Pine
William Anderson	Simon Scott
Gen. Mailenkoff	Ben Astar
Capt. William Yates	Michael St. Angel
Officer Howard	Lawrence Mann
Translator	Alex Rodine
Willie Manus	Albert Nalbandian
Lyman Mann	Tyler McVey
Sgt. Elmer K. Coxe	Roy Glenn

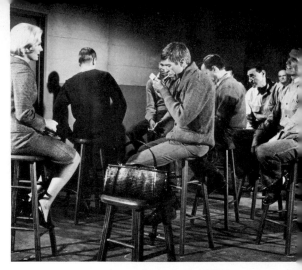

Marian Moses, James Coburn

James Coburn, Rene Paul
Above: James Coburn, Camilla Sparv

Severn Darden, James Coburn, Aldo Ray
Above: Rose-Marie, James Coburn

92

Yul Brynner, Omar Sharif, Jack Hawkins

Trevor Howard, E. G. Marshall, Nadja Tiller,
Eli Wallach

evor Howard, Senta Berger. Above: Hugh Griffith,
Yul Brynner. Right: Marcello Mastroianni,
Rita Hayworth

THE POPPY IS ALSO
A FLOWER

(COMET) Director, Terence Young; Screenplay, Jo Eisinger; Music, Georges Auric; In Eastman Color. November release.

CAST

Night Club Entertainer	Senta Berger
Benson	Stephen Boyd
Colonel Salem	Yul Brynner
Linda Benson	Angie Dickinson
Superintendent Roche	Georges Geret
Tribal Chief	Hugh Griffith
General Bahar	Jack Hawkins
Monique	Rita Hayworth
Agent Lincoln	Trevor Howard
Society Photographer	Jocelyn Lane
Trini Lopez	Trini Lopez
Agent Jones	E. G. Marshall
Inspector Mosca	Marcello Mastroianni
Capitano Dinonno	Amedeo Nazzari
Leader of Tribesmen	Jean Claude Pascal
Captain	Anthony Quayle
Marco	Gilbert Roland
Martin	Harold Sakata
Dr. Rad	Omar Sharif
Chasen	Barry Sullivan
Dr. Bronowska	Nadja Tiller
Locarno	Eli Wallach

and Luisa Rivelli, Laya Raki, Silvia Sorrente, Howard Vernon, Marilu Tolo, Violette Marceau, Gilda Dahlberg, Morteza Kazerouni, Bob Cunningham, Ali Oveisi

93

Eva Marie Saint, Evans Evans, Claude Dauphin, Yves Montand. Above (L): Francoise Hardy, Antonio Sabato, (R) Brian Bedford, Jessica Walter. Top (L): Yves Montand, Adolfo Celi, (R) Yves Montand, Genevieve Page

GRAND PRIX

(MGM) Producer, Edward Lewis; Director, John Frankenheimer; Screen Story and Screenplay, Robert Alan Aurthur; Music, Maurice Jarre; Director of Photography, Lionel Lindon; Assistant Directors, Enrico Isacco, Roger Simons, Stephan Isovesco, Sam Itzkowitch; A Douglas & Lewis Production in Cinerama, Super Panavision, and Metrocolor. December release.

CAST

Pete Aron	James Garner
Louise Frederickson	Eva Marie Saint
Jean-Pierre Sarti	Yves Montand
Izo Yamura	Toshiro Mifune
Scott Stoddard	Brian Bedford
Pat Stoddard	Jessica Walter
Lisa	Francoise Hardy
Nino Barlini	Antonio Sabato
Jeff Jordan	Jack Watson
Monique Delvaux Sari	Genevieve Page
Hugo Simon	Claude Dauphin
Augustino Manetta	Adolfo Celi
Ferrari Crew Chief (Guido)	Enzo Fiermonte
Wallace Bennett	Donal O'Brien
Mrs. Stoddard	Rachel Kempson
Mr. Stoddard	Ralph Michael
Children's father in spa	Jean Michaud
Sportscaster	Alan Fordney
Tim Randolph	Phil Hill
Bob Turner	Graham Hill
Douglas McClendon	Bruce McLaren
John Hogarth	Richie Ginther
Mrs. Tim Randolph	Evans Evans
Victor	Bernard Cahier
Photographer David	John Bryson
Claude (at Delvaux factory)	Arthur Howard
American Boy	Alain Gerard
Doctor at Monza	Tiziano Feroldi
Rafael	Gilberto Mazzi
BBC Interviewer	Raymond Baxter
Ferrari Official	Eugenio Dragoni
Japanese Interpreter	Maasaki Asukai
Doctor at Monte Carlo	Albert Remy

James Garner, Toshiro Mifune

Yves Montand, Eva Marie Saint, Tiziano Feroldi
Above: James Garner, Brian Bedford

George Maharis, Arthur O'Connell

Katy Jurado, Sidney Blackmer

A COVENANT WITH DEATH

(WARNER BROS.) Executive Producer, William Conrad; Director, Lamont Johnson; Screenplay, Larry Marcus, Saul Levitt; Based on novel by Stephen Becker; Director of Photography, Robert Burks; Music, Leonard Rosenman; Assistant Director, Gil Kissel; In Technicolor. December release.

CAST

Ben Lewis	George Maharis
Rosemary	Laura Devon
Eulalia	Katy Jurado
Bryan Talbot	Earl Holliman
Judge Hockstadter	Arthur O'Connell
Colonel Oates	Sidney Blackmer
Harmsworth	Gene Hackman
Dietrich	John Anderson
Rafaela	Wende Wagner
Ignacio	Emilio Fernandez
Parmalee	Kent Smith
Musgrave	Lonny Chapman
Digby	Jose De Vega
Chillingworth	Larry D. Mann
Bruce Donnelly	Whit Bissell
Dr. Shilling	Russell Thorson

Earl Holliman, George Maharis. Above: George Maharis, Wende Wagner. Left: George Maharis, Laura Devon

ONE OF OUR SPIES IS MISSING

Producer, Boris Ingster; Director, E. Darrell Hallenbeck; Screenplay, Howard Rodman; Story, Henry Slesar; Director of Photography, Fred Koenekamp; Music, Gerald Fried; Assistant Director, Wilbur Mosier; Associate Producer, George M. Lehr; Executive Producer, Norman Felton; Supervising Producer, David Victor; The Man From U.N.C.L.E. Theme, Jerry Goldsmith; An Arena Production in Metrocolor. December release.

CAST

Napoleon Solo	Robert Vaughn
Illya Kuryakin	David McCallum
Mr Waverly	Leo G. Carroll
Sir Norman Swickert	Maurice Evans
Madame De Sala	Vera Miles
Joanna Sweet	Ann Elder
Jordin	Bernard Fox
Lorelei Lancer	Dolores Faith
Do Do	Anna Capri
Alexander Gritsky	Harry Davis
Wanda	Yvonne Craig
Olga	Monica Keating
Fleeton	Cal Bolder
Texan	Robert Easton
Phillip Bainbridge	James Doohan
Corvy	Ollie O'Toole
Steward	Antony Eustrel
Cat Man	Richard Peel
Pet Shop Owner	Barry Bernard

Ann Elder, Robert Vaughn, Leo G. Carroll, David McCallum. Below: Maurice Evans

Duke Howard, Dean Martin, Ann-Margret
Above: Dean Martin, Karl Malden

MURDERERS' ROW

(COLUMBIA) Producer, Irving Allen; Director, Henry Levin; Screenplay, Herbert Baker; Based on Novel by Donald Hamilton; Director of Photography, Sam Leavitt; Music, Lalo Schifrin, Howard Greenfield; Assistant Director, Ray Gosnell; A Meadway-Claude Production in Technicolor. December release.

CAST

Matt Helm	Dean Martin
Suzie	Ann-Margret
Julian Wall	Karl Malden
Coco Duquette	Camilla Sparv
MacDonald	James Gregory
Lovey Kravezit	Beverly Adams
Dr. Norman Solaris	Richard Eastham
Ironhead	Tom Reese
Billy Orcutt	Duke Howard
Guard	Ted Hartley
Capt. Deveraux	Marcel Hillaire
Miss January	Corinne Cole
Dr. Rogas	Robert Terry
Themselves	Dino, Desi and Billy

ANY WEDNESDAY

(WARNER BROS.) Producer, Julius J. Epstein; Director, Robert Ellis Miller; Screenplay, Julius J. Epstein; Based on play by Muriel Resnik; Director of Photography, Harold Lipstein; Music, George Duning; Song "Any Wednesday" by George Duning, Marilyn and Alan Bergman; Assistant Director, Victor Vallejo; Costumes, Dorothy Jeakins; In Technicolor. December release.

CAST

Ellen Gordon	Jane Fonda
John Cleves	Jason Robards
Cass Henderson	Dean Jones
Dorothy Cleves	Rosemary Murphy
Miss Linsley	Ann Prentiss
Felix	Jack Fletcher

Left: Jane Fonda, Jason Robards

Jason Robards, Rosemary Murphy, Jane Fonda, Dean Jones

son Robards, Rosemary Murphy. Above: Jane
Fonda, Dean Jones, Jason Robards

Jane Fonda, also above with Dean Jones

Shirley MacLaine, Michael Caine

GAMBIT

(UNIVERSAL) Producer, Leo L. Fuchs; Director, Ronald Neame; Screenplay, Jack Davies, Alvin Sargent; Based on novel by Sidney Carroll; Director of Photography, Clifford Stine; Gowns, Jean Louis; Music, Maurice Jarre; Assistant Director, Joseph Kenny; In Technicolor. December release.

CAST

Nicole	Shirley MacLaine
Harry	Michael Caine
Shahbandar	Herbert Lom
Ram	Roger C. Carmel
Abdul	Arnold Moss
Emile	John Abbott
Colonel Salim	Richard Angarola
Hotel Clerk	Maurice Marsac

Shirley MacLaine, Michael Caine, Herbert Lom
Above: Michael Caine, Shirley MacLaine, and top
with Arnold Moss, and left with John Abbott
Left Center: Shirley MacLaine

I DEAL IN DANGER

(20th CENTURY-FOX) Executive Producer and Director, Walter Grauman; Producer, Buck Houghton; Screenplay, Larry Cohen; Music, Lalo Schiffrin, Mullendore; Directors of Photography, Sam Leavitt, Kurt Grigoleit; Assistant Directors, Ray Taylor, Hans Sommer, Wolfgang Von Schiber; A Rogo Production in De-Luxe Color. December release.

CAST

David March	Robert Goulet
Suzanne Duchard	Christine Carere
Spauling	Donald Harron
Luber	Horst Frank
Elm	Werner Peters
Gretchen Hoffman	Eva Pflug
Ericka von Lindendorf	Christiane Schmidtmer
von Lindendorf	John van Dreelan
Richter	Hans Reiser
Baroness	Margit Saad
Eckhardt	Peter Capell
Brunner	Osman Ragheb
Gorleck	John Alderson
Stolnitz	Dieter Eppler
Becker	Dieter Kirchlechner
Dr. Zimmer	Manfred Andrae
Kraus	Alexander Allerson
Submarine Pilot	Paul Glawion

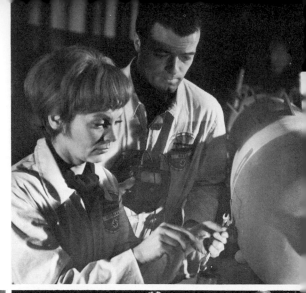

Christine Carere, Robert Goulet
Above: Horst Frank, Robert Goulet

Werner Peters, Robert Goulet, Christine Carere
Above: Robert Goulet, Eva Pflug, Horst Frank
Top: Eva Pflug, Robert Goulet

YOU'RE A BIG BOY NOW

(SEVEN ARTS) Producer, Phil Feldman; Direction and Screenplay, Francis Ford Coppola; Based on Novel by David Benedictus; Director of Photography, Andy Laszlo; Music, John Sebastian; Assistant Director, Larry Sturhahn; In PatheColor. December release.

CAST

Barbara Darling	Elizabeth Hartman
Margery Chanticleer	Geraldine Page
Miss Thing	Julie Harris
Bernard	Peter Kastner
I. H. Chanticleer	Rip Torn
Richard Mudd	Michael Dunn
Raef	Tony Bill
Amy	Karen Black
Policeman Francis Graf	Dolph Sweet
Kurt Doughty	Michael O'Sullivan

Left: Michael Dunn, Elizabeth Hartman

Rip Torn, Julie Harris. Above: Rip Torn, Geraldine Page, Karen Black, Peter Kastner

Elizabeth Hartman, Peter Kastner. Above: Dolph Sweet, Geraldine Page, Julie Harris

Jack Palance, Marie Gomez

Ralph Bellamy, Lee Marvin

Claudia Cardinale, Jack Palance

Burt Lancaster, Lee Marvin. Above: Claudia
Cardinale, Lee Marvin, Robert Ryan, Woody St

Burt Lancaster, Claudia Cardinale

Lee Marvin, Claudia Cardinale, Robert Ryan,
Woody Strode

THE PROFESSIONALS

(COLUMBIA) Direction and Screenplay, Richard Brooks; Based on novel "A Mule For The Marquesa" by Frank O'Rourke; Music, Maurice Jarre; Director of Photography, Conrad Hall; Assistant Director, Tom Shaw; A Pax Enterprises Production in Panavision and Technicolor. December release.

CAST

Dolworth	Burt Lancaster
Fardan	Lee Marvin
Ehrengard	Robert Ryan
Raza	Jack Palance
Maria	Claudia Cardinale
Grant	Ralph Bellamy
Jake	Woody Strode
Ortega	Joe De Santis
Fierro	Rafael Bertrand
Padillia	Jorge Martinez De Hoyos
Chiquita	Marie Gomez
Revolutionaries	Jose Chavez, Carlos Romero
Banker	Vaughn Taylor

Ralph Bellamy, Lee Marvin. Above: Burt Lancaster,
Robert Ryan, (L) Claudia Cardinale

THE SAND PEBBLES

(20th CENTURY-FOX) Producer-Director, Robert Wise; Associate Producer-Second Unit Director, Charles Maguire; Screenplay, Robert Anderson; From the novel by Richard McKenna; Director of Photography, Joseph MacDonald; Music, Jerry Goldsmith; Assistant Director, Ridgeway Callow; Costumes, Renie; In Panavision and DeLuxe Color. December release.

CAST

Holman	Steve McQueen
Frenchy	Richard Attenborough
Collins	Richard Crenna
Shirley	Candice Bergen
Maily	Marayat Andriane
Po-Han	Mako
Jameson	Larry Gates
Ensign Bordelles	Charles Robinson
Stawski	Simon Oakland
Harris	Ford Rainey
Bronson	Joe Turkel
Crosley	Gavin MacLeod
Shanahan	Joseph di Reda
Major Lin	Richard Loo
Franks	Barney Phillips
Restorff	Gus Trikonis
Perna	Shepherd Sanders
Farren	James Jeter
Jennings	Tom Middleton
Cho-Jen	Paul Chinpae
Chien	Tommy Lee
Haythorn	Stephen Jahn
Wilsey	Jay Allan Hopkins
Lamb	Steve Ferry
Wellbeck	Ted Fish
Coleman	Loren Janes
Waldron	Glenn Wilder

Charles Robinson, Richard Crenna, Barney Phillips
Top: Richard Attenborough, Steve McQueen

Steve McQueen, Candice Bergen,
Richard Crenna

ve McQueen, Candice Bergen. Above: Richard
Attenborough, Marayat Andriane

Steve McQueen, Richard Crenna
Above: Candice Bergen, Larry Gates

107

Chris Noel, Steve Franken, Gary Clarke
in "Wild Wild Winter"

David McCallum
in "The Big T.N.T. Show"

WILD WILD WINTER (Universal) Producer, Bart Patton; Director, Lennie Weinrib; Screenplay, David Malcolm; Director of Photography, Frank Phillips; Associate Producer, Harry R. Sherman; Costumes, Paula Giokaris; Assistant Director, Thomas J. Schmidt; Music, Jerry Long, Songs, Al Capps, Mary Dean, Chester Pitkin, Mark Gordon, Rictor Millrose, Tony Bruno, Ron Elliott; Sung by Dick and Dee Dee, Jackie and Gayle, The Astronauts, Jay and The Americans, The Beau Brummels; A Patton-Weinrib Production in Technicolor. January release. CAST: Gary Clarke, Chris Noel, Don Edmonds, Suzie Kaye, Les Brown, Jr., Vicky Albright, Jim Wellman, Steve Franken, Steve Rogers, Loren James, Jay and The Americans, Beau Brummels, Dick and Dee Dee, The Astronauts, Jackie and Gayle.

MARA OF THE WILDERNESS (Allied Artists) Producer, Brice Mack; Executive Producer, Lindsley Parsons; Director, Frank McDonald; Screenplay, Tom Blackburn; Story, Rod Scott; Music, Harry Bluestone; Director of Photography, Robert Wyckoff; Assistant Director, Wilson Shyer; A Unicorn Production in DeLuxe Color. January release. CAST: Adam West, Linda Saunders, Theo Marcuse, Denver Pyle, Sean McClory, Eve Brent, Roberto Contreras, Ed Kemmer, Stuart Walsh, Lelia Walsh.

CONQUERED CITY (American International) Director, Joseph Anthony. January release. CAST: David Niven, Ben Gazzara, Martin Balsam, Lea Massari, Michael Craig.

THE BIG T.N.T. SHOW (American International) Producer, Phil Spector; Director, Larry Peerce; Director of Photography, Robert Boatman; Assistant Director, Anthony Ray; Choreography, Ward Ellis; Associate Producer, Jerry Goldstein; Executive Producers, James H. Nicholson, Samuel Z. Arkoff, Henry G. Saperstein. January release. CAST: David McCallum, Roger Miller, Ray Charles and His Band, Joan Baez, Donovan, The Byrds, Petula Clark, The Lovin' Spoonful, The Ronettes, Ike and Tina Turner, Bo Diddley, The Modern Folk Quartet.

THE MONEY TRAP (MGM) Producers, Max E. Youngstein, David Karr; Director, Burt Kennedy; Screenplay, Walter Bernstein; From novel by Lionel White; Director of Photography, Paul Vogel; In Panavision. February release. CAST: Glenn Ford, Elke Sommer, Rita Hayworth, Ricardo Montalban, Joseph Cotten.

FRANKENSTEIN MEETS THE SPACE MONSTER (Allied Artists) Producer, Robert McCarty; Director, Robert Gaffney; Executive Producer, Alan V. Iselin; Original Story, George Garret; A Vernon Films-Seneca Production by Futurama. February release. CAST: Robert Reilly, James Karen, David Kerman, Nancy Marshall, Marilyn Hanold, Lou Cutell.

INDIAN PAINT (Eagle-International) Direction and Screenplay, Norman Foster; A Tejas Production in Color. February release. CAST: Johnny Crawford, Jay Silverheels, Robert Crawford, Jr., Pat Hogan.

Michael Craig, David Niven, Ben Gazzara
in "Conquered City"

Rita Hayworth, Glenn Ford
in "The Money Trap"

THE LOVE GODDESSES (Continental) Produced and Written by Saul J. Turell and Graeme Ferguson; Narrated by Carl King. January release. A documentary tribute to movie queens of the past and present using film clips.

WEEKEND OF FEAR (JD) Produced, Directed, and Written by Joe Danford; Director of Photography, Saul N. Leyton; Music, William H. Lockwood. February release. CAST: Micki Malone, Kenneth Washman, Tory Alburn, Ruth Trent, Dianne Danford, James Vaneck, Kurt Donsbach, Jill Banner.

RAT FINK (Cinema Distributors) A Genesis Production; Director, James Landis. February release. CAST: Schuyler Hayden.

"The Last Chapter"

Tom Drake, Jane Russell, Dana Andrews
in "Johnny Reno"

CURSE OF THE VOODOO (Allied Artists) Presented by Futurama Entertainment Corporation; A Gordon Film Production. February release. CAST: Bryant Haliday, Dennis Price, Lisa Daniely.

THE LAST CHAPTER (Ben-Lar) Producers and Directors, Benjamin and Lawrence Rothman; Screenplay, S. L. Schneiderman; Choral Selections by Farband Culture Chorus; Narrated by Theodore Bikel. February release. A documentary on the centuries of historical and cultural contributions made to Poland by its Jewish citizens.

FASTER, PUSSYCAT, KILL! KILL! (Eve) Producer, Eve Meyer; Director, Russ Meyer; Story, Jack Moran; Director of Photography, Walter Schenk; Music, Paul Sawtelle, Bert Shefter; Assistant Director, George Costello. February release. CAST: Tura Santana, Haji, Lori Williams, Susan Bernard, Stuart Lancaster, Paul Trinka, Dennis Busch, Ray Barlow, Mickey Foxx.

QUEEN OF BLOOD (American International) Producer, George Edwards; Direction and Screenplay, Curtis Harrington; Associate Producer, Stephanie Rothman; Director of Photography, Vilis Lapenieks; Music, Leonard Morand; In Pathecolor. March release. CAST: John Saxon, Basil Rathbone, Judi Meredith, Dennis Hopper, Florence Marly, Robert Boon, Don Eitner, Virgil Frye, Robert Porter, Terry Lee, Forrest Ackerman.

JOHNNY RENO (Paramount) Producer, A. C. Lyles; Director, R. G. Springsteen; Director of Photography, Hal Stine; Screenplay, Steve Fisher; Story, Steve Fisher, A. C. Lyles; Assistant Directors, Jim Rosenberger, Bob Jones; Music, Jimmie Haskell; In Techniscope and Technicolor. March release. CAST: Dana Andrews, Jane Russell, Lon Chaney, John Agar, Lyle Bettger, Tom Drake, Richard Arlen, Robert Lowery, Tracy Olsen, Paul Daniel, Dale Van Sickle.

YEAR OF THE HORSE (Dienstag-Orkin) Producers, Mildred Dienstag, Therese Orkin; Associate Producer, Jean Cantor; Direction and Screenplay, Irving Sunasky; Narrated by Mark Hubley; Director of Photography, Morton L. Heilig; In Eastman Color. March release. CAST: Gabriel Mason, Bradley Joe, Alvin Lum, Mary Mon Toy, Lorraine Wong, Mr. and Mrs. Thom, Mary Hui, Peter Wong, Dick Hanover, Burt Harris.

DEATHWATCH (Beverly) Producers, Leonard Nimoy, Vic Morrow; Director, Vic Morrow; Screenplay, Morrow and Barbara Turner; From Jean Genet play; Director of Photography, Vilis Lapenieks; Music, Gerald Fried. March release. CAST: Leonard Nimoy, Michael Forest, Paul Mazursky, Robert Ellenstein, Gavin McLeod.

John Saxon, Basil Rathbone
in "Queen Of Blood"

Henry Fonda, Peter Van Eyck
in "The Dirty Game"

BLOOD BATH (American International) Producer, Jack Hill; Direction and Screenplay, Jack Hill, Stephanie Rothman; Music, Mark Lowry; Director of Photography, Alfred Taylor. March release. CAST: William Campbell, Marrisa Mathes, Lori Saunders, Sandra Knight.

THE DIRTY GAME (American International) Executive Producer, Richard Hellman; Associate Producer, Eugene Tucherer; Directors, Terence Young, Christian-Jacque, Carlo Lizzani; Screenplay, Jo Eisinger; Music, Robert Mellin; Directors of Photography, Pierre Petit, Richard Angst, Enrico Menczer; An Unger Production. April release. CAST: Henry Fonda, Robert Ryan, Vittorio Gassman, Annie Girardot, Bourvil, Robert Hossein, Peter Van Eyck, Maria Grazia Buccela.

109

**Herman's Hermits
in "Hold On!"**

**Fernando Rey, Russ Tamblyn, Maria Granada
in "Son Of A Gunfighter"**

HOLD ON! (MGM) Producer, Sam Katzman; Director, Arthur Lubin; Screenplay, James B. Gordon; Director of Photography, Paul C. Vogel; Music, Fred Karger; Choreography, Wilda Taylor; Songs, P. F. Sloan, Steve Barri, Noel Tay, Fred Karger, Sid Wayne, Ben Weisman; Assistant Director, Al Shenberg; A Four Leaf Production in Panavision and Metrocolor. April release. CAST: Peter Blair Noone, Karl Green, Keith Hopwood, Derek Leckenby, Barry Whitwam, Shelley Fabares, Sue Ane Langdon, Herbert Anderson, Bernard Fox, Harry Hickox, Hortense Petra, Mickey Deems, Ray Kellogg, John Hart, Phil Arnold.

BILLY THE KID VS. DRACULA (Embassy) Producer, Carroll Case; Director, William Beaudine; Story and Screenplay, Carl K. Hittleman; Music, Raoul Kraushaar; Director of Photography, Lothrop Worth; Assistant Director, Max Stein; A Circle Productions Inc. presentation in Color. April release. CAST: Chuck Courtney, John Carradine, Melinda Plowman, Virginia Christine, Walter Janovitz, Bing Russell, Lennie Greer, Roy Barcroft, Olive Carey, Richard Reeves, Harry Carey, Jr., Hannie Landman, Marjorie Bennett, William Forrest, George Cisar, Max Klevin, Jack Williams, William Chalee, Charlita.

SON OF A GUNFIGHTER (MGM) Producer, Lester Welch; Director, Paul Landres; Screenplay, Clarke Reynolds; Director of Photography, Manuel Berenguer; Theme Music, Robert Mellin; Arrangements, Frank Barber; Associate Producers, Sam X. Abarbanel, Gregorio Sacristan; Assistant Director, Joe Ochoa; A Lester Welch Production in association with Zurbano Films; In Cinemascope and Metrocolor. May release. CAST: Russell Tamblyn, Kieron Moore, James Philbrook, Fernando Rey, Maria Granada, Aldo Sambrell, Antonio Casas, Barta Barri, Ralph Browne, Andy Anza, Fernando Hilbeck, Hector Quiroga, Carmen Tarrazo, Maria Jose Callado.

FAT SPY (Magna) Producer, Everett Rosenthal; Director, Joseph Cates; Screenplay, Matthew Andrews; Director of Photography, Joseph Brun; Music, Al Kasha, Joel Hirshhorn, Han Hunter; Assistant Director, George Goodman; A Phillip Productions and Magna Films Co-Production in Color. May release. CAST: Phyllis Diller, Jack E. Leonard, Brian Donlevy, Johnny Tillotson, Jayne Mansfield, Lauree Berger, Jordan Christopher, The Wild Ones, Lou Nelson, Toni Lee Shelley, Penny Roman, Chuck Alden, Eddie Wright, Tommy Graves, Tommy Trick, Linda Harrison, Deborah White, Toni Turner, Jill Bleidner, Tracy Vance, Jeanette Taylor.

**Estelita, John Lupton, Cal Bolder
in "Jesse James Meets Frankenstein's Daughter"**

**Skip Homeier, Joan Staley, Don Knotts
in "The Ghost And Mr. Chicken"**

JESSE JAMES MEETS FRANKENSTEIN'S DAUGHTER (Embassy) Producer, Carroll Case; Director, William Beaudine; Story and Screenplay, Carl H. Hittleman; Director of Photography, Lothrop Worth; Assistant Director, Max Stein; Music, Raoul Kraushaar; A Circle Productions Inc. presentation in Color. April release. CAST: John Lupton, Estelita, Cal Bolder, Narda Onyx, Steven Geray, Raymond Barnes, Jim Davis, Felipe Turich, Rosa Turich, Page Slattery, Nestor Paiva, Dan White, Roger Creed, Fred Stromsoe, William Faucett, Mark Norton.

THE GHOST AND MR. CHICKEN (Universal) Producer, Edward Montagne; Director, Alan Rafkin; Director of Photography, William Margulies; Assistant Directors, Phil Bowles, James Welch, Bill Gillmore; In Technicolor and Techniscope. May release. CAST: Don Knotts, Joan Staley, Liam Redmond, Dick Sargent, Skip Homeier, Reta Shaw, Lurene Tuttle, Philip Ober, Harry Hickox, George Chandler, Charles Lane, Jim Begg, Hope Summers, Hal Smith.

Rose Marie, Morey Amsterdam
in "Don't Worry, We'll Think Of A Title"

Jay North, Clint Walker, Sonia Sahani
in "Maya"

DON'T WORRY, WE'LL THINK OF A TITLE
(United Artists) Executive Producer, Aubrey
Schenck; Associate Producer, Hal Klein; Director,
Harmon Jones; Assistant Directors, Read Killgore,
C. M. "Babe" Florance; Director of Photography,
Brick Marquard; Screenplay, John Hart, Morey
Amsterdam; Additional Dialogue, George W.
Schenck, William Marks; Music, Richard DeSalle.
May release. CAST: Morey Amsterdam, Rose Marie,
Richard Deacon, Tim Herbert, Jackie Heller, Joey
Adams, Andy Albin, Michael Ford, January Jones.
Carmen Phillips, Henry Corden, Peggy Mondo,
Percy Helton, LaRue Farlow, Moe Howard, Yau
Shan Tung, Arline Hunter, Annazette, Gregg Am-
sterdam, Darryl Vaughan, Danny Thomas, Forrest
Tucker, Irene Ryan, Milton Berle, Steve Allen,
Carl Reiner, Slapsy Maxie Rosenbloom, Nick
Adams, Cliff Arquette.

NAVAJO RUN (American International) Producer-
Director, Johnny Seven; Screenplay, Jo Heims;
Director of Photography, Gregory Sandor; Music,
William Loose, Emil Cadkin; Co-Director, Miles
Dickson; Executive Producers, Mark Lipsky, Max-
well Rubin; Associate Producer, Edward J. Forsyth;
A Lorajon Production. May release. CAST: Johnny
Seven, Warren Kemmerling, Virginia Vincent, Ron
Soble.

MAYA (MGM) Producers, Frank King, Maurice
King; Associate Producers, Mary P. Murray, Her-
man King; Director, John Berry; Screenplay, John
Fante; Adaptation, Gilbert Wright; Based on story
"The Wild Elephant" by Jalal Din and Lois Roth;
Music, Riz Ortolani; Director of Photography, Gun-
ter Senftleben; Assistant Director, Bluey Hill; A
King Brothers Production in Technicolor and Pana-
vision. June release. CAST: Clint Walker, Jay
North, I. S. Johar, Sajid Kahn, Jairaj, Sonia Sahni,
Nana Palshikar, Uma Rao, Madhusdan Pathak.

THE CAT (Embassy) Producer-Director, Ellis
Kadison; Screenplay, William Redlin, Laird Koenig;
Associate Producer, William Schwartz; Director of
Photography, Monroe Askins; Music, Stan Worth;
Assistant Director, Grayson Rogers; A World-Cine
Associates Production in Pathecolor. June release.
CAST: Roger Perry, Peggy Ann Garner, Barry Coe,
Dwayne Redlin, George "Shug" Fisher, Ted Darby,
John Todd Roberts, Richard Webb, Les Bradley.

THE BLACK KLANSMAN (US Films) Producer-
Director, Ted V. Mikel; Screenplay, John T.
Wilson, Arthur A. Names; Presented by Joe Solo-
mon; An SGS Production. June release. CAST:
Richard Gilden, Rima Kutner, Harry Lovejoy, Max
Julien, Jake Deslonde, Jimmy Mack, Maureen Gaff-
ney, William McLenan, Gino De Agustino, Tex
Armstrong, Byrd Holland, Whitman Mayo, Frances
Williams, Ray Dennis.

Johnny Seven, Virginia Vincent
in "Navajo Run"

Roger Perry, Dwayne Redlin, Peggy Ann Garner,
Barry Coe in "The Cat"

INTIMACY (Goldstone) Producer, David Heilwell;
Director, Victor Stoloff. May release. CAST: Jack
Ging, Nancy Malone, Joan Blackman, Barry Sulli-
van, Jackie DeShannon.

INCIDENT AT PHANTOM HILL (Universal) Producer, Harry Tatelman; Director, Earl Bellamy;
Director of Photography, Manny Nathan; Assistant
Directors, Mike Moder, Wendell Franklin; In Technicolor. July release. CAST: Robert Fuller, Jocelyn Lane, Dan Duryea, Claude Akins, Noah Beery,
Linden Chiles, Tom Simcox, Paul Fix.

Nancy Kovack, Francisco Riquerio, Mike Henry in "Tarzan And The Valley Of Gold"

Yvonne De Carlo, Butch Patrick, Fred Gwynne, Al Lewis, Debbie Watson in "Munster, Go Home"

TARZAN AND THE VALLEY OF GOLD (American International) Producer, Sy Weintraub; Director, Robert Day; Associate Producer, Steve Shagan; Assistant Directors, Max Stein, Mario Cisneros; Director of Photography, Irving Lippman; Screenplay, Clair Huffaker; Based on characters created by Edgar Rice Burroughs; Music, Val Alexander; In Panavision and Color. July release. CAST: Mike Henry, David Opatashu, Manuel Padilla, Jr., Nancy Kovack, Don Megowan, Frank Brandstetter, Eduardo Noriega, Enrique Lucero, Francisco Riquerio.

THE TRAMPLERS (Embassy) Producer-Director, Albert Band; Screenplay, Ugo Liberatore, Albert Band; Based on novel "Guns of North Texas" by Will Cook; Director of Photography, Silvano Ippolito; Assistant Directors, Franco Prosperi, Francois Dupont-Midy; Costumes, Sergio Selli; In Color and Wide Screen. July release. CAST: Joseph Cotten, Gordon Scott, James Mitchum, Ilaria Occhini, Franco Nero, Emma Vannoni, Georges Lycan. Muriel Franklin, Aldo Cecconi, Franco Balducci, Claudio Gora, Romano Puppo, Dario Michaelis, Ivan Scratuglia, Carla Calo, Dino Desmond, Silla Bettina, Edith Peters.

MUNSTER, GO HOME (Universal) Producer, Joe Connelly; Director, Earl Bellamy; Director of Photography, Benny Kline; Assistant Directors, Dolph Zimmer, Wendell Franklin; In Technicolor. July release. CAST: Fred Gwynne, Yvonne De Carlo, Al Lewis, Butch Patrick, Debbie Watson, Terry-Thomas, Hermione Gingold, Jeanne Arnold, Robert Pine, Maria Lennard, Arthur Malet, Richard Dawson, John Carradine, Bernard Fox, Diane Chesney.

THE NIGHT OF THE GRIZZLY (Paramount) Producer, Burt Dunne; Director, Joseph Pevney; Screenplay, Warren Douglas; Assistant Director, Howard Roessel; Directors of Photography, Harold Lipstein, Loyal Griggs; Music, Leith Stevens; Song "Angela", Jay Livingston, Ray Evans; In Techniscope and Technicolor. July release. CAST: Clint Walker, Martha Hyer, Keenan Wynn, Nancy Kulp, Kevin Brodie, Ellen Corby, Jack Elam, Ron Ely, Med Flory, Leo Gordon, Don Haggerty, Sammy Jackson, Victoria Paige Meyerink, Candy Moore, Regis Toomey.

THE ENDLESS SUMMER (Cinema 5) A documentary about the seemingly casual and carefree world of surfing around the world. Produced, Directed, Photographed, Documented, and Narrated by Bruce Brown. Musical Theme written and played by The Sandals; Filmed in Color. July release. CAST: Mike Hyson, Robert August.

Audie Murphy, Buster Crabbe in "Arizona Raiders"

Gordon Scott, James Mitchum in "The Tramplers"

ARIZONA RAIDERS (Columbia) Producer, Grant Whytock; Director, William Witney; Screenplay, Alex Gottlieb, Mary and Willard Willingham; Story, Frank Gruber, Richard Schayer; An Admiral Pictures Production in Technicolor and Techniscope. July release. CAST: Audie Murphy, Michael Dante, Ben Cooper, Buster Crabbe, Gloria Talbot.

A PILGRIMAGE FOR PEACE: POPE PAUL VI VISITS AMERICA (Roberts) Producer, Joseph L. Roberts; Written and Directed by Carl Allensworth; Narrated by Phil Tonkin; In Color. July release. A documentary of the Pope's visit to New York in 1965.

Clint Walker, Martha Hyer, Kevin Brodie
in "The Night Of The Grizzly"

Rip Torn, Dorothy Provine, David McCallum
in "One Spy Too Many"

THAT MAN FLINTSTONE (Columbia) Formerly "The Man Called Flintstone." Produced and Directed by Joseph Barbera and William Hanna; Screenplay, Harvey Bullock, Ray Allen; Music, Marty Paich, Ted Nichols; Songs, John McCarthy, Doug Goodwin; "Pensate Amore" sung by Louis Prima; Animation Director, Charles A. Nichols; Filmed in Eastman Color by Pathe. August release. CAST: Voices of Alan Reed, Mel Blanc, Jean Vander Pyl, Gerry Johnson, Don Messick, Janet Waldo, Paul Frees, Harvey Korman, John Stephenson, June Foray.

BIRDS DO IT (Columbia) Producer, Stanley Colbert; Director, Andrew Marton; Screenplay, Arnie Kogen, Art Arthur; Story, Leonard Kaufman; Executive Producer, Ivan Tors; Music, Samuel Matlovsky; Title Song, Howard Greenfield, Jack Keller; Director of Photography, Howard Winner; Assistant Director, James Gordon MacLean: In Pathe Color. August release. CAST: Soupy Sales, Tab Hunter, Arthur O'Connell, Edward Andrews, Doris Dowling, Beverly Adams, Louis Quinn, Frank Nastasi, Burt Taylor, Courtney Brown, Russell Saunders, Julian Voloshin, Bob Bersell, Warren Day, Jay Laskay, Burt Leigh.

ONE SPY TOO MANY (MGM) Producer, David Victor; Director, Joseph Sargent; Screenplay, Dean Hargrove; Developed by Sam Rolfe; Music, Gerald Fried; Director of Photography, Fred Koenekamp; Executive Producer, Norman Felton; Associate Producer, Mort Abrahams; Assistant Director, E. Darrell Hallenbeck; "The Man From U.N.C.L.E." Theme, Jerry Goldsmith; An Arena Production in Metrocolor. September release. CAST: Robert Vaughn, David McCallum, Rip Torn, Dorothy Provine, Leo G. Carroll, Yvonne Craig, David Opatoshu, David Sheiner, Donna Michelle, Leon Lontoc, Robert Karnes, Clarke Gordon, James Hong, Cal Bolder, Carole Williams, Teru Shimada, Arthur Wong, Robert Gibbons.

SMOKY (20th Century-Fox) Producer, Aaron Rosenberg; Director, George Sherman; Screenplay, Harold Medford; Based on screenplay by Lillie Hayward, Dwight Cummins, Dorothy Yost; From novel by Will James; Music, Leith Stevens; Title Song by Ernie Sheldon and Leith Stevens; Sung by Hank Thompson; Additional Songs by Hoyt Axton; Director of Photography, Jack Swain; Assistant Director, Ted Schilz; In DeLuxe Color. September release. CAST: Fess Parker, Diana Hyland, Katy Jurado, Hoyt Axton, Robert Wilke, Armando Silvestre, Jose Hector Galindo, Jorge Martinez de Hoyos, Ted White, Chuck Roberson, Robert Terhune, Jack Williams.

Bruce Brown
in "The Endless Summer"

Beverly Adams, Soupy Sales, Frank Nastasi
in "Birds Do It"

THE STREET IS MY BEAT (Emerson) Producers, Alan P. Magerman, Jack Paller, Irvin Berwick; Director, Irvin Berwick; Screenplay, Harold Livingston, Berwick; Director of Photography, Joseph V. Mascelli; Music, Harrose; Title Song sung by Marilyn Michaels. August release. CAST: Shary Marshall, Todd Lasswell, John Harmon, Anne MacAdams, Tom Irish, Beverly Oliver, Bob Brown, Susan Cummings, J. Edward McKinley.

RUN, APPALOOSA, RUN (Buena Vista) Producer, Walt Disney; Co-Producer-Director, Larry Lansburgh; Screenplay, Janet Lansburgh; Based on Story by Larry Lansburgh; Narration and Title Song sung by Rex Allen; In Technicolor. September release. CAST: Adele Palacios, Wilbur Plaugher, Jerry Gatlin, Walter Cloud, Ray Patnaude.

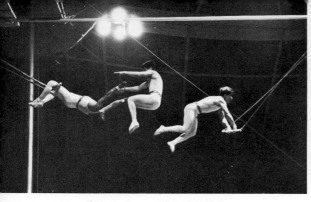

"Rings Around The World"

Edward Albert, Anthony Perkins
in "Violent Journey"

RINGS AROUND THE WORLD (Columbia) Producer-Director, Gilbert Gates; Screenplay, Victor Wolfson; Music, Jacques Belasco; In Eastman Color. September release. Narrated by Don Ameche.

THE PLAINSMAN (Universal) Producer, Richard E. Lyons; Director, David Lowell Rich; Screenplay, Michael Blankfort; Director of Photography, Bud Thackery; Associate Producer, Jack Leewood; Costumes, Helen Colvig; Assistant Director, Edward K. Dodds; Music, Johnny Williams; In color. September release. CAST: Don Murray, Guy Stockwell, Abby Dalton, Bradford Dillman. Henry Silva, Simon Oakland, Leslie Nielsen, Edward Binns, Michael Evans, Percy Rodriguez, Terry Wilson, Walter Burke, Emily Banks.

RAT PFINK AND BOO BOO (Craddock) Produced, Directed, Photographed, and Written by Ray Dennis Steckler; Screenplay, Ronald Haydock; From Story by Steckler; Music, Henry Price; A Morgan Pictures production. September release. CAST: Carolyn Brandt, Vin Saxon, Titus Moede, George Caldwell, Mike Kannon, James Bowie, Keith Wester, Mary Jo Curtis, Romeo Barrymore, Dean Danger, Kogar.

VIOLENT JOURNEY (American International) Formerly "The Fool Killer"; Producer, David Friedkin; Executive Producer, Worthington Miner; Director, Servando Gonzalez; Screenplay, Morton Fine, David Friedkin; Based on novel by Helen Eustis; Director of Photography, Alex Phillips, Jr.; Music, Gustavo C. Carreon; Associate Producers, Harrison Starr, Alfred Markim; Costumes, Dorothy Jeakins. October release. CAST: Anthony Perkins, Dana Elcar, Edward Albert, Henry Hull, Salome Jens, Charlotte Jones, Arnold Moss, Sindee Anne Richards, Frances Gaar, Wendell Phillips.

THAT TENNESSEE BEAT (20th Century-Fox) Producer-Director, Richard Brill; Screenplay, Paul Schneider; Director of Photography, Jack Steeley; Songs, Merle Travis; Theme Song sung by Merle Travis; A Robert L. Lippert Presentation. October release. CAST: Sharon DeBord, Earl Richards, Dolores Faith, Minnie Pearl, Merle Travis, Jim Reader, Cecil Scaife, Rink Hardin, Lightnin' Chance, Sam Tarpley, Buddy Mize, Ed Livingston, Ernest Keller, Maurice Dembsky, The Statler Brothers, Boots Randolph, Stony Mountain Cloggers, Pete Drake.

Adele Palacios
in "Run, Apaloosa, Run"

Don Murray, Abby Dalton, Guy Stockwell
in "The Plainsman"

MOONLIGHTING WIVES (Craddock) Direction and Screenplay, Joe Sarno; Director of Photography, Jerry Kalogeratos; Music, Stan Free; A Morgan Pictures production in DeLuxe Color. September release. CAST: Diane Vivienne, Joan Nash, John Aristedes, Fatima.

NIGHT TRAIN TO MUNDO FINE (Hollywood Star) Producers, Anthony Cardoza, Coleman Francis; Direction and Screenplay, Coleman Francis; Director of Photography, Herb Roberts; Music, John Bath; Title Song, Ray Gregory. November release. CAST: Coleman Francis. Anthony Cardoza, Harold Saunders, John Carradine, John Morrison, George Prince, Lanell Cado, Tom Hanson, Julian Baker, Charles Harter, Elaine Gibford, Bruce Love, Nick Raymond, Clarence Walker, Richard Lance.

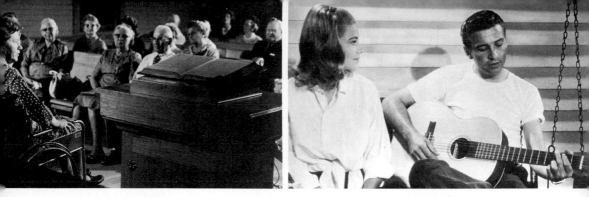

Minnie Pearl
in "That Tennessee Beat"

Mary Frann, Waylon Jennings
in "Nashville Rebel"

DOOR-TO-DOOR MANIAC (American International) Producer, James Ellsworth; Director, Bill Karn; Screenplay, M. K. Forester; Based on story by Palmer Thompson; Adapted by Robert Joseph; Director of Photography, Carl Guthrie; Music, Gene Kauer; Songs, Johnny Cash; Executive Producer, Ludlow Flower; Associate Producer, William Mace. November release. CAST: Johnny Cash, Donald Woods, Cay Forester, Pamela Mason, Midge Ware, Vic Tayback, Ronnie Howard, Merle Travis, Howard Wright, Norma Varden.

THE NAVY VS. THE NIGHT MONSTERS (Realart) Producer, George Edwards; Direction and Screenplay, Michael Hoey; Director of Photography, Stanley Cortez; Assistant Director, Dick Dixon; In DeLuxe Color. November release. CAST: Mamie Van Doren, Anthony Eisley, Pamela Mason, Bill Gray, Bobby Van, Walter Sande, Edward Faulkner, Phillip Terry.

WOMEN OF THE PREHISTORIC PLANET (Realart) Producer, George Edwards; Direction and Screenplay, Arthur Pierce; Director of Photography, Archie Dalzell; Assistant Director, Jack Voglin; In DeLuxe Color. November release. CAST: Wendell Corey, Keith Larsen, John Agar, Paul Gilbert, Merry Anders, Irene Tsu.

NASHVILLE REBEL (American International) Producer, Fred A. Niles; Director, Jay J. Sheridan; Screenplay, Ira Kerns, Jay J. Sheridan; Story, Click Weston; Associate Producer, Jane Dowden; Music, Robert Blanford; Director of Photography, John Elsenback; Presented by Fred A. Niles Productions in association with Show Biz Inc. December release. CAST: Waylon Jennings, Tex Ritter, Sonny James, Faron Young, Loretta Lynn, Porter Wagoner, The Wilburn Brothers, Henny Youngman, Gordon Oas-Heim, Mary Fran, Ce Ce Whitney, Cousin Jody, Archie Campbell.

HALLUCINATION GENERATION (American International) Executive Producer, Robert D. Weinbach; Producer, Nigel Cox; Direction and Screenplay. Edward Mann; Associate Producers, Jerome A. Siegel, Morton M. Rosenfeld; Music, Bernardo Segall; Director of Photography, Francisco Sempere; Presented by Herbert R. Steinmann. December release. CAST: George Montgomery, Danny Stone, Tom Baker, Renate Kasche, Marianne Kanter, Steve Rowland.

Jose Spinosa, Armando Silvestre, Glenn Ford,
Stella Stevens in "Rage"

George Montgomery
in "Hallucination Generation"

RAGE (Columbia) Producer-Director, Gilberto Gazcon; Screenplay, Teddi Sherman, Gilberto Gazcon, Fernando Mendez; Executive Producer, Richard Goldstone; A Cinematografica Jalisco-Joseph M. Schenck Enterprises Production in Color. December release. CAST: Glenn Ford, Stella Stevens, David Reynoso, Armando Silvestre, Ariadna Welter, Jose Elias Moreno, Dacia Gonzalez, Pancho Cordova, Susana Cabrera, David Silva, Quentin Bulnes, Valentin Trujillo.

THE CHELSEA GIRLS (Film-makers') Produced, Directed, Written, and Filmed by Andy Warhol; In black and white, and color. December release. CAST: Nico, Gerard Malanga, Pope Ondine, Ingrid Superstar, Marie Menken, International Velvet, The Dutchess, Mario Montez.

115

Alan Arkin

Candice Bergen

Sandy Dennis

Brian Bedford

PROMISING PERSONALITIES OF 1966

Alex Cord

Vanessa Redgrave

Camilla Sparv

Christopher Jordan

Sean Garrison

Jessica Walter

Raquel Welch

Guy Stockwell

118

Lynn Redgrave

| Mary Pickford | Spencer Tracy | Norma Shearer | James Stewart | Bette Davis |

ACADEMY AWARD WINNERS

(1) Best Picture, (2) Actor, (3) Actress, (4) Supporting Actor, (5) Supporting Actress, (6) Director, (7) Special Award, (8) Best Foreign Film

1927-28: (1) "Wings", (2) Emil Jannings in "The Way Of All Flesh", (3) Janet Gaynor in "Seventh Heaven", (6) Frank Borzage for "Seventh Heaven", (7) Charles Chaplin.

1928-29: (1) "Broadway Melody", (2) Warner Baxter in "Old Arizona", (3) Mary Pickford in "Coquette", (6) Frank Lloyd for "The Divine Lady".

1929-30: (1) "All Quiet On The Western Front", (2) George Arliss in "Disraeli", (3) Norma Shearer in "The Divorcee", (6) Lewis Milestone for "All Quiet On The Western Front".

1930-31: (1) "Cimarron", (2) Lionel Barrymore in "A Free Soul", (3) Marie Dressler in "Min and Bill", (6) Norman Taurog for "Skippy".

1931-32: (1) "Grand Hotel", (2) Fredric March in "Dr. Jekyll and Mr. Hyde", (3) Helen Hayes in "The Sin of Madelon Claudet", (6) Frank Borzage for "Bad Girl".

1932-33: (1) "Cavalcade", (2) Charles Laughton in "The Private Life of Henry VIII", (3) Katharine Hepburn in "Morning Glory", (6) Frank Lloyd for "Cavalcade".

1934: (1) "It Happened One Night", (2) Clark Gable in "It Happened One Night", (3) Claudette Colbert in "It Happened One Night", (6) Frank Capra for "It Happened One Night", (7) Shirley Temple.

1935: (1) "Mutiny On The Bounty", (2) Victor McLaglen in "The Informer", (3) Bette Davis in "Dangerous", (6) John Ford for "The Informer", (7) D. W. Griffith.

1936: (1) "The Great Ziegfeld", (2) Paul Muni in "The Story of Louis Pasteur", (3) Luise Rainer, in "The Great Ziegfeld", (4) Walter Brennan in "Come and Get It", (5) Gale Sondergaard in "Anthony Adverse", (6) Frank Capra for "Mr. Deeds Goes To Town".

1937: (1) "The Life of Emile Zola", (2) Spencer Tracy in "Captains Courageous", (3) Luise Rainer in "The Good Earth", (4) Joseph Schildkraut in "The Life of Emile Zola", (5) Alice Brady in "In Old Chicago", (6) Leo McCarey for "The Awful Truth", (7) Mack Sennett, Edgar Bergen.

1938: (1) "You Can't Take It With You", (2) Spencer Tracy in "Boys Town", (3) Bette Davis in "Jezebel", (4) Walter Brennan in "Kentucky", (5) Fay Bainter in "Jezebel", (6) Frank Capra for "You Can't Take It With You", (7) Deanna Durbin, Mickey Rooney, Harry M. Warner, Walt Disney.

1939: (1) "Gone With The Wind", (2) Robert Donat in "Goodbye, Mr. Chips", (3) Vivien Leigh in "Gone With The Wind", (4) Thomas Mitchell in "Stagecoach", (5) Hattie McDaniel in "Gone With The Wind", (6) Victor Fleming for "Gone With The Wind", (7) Douglas Fairbanks, Judy Garland.

1940: (1) "Rebecca", (2) James Stewart in "The Philadelphia Story", (3) Ginger Rogers in "Kitty Foyle", (4) Walter Brennan in "The Westerner", (5) Jane Darwell in "The Grapes of Wrath", (6) John Ford for "The Grapes of Wrath", (7) Bob Hope.

1941: (1) "How Green Was My Valley", (2) Gary Cooper in "Sergeant York", (3) Joan Fontaine in "Suspicion", (4) Donald Crisp in "How Green Was My Valley", (5) Mary Astor in "The Great Lie", (6) John Ford for "How Green Was My Valley", (7) Leopold Stokowski, Walt Disney.

1942: (1) "Mrs. Miniver", (2) James Cagney in "Yankee Doodle Dandy", (3) Greer Garson in "Mrs. Miniver", (4) Van Heflin in "Johnny Eager", (5) Teresa Wright in "Mrs. Miniver", (6) William Wyler for "Mrs. Miniver", (7) Charles Boyer, Noel Coward.

1943: (1) "Casablanca", (2) Paul Lukas in "Watch On The Rhine", (3) Jennifer Jones in "The Song of Bernadette", (4) Charles Coburn in "The More The Merrier", (5) Katina Paxinou in "For Whom The Bell Tolls", (6) Michael Curtiz for "Casablanca".

1944: (1) "Going My Way", (2) Bing Crosby in "Going My Way", (3) Ingrid Bergman in "Gaslight", (4) Barry Fitzgerald in "Going My Way", (5) Ethel Barrymore in "None But The Lonely Heart", (6) Leo McCarey for "Going My Way", (7) Margaret O'Brien, Bob Hope.

1945: (1) "The Lost Weekend", (2) Ray Milland in "The Lost Weekend", (3) Joan Crawford in "Mildred Pierce", (4) James Dunn in "A Tree Grows in Brooklyn", (5) Anne Revere in "National Velvet", (6) Billy Wilder for "The Lost Weekend", (7) Walter Wanger, Peggy Ann Garner.

1946: (1) "The Best Years of Our Lives", (2) Fredric March in "The Best Years of Our Lives", (3) Olivia de Havilland in "To Each His Own", (4) Harold Russell in "The Best Years of Our Lives", (5) Anne Baxter in "The Razor's Edge", (6) William Wyler for "The Best Years of Our Lives", (7) Laurence Olivier, Harold Russell, Ernst Lubitsch, Claude Jarman, Jr.

1947: (1) "Gentleman's Agreement", (2) Ronald Colman in "A Double Life", (3) Loretta Young in "The Farmer's Daughter", (4) Edmund Gwenn in "Miracle On 34th Street", (5) Celeste Holm in "Gentleman's Agreement", (6) Elia Kazan for "Gentleman's Agreement", (7) James Baskette.

1948: (1) "Hamlet", (2) Laurence Olivier in "Hamlet", (3) Jane Wyman in "Johnny Belinda", (4) Walter Huston in "The Treasure of The Sierra Madre", (5) Claire Trevor in "Key Largo", (6) John Huston for "The Treasure of The Sierra Madre", (7) Ivan Jandl, Sid Grauman, Adolph Zukor, Walter Wanger.

1949: (1) "All The King's Men", (2) Broderick Crawford in "All The King's Men", (3) Olivia de Havilland in "The Heiress", (4) Dean Jagger in "Twelve O'Clock High", (5) Mercedes McCambridge in "All The King's Men", (6) Joseph L. Mankiewicz for "A Letter To Three Wives", (7) Bobby Driscoll, Fred Astaire, Cecil B. DeMille, Jean Hersholt.

1950: (1) "All About Eve", (2) Jose Ferrer in "Cyrano de Bergerac", (3) Judy Holliday in "Born Yesterday", (4) George Sanders in "All About Eve", (5) Josephine Hull in "Harvey", (6) Joseph L. Mankiewicz for "All About Eve", (7) George Murphy, Louis B. Mayer.

Van Heflin **Vivien Leigh** **Bing Crosby** **Joan Fontaine** **James Dunn**

1951: (1) "An American in Paris", (2) Humphrey Bogart in "The African Queen", (3) Vivien Leigh in "A Streetcar Named Desire", (4) Karl Malden in "A Streetcar Named Desire", (5) Kim Hunter in "A Streetcar Named Desire", (6) George Stevens for "A Place In The Sun", (7) Gene Kelly.

1952: (1) "The Greatest Show On Earth", (2) Gary Cooper in "High Noon", (3) Shirley Booth in "Come Back, Little Sheba", (4) Anthony Quinn in "Viva Zapata", (5) Gloria Grahame in "The Bad and the Beautiful", (6) John Ford for "The Quiet Man", (7) Joseph M. Schenck, Merian C. Cooper, Harold Lloyd, Bob Hope, George Alfred Mitchell.

1953: (1) "From Here To Eternity", (2) William Holden in "Stalag 17", (3) Audrey Hepburn in "Roman Holiday", (4) Frank Sinatra in "From Here To Eternity", (5) Donna Reed in "From Here To Eternity", (6) Fred Zinnemann for "From Here To Eternity", (7) Pete Smith.

1954: (1) "On The Waterfront", (2) Marlon Brando in "On The Waterfront", (3) Grace Kelly in "The Country Girl", (4) Edmond O'Brien in "The Barefoot Contessa", (5) Eva Marie Saint in "On The Waterfront", (6) Elia Kazan for "On The Waterfront", (7) Greta Garbo, Danny Kaye, Jon Whitely, Vincent Winter, (8) "Gate of Hell."

1955: (1) "Marty", (2) Ernest Borgnine in "Marty", (3) Anna Magnani in "The Rose Tattoo", (4) Jack Lemmon in "Mister Roberts", (5) Jo Van Fleet in "East of Eden", (6) Delbert Mann for "Marty", (7) "Samurai."

1956: (1) "Around The World in 80 Days", (2) Yul Brynner in "The King and I", (3) Ingrid Bergman in "Anastasia", (4) Anthony Quinn in "Lust For Life", (5) Dorothy Malone in "Written On The Wind", (6) George Stevens for "Giant", (7) Eddie Cantor, (8) "La Strada."

1957: (1) "The Bridge On The River Kwai", (2) Alec Guinness in "The Bridge On The River Kwai", (3) Joanne Woodward in "The Three Faces of Eve", (4) Red Buttons in "Sayonara", (5) Miyoshi Umeki in "Sayonara", (6) David Lean for "The Bridge On The River Kwai", (7) Charles Brackett, B. B. Kahane, Gilbert M. (Broncho Billy) Anderson, (8) "The Nights of Cabiria."

1958: (1) "Gigi", (2) David Niven in "Separate Tables", (3) Susan Hayward in "I Want To Live", (4) Burl Ives in "The Big Country", (5) Wendy Hiller in "Separate Tables", (6) Vincente Minnelli for "Gigi", (7) Maurice Chevalier, (8) "My Uncle."

1959: (1) "Ben-Hur", (2) Charlton Heston in "Ben-Hur", (3) Simone Signoret in "Room At The Top", (4) Hugh Griffith in "Ben-Hur", (5) Shelley Winters in "The Diary of Anne Frank", (6) William Wyler for "Ben-Hur", (7) Lee de Forest, Buster Keaton, (8) "Black Orpheus."

1960: (1) "The Apartment", (2) Burt Lancaster in "Elmer Gantry", (3) Elizabeth Taylor in "Butterfield 8", (4) Peter Ustinov in "Spartacus", (5) Shirley Jones in "Elmer Gantry", (6) Billy Wilder for "The Apartment", (7) Gary Cooper, Stan Laurel, Hayley Mills, (8) "The Virgin Spring."

1961: (1) "West Side Story", (2) Maximilian Schell in "Judgment At Nuremberg", (3) Sophia Loren in "Two Women", (4) George Chakiris in "West Side Story", (5) Rita Moreno in "West Side Story", (6) Robert Wise for "West Side Story", (7) Jerome Robbins, Fred L. Metzler, (8) "Through A Glass Darkly."

1962: (1) 'Lawrence of Arabia", (2) Gregory Peck in "To Kill A Mockingbird", (3) Anne Bancroft in "The Miracle Worker", (4) Ed Begley in "Sweet Bird of Youth", (5) Patty Duke in "The Miracle Worker", (6) David Lean for "Lawrence of Arabia", (8) "Sundays and Cybele."

1963: (1) "Tom Jones", (2) Sidney Poitier in "Lilies of The Field", (3) Patricia Neal in "Hud", (4) Melvyn Douglas in "Hud", (5) Margaret Rutherford in "The V.I.P.'s", (6) Tony Richardson for "Tom Jones", (8) "8½."

1964: (1) "My Fair Lady", (2) Rex Harrison in "My Fair Lady", (3) Julie Andrews in "Mary Poppins", (4) Peter Ustinov in "Topkapi", (5) Lila Kedrova in "Zorba The Greek", (6) George Cukor for "My Fair Lady", (7) William Tuttle, (8) "Yesterday, Today and Tomorrow."

1965: (1) "The Sound Of Music", (2) Lee Marvin in "Cat Ballou", (3) Julie Christie in "Darling", (4) Martin Balsam in "A Thousand Clowns", (5) Shelley Winters in "A Patch Of Blue", (6) Robert Wise for "The Sound Of Music", (7) Bob Hope, (8) "The Shop On Main Street".

Mary Astor **Laurence Olivier** **Teresa Wright** **Broderick Crawford** **Katina Paxinou**

Julie Christie
in "Darling"

Lee Marvin
in "Cat Ballou"

Martin Balsam
in "A Thousand Clowns"

Shelley Winters
in "A Patch Of Blue"

ACADEMY AWARD WINNERS FOR 1965

Ida Kaminska
in
"THE SHOP ON MAIN STREET"

FOREIGN FILMS

THE SHOP ON MAIN STREET

(PROMINENT) Directors, Jan Kadar, Elmar Klos; A Barrandov Studios Production. January release.

CAST

Tono Brtko	Josef Kroner
Rosalie Lautmann	Ida Kaminska
Evelina Brtko	Hana Slivkova
Marcus Kolkotsky	Frantisek Zvarik
Rose Kolkotsky	Helen Zvarikova
Imro Kuchar	Martin Holly
Katz	Martin Gregor

Ida Kaminska. Right: Josef Kroner
Top: Josef Kroner, Ida Kaminska

da Kaminska. Top: Hana Slivkova, Josef
Kroner, Helen Zvarikova, Frantisek Zvarik

Josef Kroner (R)

WHERE THE SPIES ARE

(MGM) Executive Producer, Stephen Pallos; Producer-Director, Val Guest; Screenplay, Val Guest, Wolf Mankowitz; Based on novel "Passport To Oblivion" by James Leasor; Music, Brian Fahey; In Panavision and Color. January release.

CAST

Dr. Jason Love	David Niven
Vikki	Francoise Dorleac
Col. MacGillivray	John LeMesurier
Rosser	Cyril Cusack
Farouk	Eric Pohlmann
Josef	Richard Marner
Simmias	Paul Stassino
First Man	George Pravda
Mr. Kahn	Reginald Beckwith
Assassin	George Mikell
Parkington	Nigel Davenport
Second Man	Gabor Baraker
Stanislaus	Ronald Radd

Francois Dorleac. Above: David Niven (L)

126

David Niven, unidentified, Nigel Davenport. Above (and top): Francois Dorleac, David Niven

McGUIRE, GO HOME!

(CONTINENTAL) Producer, Betty E. Box; Director, Ralph Thomas; Screenplay, Ian Stuart Black; Music, Angelo Lavagnino; Director of Photography, Ernest Steward; Assistant Directors, Simon Relph, Leon Lenoir; Costumes, Yvonne Caffin; Executive Producer, Earl St. John; A J. Arthur Rank Production. January release.

CAST

Major McGuire	Dirk Bogarde
Haghios	George Chakiris
Juno Kozani	Susan Strasberg
Baker	Denholm Elliott
Skyros	Gregoire Aslan
Emile	Colin Campbell
Dr. Andros	Joseph Furst
Mrs. Andros	Katherine Kath
Prinos	George Pastell
Alkis	Paul Stassino
Colonel Park	Nigel Stock

Susan Strasberg, Dirk Bogarde. Above (L): Susan Strasberg. Right: Susan Strasberg, Dirk Bogarde. Top: George Chakiris, Joseph Furst, Susan Strasberg

Wilfrid Hyde-White, Daliah Lavi, Dennis Price

Shirley Eaton, Hugh O'Brian, Daliah Lavi

TEN LITTLE INDIANS

(SEVEN ARTS) Producer, Oliver A. Unger; Director, George Pollock; Screenplay, Peter Yeldman, Peter Welbeck; Music, Malcolm Lockyer; Director of Photography, Ernie Steward; Assistant Director, Barrie Melrose; Based on novel by Agatha Christie; A Tenlit Films Production in association with Harry M. Popkin. January release.

CAST

Hugh Lombard	Hugh O'Brian
Ann Clyde	Shirley Eaton
Mike Raven	Fabian
General Mandrake	Leo Genn
William Blore	Stanley Holloway
Frau Grohmann	Marianne Hoppe
Judge Cannon	Wilfrid Hyde-White
Ilona Bergen	Daliah Lavi
Dr. Armstrong	Dennis Price
Herr Grohmann	Mario Adorf

Mario Adorf, Hugh O'Brian, Stanley Holloway, Dennis Price, Shirley Eaton, Wilfrid Hyde-White
Above: Hugh O'Brian, Stanley Holloway
Left: Shirley Eaton, Hugh O'Brian

SPY IN YOUR EYE

(AMERICAN INTERNATIONAL) Director, Vittorio Sala; Screenplay, Romano Ferraro, Adriano Baracco, Adriano Bolzoni; In Pathecolor. January release.

CAST

Paula Krauss	Pier Angeli
Colonel Lancaster	Dana Andrews
Bert Morris	Brett Halsey

Right: Dana Andrews, Brett Halsey

TIME OF INDIFFERENCE

(CONTINENTAL) Producer, Franco Cristaldi; Direction and Screenplay, Francesco Maselli; Adapted from Alberto Moravia's novel by Suso Cecchi D'Amico; Director of Photography, Gianni Di Venanzo; Music, Giovanni Fusco; Costumes, Marcel Escoffier; A Walter Reade-Sterling release of a Lux-Ultra-Vides (Roma) Film. January release.

CAST

Leo	Rod Steiger
Carla	Claudia Cardinale
Lisa	Shelley Winters
Mariagrazia	Paulette Goddard
Michele	Tomas Milian

...helley Winters, Paulette Goddard, Rod Steiger, ...Claudia Cardinale. Above: Shelley Winters, ...as Milian. Right: Rod Steiger, Paulette Goddard

THE RAILROAD MAN

(CONTINENTAL) Produced, Directed, and Written by Pietro Germi. January release.

CAST

Andrea Marcocci .... Pietro Germi
Sara Marcocci .... Luisa Della Noce
Giulia .... Sylva Koscina
Liverani .... Saro Urzi
Marcello .... Carlo Giuffre
Renato .... Renato Speziali

Pietro Germi (also above), Sylva Koscina,
Luisa Della Noce

Pietro Germi (L), Saro Urzi (R)
Above: Pietro Germi, Luisa Della Noce

WALK IN THE SHADOW

(CONTINENTAL) Producer, Michael Relph; Director, Basil Dearden; Screenplay, Janet Green, John McCormick; Music, William Alwyn; Director of Photography, Otto Heller; Assistant Director, Anthony Waye; A J. Arthur Rank Production. February release.

CAST

John Harris	Michael Craig
Dr. Brown	Patrick McGoohan
Pat Harris	Janet Munro
Hart Jacobs	Paul Rogers
Mrs. Gordon	Megs Jenkins
Teddy's Mother	Maureen Pryor
Mr. Gordon	John Barrie
Mapleton	Basil Dignam
Clyde	Leslie Sands
Duty Sister	Ellen MacIntosh
Teddy's Father	Frank Finlay
Harvard	Michael Aldridge
John's Father	Malcolm Keen
Ruth	Lynn Taylor
Teddy	Freddy Ramsey
John's Counsel	Michael Bryant
Crown Counsel	Norman Wooland

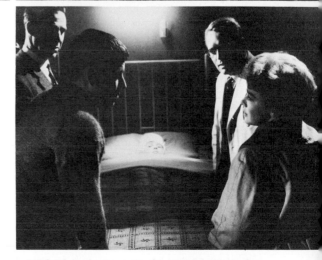

Michael Craig, Lynn Taylor, Patrick McGoohan, Janet Munro. Above: Michael Craig, Janet Munro Left Center: Janet Munro, Patrick McGoohan Above: Janet Munro, Michael Craig

131

THE SLEEPING CAR MURDER

(SEVEN ARTS) Producer, Julien Derode; Direction and Screenplay, Costa Gavras; From novel by Sebastien Japrisot; Adapted by Costa Gavras; Director of Photography, Jean Tournier; Music, Michel Magne. February release.

CAST

Eliane Darres	Simone Signoret
Inspector Grazzi	Yves Montand
La Patron	Pierre Mondy
Bambi	Catherine Allegret
Georgette Thomas	Pascale Roberts
Daniel	Jacques Perrin
Cabourg	Michel Piccoli
Eric	Jean-Louis Trintignant
Bob	Charles Denner
Jean-Lou	Claude Mann
Madame Grazzi	Nadine Alari

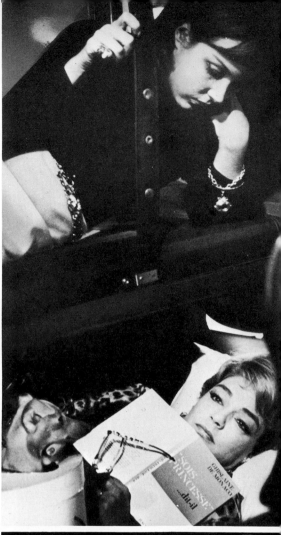

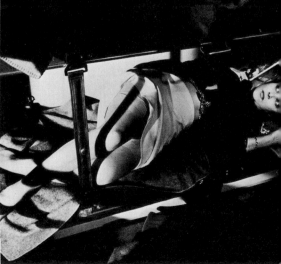

Simone Signoret, Jean-Louis Trintignant
Above: Charles Denner, Pascale Roberts

Pascale Roberts, also above with Simone Signoret

Catherine Allegret, Jacques Perrin
Above: Pierre Mondy, Yves Montand

Michel Piccoli. Above: Yves Montand, Claude
Dauphin. Top: Yves Montand, Claude Mann   133

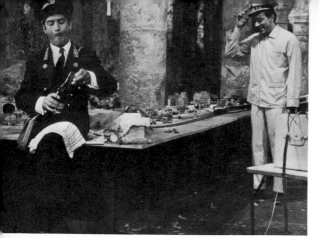

MALE COMPANION

(INTERNATIONAL CLASSICS) Producer, Julien Derode; Director, Philippe de Broca; Screenplay, Henri Lanoe; From book by Andre Couteaux; Adaptation, Henri Lanoe, Philippe de Broca; Director of Photography, Raoul Coutard; Music, Georges Delerue; A Co-Production of Julien Derode, Les Films du Siecle, and Dear Rome. February release.

CAST

Antoine	Jean-Pierre Cassel
Isabelle	Catherine Deneuve
Balthazar	Jean-Pierre Marielle
Nicole	Irina Demick
Clara	Annie Girardot
Maria	Sandra Milo
Krieg von Spiel	Dalio
The Prince	Jean-Claude Brialy
Grandfather	Andre Luguet
Louisette	Valerie Lagrange
Professor Gaetano	Paolo Stoppa
Benvenuto	Adolfo Celi

Jean-Pierre Cassel, Catherine Deneuve
Above: Annie Girardot, Jean-Pierre Cassel
Top: Jean-Claude Brialy, Jean-Pierre Cassel

Jean-Pierre Marielle, Irina Demick, Jean-Pierre Cassel. Above: Sandra Milo, Jean-Pierre Cassel

MOZAMBIQUE

(SEVEN ARTS) Producer, Oliver A. Unger; Director, Robert Lynn; In Color. February release.

CAST
Brad Webster .... Steve Cochran
Ilona Valdez .... Hildegarde Neff
Commarro .... Paul Hubschmid
Christina .... Vivi Bach
Da Silva .... Martin Benson
Henderson .... Dietmar Schoenherr
The Arab .... Gert van den Bergh

Right: Gert van den Bergh, Steve Cochran, Hildegarde Neff. Below: Steve Cochran, Hildegarde Neff

Sylva Koscina, Gustavo Re, Horst Buchholz
Above: Horst Buchholz, Sylva Koscina

THAT MAN IN ISTANBUL

(COLUMBIA) Producer, Nat Wachsberger; Director, Antonio Isasi; Screenplay, Giovanni Simonelli, Luis Comeron, Antonio Isasi, R. Illa; Music, Geroges Garvarentz; Director of Photography, Juan Gelpi; Assistant Director, Luis Garcia; In Techniscope and Color. February release.

CAST
Tony .... Horst Buchholz
Kenny .... Sylva Koscina
Bill .... Mario Adorf
Elisabeth .... Perette Pradier
Schenck .... Klaus Kinski
Bogo .... Alvaro de Luna
Brain .... Gustavo Re
Josette .... Christine Maybach
Charly .... Gerard Tychy
Jonny .... Augustin Gonzalez
Chinese .... Rocha

Hans Verner (second from left), Sophia Loren

Ziporah Peled, Sophia Loren. Above: Sophia Loren
Right: Peter Finch, Sophia Loren

JUDITH

(PARAMOUNT) Producer, Kurt Unger; Director, Daniel Mann; Screenplay, John Michael Hayes; Story, Lawrence Durrell; Associate Producer, Phil Breen; Director of Photography, John Wilcox; Music, Sol Kaplan; Costumes, Yvonne Blake, Gaia Romanini; Assistant Directors, Gerry O'Hara, Yoel Silberg, Ivan Lengyel; In Panavision and Technicolor. February release.

CAST

Judith	Sophia Loren
Aaron Stein	Peter Finch
Major Lawton	Jack Hawkins
Gustav Schiller	Hans Verner
Rachel	Zharira Charifai
Nathan	Shraga Friedman
Chaim	Andre Morell
Elie	Frank Wolff
Interrogator	Arnaldo Foa
Yaneck	Joseph Gross
Zeev	Roger Beaumont
Hannah	Zipora Peled
Lt. Carstairs	Terence Alexander
Dubin	Gilad Konstantiner
Arab Guide	Daniel Ocko
Aba	Roland Bartrop
Conklin	Peter Burton
Researcher	John Stacy

Peter Finch, Frank Wolff, Andre Morell   Peter Finch, Zharira Charifai, Hans Verner

Arnaldo Foa, Peter Finch, Frank Wolff. Above: Sophia Loren, Shraga Friedman
Terence Alexander, Sophia Loren, Jack Hawkins   Above: Peter Finch, Jack Hawkins   137

THE GOSPEL ACCORDING TO ST. MATTHEW

(CONTINENTAL) Producer-Director, Pier Paolo Pasolini; Screenplay adapted from the Gospel of St. Matthew by Pier Paolo Pasolini. February release.

CAST

Christ .... Enrique Irazoqui
Mary (in youth) .... Margherita Caruso
Mary (later) .... Susanna Pasolini
Joseph .... Marcello Morante
John the Baptist .... Mario Socrate
Peter .... Settimo Di Porto
Judas .... Otello Sestili
Matthew .... Ferruccio Nuzzo
John .... Giacomo Morante
Andrew .... Alfonso Gatto
Simon .... Enzo Siciliano
Philip .... Giorgio Agamben
Bartholomew .... Guido Cerretani

Otello Sestili, Enrique Irazoqui
138 Above: Christ with disciples at The Last Supper

Enrique Irazoqui, also above
Top: Marcello Morante, Margherita Caruso

THE TSAR'S BRIDE

(ARTKINO) Producer-Director, Vladimir Gorikker; Opera by Rimsky-Korsakov sung by the Bolshoi Opera; Music played by Bolshoi Orchestra conducted by Yevgeni Svetlanov. March release.

CAST

Tsar Ivan The Terrible	Pyotr Glebov
Martha	Raissa Nedashkovskaya
Gryaznoi	Otar Koberidze
Lyubasha	Natalya Rudnaya

Right: Otar Koberidze, Natalya Rudnaya
Below: Pyotr Glebov

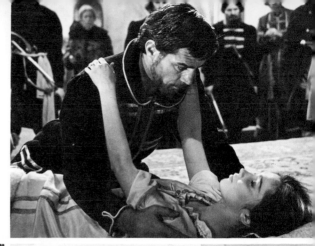

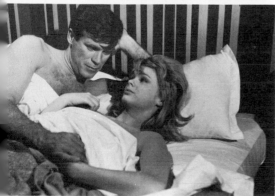

Christopher George, Lynda Day (also above)

THE GENTLE RAIN

(COMET) Executive Producer, Bert Caudle; Producer-Director, Burt Balaban; Screenplay, Robert Cream; Music, Luiz Bonfa; Director of Photography, Mario Di Leo; In Eastman Color. February release.

CAST

Bill Patterson	Christopher George
Judy Reynolds	Lynda Day
Nancy Masters	Fay Spain
Gloria	Maria Helena Diaz
Harry Masters	Lon Clark
Girl Friend	Barbara Williams
Hotel Manager	Robert Assumpaco
Jimmy	Herbert Moss
Jewelry Girl	Lorena
Nightclub Girl	Nadyr Fernandes

LA FUGA

(INTERNATIONAL CLASSICS) Producers, Vittorio Musy Glori, Alberto Casati, Mario Mariani; Director, Paolo Spinola; Screenplay, Sergio Amidei, Piero Bellanova; From an idea by Paolo Spinola, Carla Conti; Music, Piero Piccioni; Director of Photography, Marcello Gatti; Costumes, Piero Gherardi; "Topless" sung by Peppino di Capri; "La Tua Stagione" sung by Milva; A Cine 3 Production. March release.

CAST

Piera	Giovanna Ralli
Luisa	Anouk Aimee
Andrea Fabri	Paul Guers
The Psychoanalyst	Enrico Maria Salerno
The Mother	Jone Salinas Musu

**Left: Giovanna Ralli, Anouk Aimee
Below: Enrico Maria Salerno, Giovanna Ralli**

THE ALPHABET MURDERS

(MGM) Producer, Lawrence P. Bachmann; Director, Frank Tashlin; Screenplay, David Pursall, Jack Seddon; Based on Novel "The A.B.C. Murders" by Agatha Christie; Director of Photography, Desmond Dickinson; Music, Ron Goodwin; Song "Amanda" by Brian Fahey, Norman Newell; Sung by Ray Peterson; Gowns, Hardy Amies; Assistant Director, David Tomblin. March release.

CAST

Hercule Poirot	Tony Randall
Amanda Beatrice Cross	Anita Ekberg
Hastings	Robert Morley
Japp	Maurice Denham
Duncan Doncaster	Guy Rolfe
Lady Diane	Sheila Allen
Franklin	James Villiers
Don Fortune	Julian Glover
Betty Bernard	Grazina Frame
"X"	Clive Morton
Sir Carmichael Clarke	Cyril Luckham
Wolf	Richard Wattis
Sergeant	David Lodge
Cracknell	Patrick Newell
Judson	Austin Trevor
Miss Sparks	Alison Seebohm
Dragbot	Windsor Davies
Mrs. Fortune	Sheila Reid

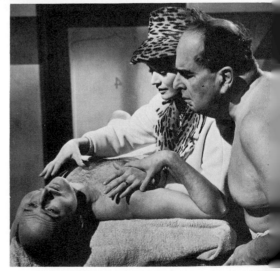

**Tony Randall, Anita Ekberg, Robert Morley
Above: Tony Randall, Grazina Frame**

HAMLET

(**LOPERT**) Direction and Screenplay, Grigori Kozintsev; From the play by William Shakespeare; Translated into Russian by Boris Pasternak; Director of Photography, Ionas Gritsius; Music, Dmitri Shostakovich; A Lenfilm Production. March release.

CAST

Hamlet	Innokenti Smoktunovsky
King	Nikhail Nazvanov
Queen	Elsa Radzin
Polonius	Yuri Tolubeyev
Ophelia	Anastasia Vertinskaya
Horatio	V. Erenberg
Laertes	C. Olesenko
Guildenstern	V. Medvedev
Rosencrantz	I. Dmitriev
Fortinbras	A. Krevalid
Gravedigger	V. Chekoerski

Innokenti Smoktunovsky, Anastasia Vertinskaya (also at top right)

DEAR JOHN

(SIGMA III) Directed and Written by Lars Magnus Lindgren; Based on novel by Olle Lansberg; An AB Sandrew-Ateljeerna Production. March release.

CAST

John	Jarl Kulle
Anita	Christina Schollin
Helene	Helena Nilsson
Raymond	Morgan Anderson
Dagny	Synnove Liljeback
Lindgren	Erik Hell
Mrs. Lindgren	Emy Storm
Erwin	Hakan Serner
Elon	Hans Wigren

Right: Helena Nilsson, Jarl Kulle, Christina Schollin

Jarl Kulle, Christina Schollin

A BALLAD OF LOVE

(ARTKINO) Director, Mikhail Bogin; Screenplay, Mikhail Bogin, Yuri Chulyukin; Camera, Richard Pieck, Heinrich Pilipson; Riga Film Studios Production. March release.

CAST

The Girl	Victoria Fyodorova
The Boy	Valentin Smirnitsky

Left: Victoria Fyodorova

Victoria Fyodorova, Valentin Smirnitsky

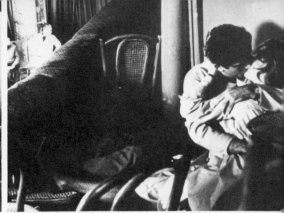

SHAKESPEARE WALLAH

(**CONTINENTAL**) Producer, Ismail Merchant;
Director, James Ivory. March release.

CAST

Sanju	Shashi Kapoor
Lizzie Buckingham	Felicity Kendal
Manjula	Madhur Jaffrey
Mr. Buckingham	Geoffrey Kendal
Mrs. Buckingham	Laura Liddell
The Maharaja	Utpal Dutt
Didi	Parveen Paul
Bobby	Jim Tytler
Sharmaji	Prayag Raaj
Guptaji	Pincho Kapoor
Aslam	Partap Sharma
Headmaster's Brother	Hamid Sayani
Director	Sudershan
Mrs. Bowen	Jennifer Kapoor

Felicity Kendal, Shashi Kapoor (also at top)
Above: Madhur Jaffrey. Left: Shashi Kapoor
Top Left: Geoffrey Kendal (C)

FANTOMAS

(LOPERT) Director, Andre Hanebelle; Dialogue and Screenplay, Jean Halain; Music, Michel Magne; In Widescreen and Color. April release.

CAST

Fantomas, and Fandor	Jean Marais
Commissioner Juve	Louis De Funes
Helene	Mylene Demongeot
Lady Beltham	Marie-Helene Arnaud
Juve's Assistant	Jacques Dynam
Newspaper Editor	Robert Dalban
Chief Inspector	Christian Toma

Right: Jean Marais in dual role
Below: Jean Marais with Mylene Demongeot

Tania Fedor. Above: Claude Jutra

TAKE IT ALL
(A Tout Prendre)

(LOPERT) Created and Directed by Claude Jutra; Additional Dialogue, Johanne, Victor Desy; Photography, Michel Brault, Jean-Claude Labrecque, Bernard Gosselin; Music: Theme, Jean Cousineau, Choir, Maurice Blackburn, Jazz, Serge Garant; A Films Cassiopee and Orion Films Production. April release.

CAST

Johanne	Johanne
Claude	Claude Jutra
Victor	Victor Desy
Mother	Tania Fedor
Priest	Guy Hoffmann
Monique	Monique Joly
Barbara	Monique Mercure
Nicolas	Patrick Straram
Actor	Francois Tasse

FATHER OF A SOLDIER

(ARTKINO) Director, Rezo Chkeidze; Screenplay, Suliko Zhgenti; Director of Photography, Lev Sukhov; A Gruzia Film Studios Production. April release.

CAST

Georgi Makharashvili .... Sergo Zakariadze and Keto Bochorishvili, Guia Kobakhidze, Vladimir Privaltsev

Left: Sergo Zakariadze

Sergo Zakariadze

THE NAKED PREY

(PARAMOUNT) Producer-Director, Cornel Wilde; Co-Producer, Sven Persson; Screenplay, Clint Johnston, Don Peters; Director of Photography, H. A. R. Thomson; Assistant Director, Bert Batt; A Theodora Production in co-production with Sven Persson Films Ltd.; In Panavision and Technicolor. April release.

CAST
Man .... Cornel Wilde
Second Man .... Gert Van Der Berg
Leader of Warriors .... Ken Gampu
Safari Overseer .... Patrick Mynhardt
Little Girl .... Bella Randels

Left (also below) Ken Gampu, Cornel Wilde

RASPUTIN—THE MAD MONK

(20th CENTURY-FOX) Producer, Anthony Nelson Keys; Director, Don Sharp; Screenplay, John Elder; Music, Don Banks; Director of Photography, Michael Reed; Assistant Director, Bert Batt; A Seven Arts-Hammer Production in DeLuxe Color. April release.

CAST
Rasputin .... Christopher Lee
Sonia .... Barbara Shelley
Dr. Zargo .... Richard Pasco
Ivan .... Francis Matthews
Vanessa .... Suzan Farmer
Peter .... Nicholas Pennell
Tsarina .... Renne Asherson
Innkeeper .... Derek Francis
Patron .... Alan Tilvern
Bishop .... Jess Ackland
Abbott .... John Welsh
Tsarvitch .... Robert Duncan
Court Physician .... John Bailey

Christopher Lee, Barbara Shelley
Above: Christopher Lee

147

CLOPORTES

(INTERNATIONAL CLASSICS) Producer, Bertrand Javal; Director, Pierre Granier-Deferre; Based on novel by Alphonse Boudard; Adaptation, Albert Simonin; Music, Jimmy Smith; Director of Photography, Nicolas Hayer; In Cinemascope.

CAST

Alphonse	Lino Ventura
Edmond	Charles Aznavour
Catherine	Irina Demick
Arthur	Maurice Biraud
Rouquemoute	Georges Geret
Tonton	Pierre Brasseur
Gertrude	Francoise Rosay
Leone	Annie Fratellini
Omar	Georges Blaness
First Inspector	Francois Mirante
Second Inspector	Francois Dalou
Elizabeth	Patricia Scott
Mme. Clancul	Marie-Helene Daste
Lescure	Daniel Ceccaldi
Clancul	Georges Chamarat

Francoise Rosay (L). Above: Pierre Brasseur, Irina Demick. Top: Maurice Biraud, Lino Ventura, Georges Geret, Charles Aznavour. Left: Irina Demick, Lino Ventura

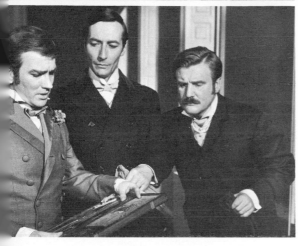

A STUDY IN TERROR

(COLUMBIA) Executive Producer, Herman Cohen; Producer, Henry E. Lester; Director, James Hill; Story and Screenplay, Donald and Derek Ford; Based on characters created by Sir Arthur Conan Doyle; Music, John Scott; Director of Photography, Desmond Dickinson; Costumes, Motley; Assistant Director, Barry Langley; A Compton-Sir Nigel Films Production in Eastman Color. April release.

CAST

Sherlock Holmes	John Neville
Doctor Watson	Donald Houston
Lord Carfax	John Fraser
Doctor Murray	Anthony Quayle
Mycroft Holmes	Robert Morley
Annie Chapman	Barbara Windsor
Angela	Adrienne Corri
Inspector Lestrade	Frank Finlay
Sally	Judi Dench
Prime Minister	Cecil Parker
Singer	Georgia Brown
Duke of Shires	Barry Jones
Cathy Eddowes	Kay Walsh
Mary Kelly	Edina Ronay
Chunky	Terry Downes

John Fraser, John Neville, Donald Houston. Above: John Neville, Robert Morley. Top: Anthony Quayle, John Neville. Right: John Neville

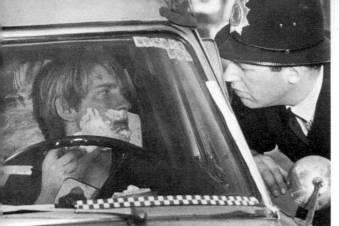

MORGAN!

(CINEMA V) Producer, Leon Clore; Director, Karel Reisz; Screenplay, David Mercer; Director of Photography, Larry Pizer; Music, Johnny Dankworth; A British Lion-Quintra Film Production. April release.

CAST

Leonie	Vanessa Redgrave
Morgan	David Warner
Napier	Robert Stephens
Mrs. Delt	Irene Handl
Mr. Henderson	Newton Blick
Mrs. Henderson	Nan Munro
Policeman	Bernard Bresslaw
Wally	Arthur Mullard
Counsel	Graham Crowden
Second Counsel	Peter Collier
Judge	John Rae
Best Man	Angus Mackay

Vanessa Redgrave. Top Left: David Warner

David Warner, also above and top

Robert Stephens, Vanessa Redgrave
Top: Vanessa Redgrave

THE SLEEPING BEAUTY

(ROYAL) A Lenfilm Production; Directors, Appolinari Dudka, Konstantin Sergeyev; Screenplay, Dudka, Sergeyev, Iosif Shapiro; Director of Photography, Anatoli Nasarov; Choreography, Konstantin Sergeyev; Music, Tchaikovsky. In Techniscope and Color. April release.

CAST

Princess Aurora _____ Alla Sizov
Prince Desire _____ Yuri Solovie
Wicked Fairy _____ Natalia Dudinskay
Lilac Fairy _____ Irina Bazhenov
King _____ Veevolod Ukho
Queen _____ O. Zabetkin
Master of Ceremonies _____ V. Riazano
Princess Florine _____ M. Makasov
The Bluebird _____ V. Pano
and members of the Kiev Ballet

Millicent Martin, Tony Tanner
in
"STOP THE WORLD—I WANT TO GET OFF"

STOP THE WORLD—
I WANT TO GET OFF

(WARNER BROS.) Producer, Bill Sargent; Film Director, Philip Saville; Stage Director, Michael Lindsay-Hogg; Mime Director, Tutte Lemkow; Assistant Director, Robert Lynn; Book, Music, and Lyrics, Anthony Newley, Leslie Bricusse; Director of Photography, Oswald Morris; In Technicolor and Mitchell System 35. May release.

CAST

Littlechap .... Tony Tanner
Evie, Anya, Ara, Ginnie .... Millicent Martin
Susan .... Leila Croft
Jane .... Valerie Croft
Little Littlechap .... Neil Hawley
Dancers-Singers .... Georgina Allen, Natasha Ashton, Carlotta Barrow, Sandra Burville, Christy Carroll, Vivyen Dunbar, Margaret Frost, Lix Gold, Sarah Hardenburg, Pak Hart, Katharine Holden, Ann Holloway, Marion Horton, Dorina House, Carolyn Irving, Pam Jones, Kay Korda, Judith McGilligan, Rosemary Philips, Julia Pitcher, Jo Anna Short, Heather Sims, Liz White

Leila Croft, Tony Tanner, Neil Hawley, Millicent Martin, Valerie Croft, also above

UP TO HIS EARS

(LOPERT) Producers, Alexandre Mnouchkine; Georges Dancigers; Director, Philippe De Broca; Screenplay, Daniel Boulanger; Based on novel by Jules Verne; Director of Photography, Edmond Sechan; Assistant Director, Claude Pinoteau; A Franco-Italian Co-Production in EastmanColor. May release.

CAST

Arthur Lempereur	Jean-Paul Belmondo
Alexandrine Pinardel	Ursula Andress
Suzy	Maria Pacome
Alice Ponchabert	Valerie Lagrange
Cornelius	Jess Hahn
Mr. Goh	Valery Inkijinoff
Leon	Jean Rochefort
Biscoton	Darry Cowl

and Paul Preboist, Mario David

Valery Inkijinoff, Jean-Paul Belmondo
Above: Jean-Paul Belmondo

Jean-Paul Belmondo, and top with Jean Rochefort, Valerie Lagrange, Jess Hahn

THE GARNET BRACELET

(ARTKINO) Director, Abram Room; Screenplay, A. Granberg, Abram Room; Director of Photography, L. Krainenkov; Pianist, Stanislav Neuhaus; Violinist, David Ashkenazi; Theme Music, Beethoven's Appassionata, Sonata No. 2; Adapted from novel by Alexander Kuprin; A Mosfilm Studio Production in Widescreen and MagiColor. May release.

CAST

Vera Nikolayevna	Ariadna Shengelaya
Zheltkov	Igor Ozerov
Vasili Lvovich	O. Basilashvili
Nikolai Nikolayevich	V. Strzhelchik
Anna Nikolayevna	N. Malyavina
Von Friese	Y. Averin
Madam Zarzhitzkaya	O. Zhizneva
Kuprin	G. Gai

Right: Ariadna Shengelaya

UNDER COVER ROGUE
(formerly "White Voices")

(RIZZOLI) Executive Producers, Nello Meniconi, Luciano Perugia; Directors, Pasquale Festa Campanile, Massimo Franciosa; Screenplay, Festa Campanile, Franciosa, Luigi Magni; Director of Photography, Ennio Guarnieri; Music, Gino Marinuzzi, Jr.; In Techniscope and Technicolor. May release.

CAST

Meo	Paolo Ferrari
Teresa	Graziella Granata
Lorenza	Anouk Aimee
Carolina	Sandra Milo
Guilia	Barbara Steele

and Vittorio Caprioli, Claudio Gora, Philippe LeRoy, Jacqueline Sassard, Jean Tissier, Leopoldo Trieste, Jeanne Valerie, Alfredo Bianchini, Luigi Basagaluppi, Giulio Battiferri, Anita Durante, Francesco Mule, Jacques Herlin, Guglielmo Spoletini, Filippo Spoletini

Paolo Ferrari, Barbara Steele
Left: Paolo Ferrari, Sandra Milo

ENOUGH ROPE

(ARTIXO) Executive Producer, Yvon Guezel; Director, Claude Autant-Lara; Screenplay, Jean Aurenche, Pierre Bost; Based on novel "The Blunderer" by Patricia Highsmith; Director of Photography, Jacques Natteau; Music, Rene Cloerec; In Widescreen; Presented by Artie Shaw. May release.

CAST

Kimmel	Gert Frobe
Ellie	Marina Vlady
Corby	Robert Hossein
Walter Saccard	Maurice Ronet
Clara Saccard	Yvonne Furneaux
Mme. Kimmel	Paulette Dubost
Tony	Harry Mayen
Police Commissioner	Jacques Monod

Right: Marina Vlady (L)

Gert Frobe (R)

THE PSYCHOPATH

(PARAMOUNT) Producers, Max J. Rosenberg, Milton Subotsky; Director, Freddie Francis; Screenplay, Robert Bloch; Assistant Director, Peter Price; Director of Photography, John Wilcox; Music, Phil Martel; An Amicus Production in Technicolor and Techniscope. May release.

CAST

Inspector Holloway	Patrick Wymark
Mrs. Von Sturm	Margaret Johnston
Mark Von Sturm	John Standing
Frank Saville	Alexander Knox
Louise Saville	Judy Huxtable
Donald Loftis	Don Borisenko
Dr. Glyn	Colin Gordon
Martin Roth	Thorley Walters
Victor Ledoux	Robert Crewdson
Morgan	Tim Barrett
Tucker	Frank Forsyth
Mary	Olive Gregg
Briggs	Harold Lang
Reinhardt Klermer	John Harvey
Cigarette Girl	Greta Farrer

Thorley Walters, Alexander Knox, Robert Crewdson
Above: Margaret Johnston, Judy Huxtable
158 Top: Patrick Wymark, Margaret Johnston

Alexander Knox, Patrick Wymark, Judy Huxtable, Don Borisenko. Above: John Standing, Margaret Johnston

TIKO AND THE SHARK

(MGM) Producer, Goffredo Lombardo; Director, Folco Auilici; Screenplay, Folco Quilici, Ottavio Alessi, A. Frassinet; Story, Italo Calvino; Based on Novel by Clement Richer; Music, Francesco De Masi; Director of Photography, Pier Ludovico Pavoni; A Titanus-Metro Production in Eastmancolor. June release.

CAST

Diana	Marlene Among
Tiko	Al Kauwe
Tiko as a child	Denis Pouira
Diana as a child	Diane Samsoi
Cocoyo	Roau

Right: Marlene Among, Al Kauwe

THE GREAT SPY CHASE

(AMERICAN INTERNATIONAL) Executive Producer, Alain Poire; Producer-Director, Georges Lautner; Original Script, Michel Audiard, Albert Simonin; Dialogue, Michel Audiard; Director of Photography, Maurice Fellous; Music, Michel Magne. May release.

CAST

Lagneau	Lino Ventura
Lafarelli	Bernard Blair
Cassilieff	Francis Blanche
Amaranthe	Mireille Darc
Muller	Charles Millot
Rossini	Andre Weber
O'Brien	Jess Hahn
Le Douanier	Jacques Balutin
Le Camionneur	Robert Dalban
Rosalinde	Michele Marceau

Lino Ventura, Bernard Blair, Charles Millot, Francis Blanche, also above, Left: Michele Marceau, Mireille Darc 159

A MAN AND A WOMAN

(ALLIED ARTISTS) Direction and Story, Claude Lelouch; Adaptation and Dialogue, Pierre Uytterhoeven, Claude Lelouch; Director of Photography, Claude Lelouch; Music, Frais Lai; Lyrics, Pierre Barouh; A Les Films 13 Production in EastmanColor. June release.

CAST

Anne Gauthier	Anouk Aimee
Jean-Louis Duroc	Jean-Louis Trintignant
Pierre Gauthier	Pierre Barouh
Valerie Duroc	Valerie Lagrange
Head Mistress	Simone Paris
Antoine Duroc	Antoine Sire
Francoise Gauthier	Souad Amidou
Mistress of Jean-Louis	Yane Barry

Left Center and Top: Anouk Aimee, Jean-Louis Trintignant

THE GIRL GETTERS

(AMERICAN INTERNATIONAL) Producer, Kenneth Shipman; Director, Michael Winner; Screenplay, Peter Draper; Director of Photography, Nicolas Roeg; Associate Producer, George Fowler; Assistant Director, Peter Price; Music, Stanley Black. June release.

CAST

Tinker	Oliver Reed
Nicola	Jane Merrow
Suzy	Barbara Ferris
Lorna	Julia Foster
Larsey	Harry Andrews
Ella	Ann Lynn
Philip	Guy Doleman
Willy	Andrew Ray
Grib	John Porter Davison
Sneakers	Clive Colin Bowler
Sammy	Iain Gregory
David	David Hemmings
Nidge	John Alderton
Ivor	Jeremy Burnham
Michael	Mark Burns
James	Derek Nimmo
Sylvie	Pauline Munro
Alfred	Derek Newark
Marianne	Stephanie Beaumont
Helga	Talitha Pol
Ingrid	Dora Reisser
Jasmin	Susan Burnet

Right: Clive Colin Bowler, David Hemmings, Oliver Reed, Iain Gregory, Andrew Ray
Above: Oliver Reed (L)

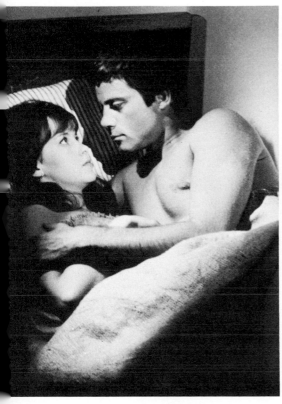

Jane Merrow, Oliver Reed

Julia Foster, Oliver Reed

MADAME BUTTERFLY

(RIZZOLI) Director, Carmine Gallone; Opera based on book of John L. Long and play by David Belasco; Music, Giacomo Puccini; A Rizzoli-Toho-Gallone Production in Technicolor. June release.

CAST

Cio Cio San .... Kaoru Yachigusa
Suzuki .... Michiko Tanaka
Pinkerton .... Nicola Filacuridi
Sharpless .... Ferdinando Lidonni
Goro .... Kiyoshi Takagi
Yamadori .... Satoshi Nakamura
Zio Bonzo .... Yoshio Kosugi
and The Takarazuka Ballet

Left: Michiko Tanaka, Kaoru Yachigusa, Nicola Filacuridi

Kaoru Yachigusa (Center and above)

Nicola Filacuridi, Kaoru Yachigusa

THE MAIN CHANCE

(EMBASSY) Producer, Jack Greenwood; Director, John Knight; Screenplay, Richard Harris; Based on Novel by Edgar Wallace. June release.

CAST

Potter .... Gregoire Aslan
Christine .... Tracy Reed
Michael Blake .... Edward De Souza
Joe Hayes .... Stanley Meadows
Ross .... Jack Smethurst

Right: Gregoire Aslan, Tracy Reed, Edward De Souza

Tracy Reed

Edward De Souza, Gregoire Aslan
Above: Gregoire Aslan, Tracy Reed

THE BLUE MAX

(20th CENTURY-FOX) Executive Producer, Elmo Williams; Producer, Christian Ferry; Director, John Guillermin; Screenplay, Gerald Hanley, David Pursall, Jack Seddon; Based on novel by Jack D. Hunter; Adaptation, Ben Barzman, Basilio Franchina; Director of Photography, Douglas Slocombe; Music, Jerry Goldsmith; Assistant Directors, Jack Causey, Derek Cracknell; In Cinemascope and DeLuxe Color. June release.

CAST

Bruno Stachel	George Peppard
Count von Klugermann	James Mason
Countess Kasti	Ursula Andress
Willi Von Klugermann	Jeremy Kemp
Richthofen	Carl Schell
Heidemann	Karl Michael Vogler
Elfi Heidemann	Loni Von Friedl
Holbach	Anton Diffring
Rupp	Peter Woodthorpe
Kettering	Harry Towb
Ziegel	Derek Newark
Fabian	Derren Nesbitt
Field Marshal Von Lenndorf	Friedrich Ledebur
Crown Prince	Roger Ostime
Hans	Hugo Schuster
Pilots	Tim Parkes, Ian Kingsley, Ray Browne

Jeremy Kemp, James Mason. Above: George Peppard
Right Center: James Mason

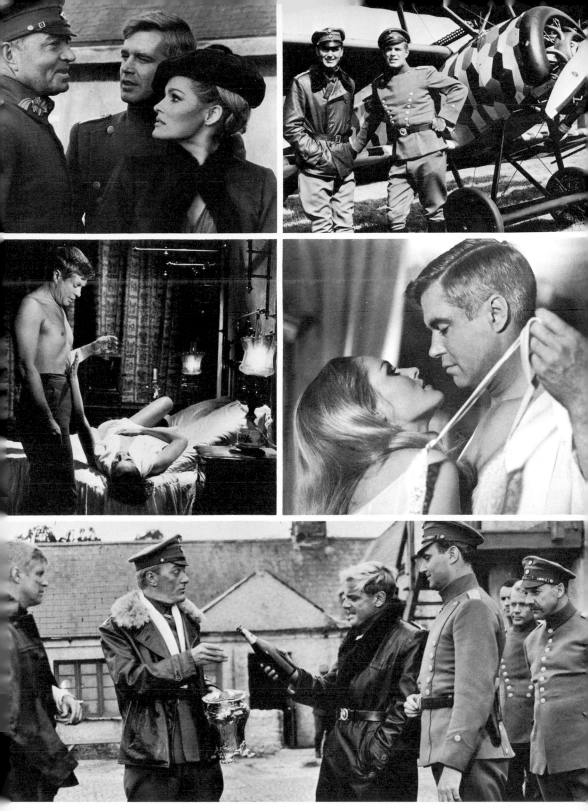

George Peppard, Jeremy Kemp, Carl Schell, Karl Michael Vogler. Above: George Peppard, Ursula Andress. Top (L): James Mason, George Peppard, Ursula Andress (R) Karl Michael Vogler, George Peppard

MODESTY BLAISE

(20th CENTURY-FOX) Producer, Joseph Janni; Director, Joseph Losey; Screenplay, Evan Jones; Based on comic strip created by Peter O'Donnell and Jim Holdaway; Director of Photography, Jack Hildyard; Associate Producers, Norman Priggen, Michael Birkett; Assistant Directors, Gavrik Losey, Claude Watson; Music, John Dankworth; Songs, Benny Green, Evan Jones; Performed by David and Jonathan; In DeLuxe Color. June release.

CAST

Modesty Blaise	Monica Vitti
Willie Garvin	Terence Stamp
Gabriel	Dirk Bogarde
Sir Gerald Tarrant	Harry Andrews
Paul Hagan	Michael Craig
Melina	Scilla Gabel
Nicole	Tina Marquand
McWhirter	Clive Revill
Mrs. Fothergill	Rossella Falk
Crevier	Joe Melia
Walter	Lex Schoorel
Pacco	Sylvan
Hans	Jon Bluming
Enrico	Roberto Bisacco
Basilio	Sara Urzi
Friar	Guiseppe Paganelli
Minister	Alexander Knox

Monica Vitti. Top Right: Harry Andrews, Terence Stamp, Monica Vitti

Michael Craig, Monica Vitti. Above: Dirk Bogarde, Monica Vitti, Terence Stamp

THE SUCKER

(ROYAL) Produced, Directed, Written, and Photographed by Gerard Oury; In Color. June release.

CAST

Antoine Marechal	Bourvil
Leopold Saroyan	Luis De Funes
Mario Costa	Pierre Roussel
Ursela	Beba Loncar
La Souris	Walter Chiari
Gina	Daniella Rocca
Lino	Nanbo Buzzanca

Bourvil, also above, and top with Luis De Funes
Right Center: Walter Chiari

LADY L

(MGM) Producer, Carlo Ponti; Director, Peter
Ustinov; Screenplay, Peter Ustinov; Based on
novel by Romain Gary; In Panavision and
Color. July release.

CAST

Lady L (Lady Lendale)	Sophia Loren
Armand	Paul Newman
Dicky (Lord Lendale)	David Niven
Inspector Mercier	Claude Dauphin
Gerome	Phillipe Noiret
Lecoeur	Michel Piccoli
Sapper	Marcel Dalio
Sir Percy	Cecil Parker
Krajewski	Jean Wiener
Kobeleff	Daniel Emilfork
Koenigstein	Eugene Deckers
Beala	Jacques Duphilo
Agneau	Tanya Lopert
Pantoufle	Catherine Allegret
Prince Otto	Peter Ustinov

Paul Newman, Sophia Loren, also Right Center
Above: Sophia Loren, David Niven

GYPSY GIRL

(CONTINENTAL) Producer, Jack Hanbury; Director, John Mills; Screenplay, Mary Hayley Bell, John Prebble; Story, Mary Hayley Bell; Director of Photography, Arthur Ibbetson; A Rank Presentation in Color. July release.

CAST

Brydie White .... Hayley Mills
Roibin .... Ian McShane
Edwid Dacres .... Laurence Naismith
Phillip Moss .... Geoffrey Bayldon
Mrs. White .... Annette Crosbie
and Norman Bird, Hamilton Dyce, Pauline Jameson, Rachel Thomas, Judith Furse, Anne Blake, June Ellis

Right: Hayley Mills, Annette Crosbie

Hayley Mills, Geoffrey Bayldon
Above: Laurence Naismith, Hayley Mills

Ian McShane, Hayley Mills (also above)

Jose Marco Davo, Angel Peralta, Marisol
Left: Marisol, Rafael De Cordova

EVERY DAY IS A HOLIDAY

(COLUMBIA) Producer-Director, Mel Ferrer; Associate Producer, Manuel J. Goyanes; Screenplay, Mel Ferrer, Jose Maria Palacio; Story, Mel Ferrer; Director of Photography, Antonio L. Ballesteros; In Color. July release.

CAST

Chica .... Marisol
Angel .... Angel Peralta
Dancer .... Rafael De Cordova
Impresario .... Jose Marco Davo
Femme Fatale .... Vala Clifton
Manolo .... Pedro Mari Sanchez
and Jesus Guzman, Jose Sepulveda, Francisco Camoiras, Jose Maria Labernie, Luis Barbero, Toni Canal, Jack Gasins

Angel Peralta, Marisol. Above and Left: Marisol

BANG, BANG, YOU'RE DEAD!

(AMERICAN INTERNATIONAL) Executive Producer, Oliver A. Unger; Producer, Harry Alan Towers; Director, Don Sharp; Screenplay, Peter Yeldam; Director of Photography, John Von Kotze; Music, Malcolm Lockyer; Assistant Director, Barrie Melrose; A Landau-Unger Presentation in Color. August release.

CAST

Andrew Jessel	Tony Randall
Kyra Stanovy	Senta Berger
El Caid	Terry-Thomas
Mr. Casimir	Herbert Lom
Arthur Fairbrother	Wilfrid Hyde-White
Achmed	Gregoire Aslan
George Lillywhite	John Le Mesurier
Jonquil	Klaus Kinski
Samia Voss	Margaret Lee
Hotel Clerk	Emil Stemmler
Madame Bouseny	Helen Sanguineti
Martinez	Sanchez Francisco
Police Chief	William Sanguineti
Motorcycle Policeman	Hassan Essakali
Philippe	Keith Peacock
Export Manager	Burt Kwouk

Right: Terry-Thomas, Senta Berger

THE IDOL

(EMBASSY) Producer, Leonard Lightstone; Executive Producer, Joseph E. Levine; Director, Daniel Petrie; Associate Producer, Robert Porter; Screenplay, Millard Lampell; Based on story by Ugo Liberatore; Music, John Dankworth; Director of Photography, Ken Higgins; Assistant Director, Bryan Coates. August release.

CAST

Carol	Jennifer Jones
Marco	Michael Parks
Timothy	John Leyton
Sarah	Jennifer Hilary
Martin Livesey	Guy Doleman
Rosalind	Natasha Pyne
Lewis	Jeremy Bulloch
Barmaid	Fanny Carby
Second Woman at party	Caroline Blakiston
Man at party	Vernon Dobtcheff
Boy	Michael Gordon
Simon	Gordon Gostelow
Policeman	Ken Haward
Woman at party	Renee Houston
Rosie	Priscilla Morgan
Mrs. Muller	Edna Morris
Tommy	Peter Porteous
Laborers	Terry Richards, Derek Ware
Police Inspector	Jack Watson
Landlay	Rita Webb
Dorothea	Tina Williams

Jennifer Hilary, Michael Parks, Jennifer Jones, John Leyton. Above: Jennifer Jones, Michael Parks Left: Jennifer Jones, John Leyton

171

THE WRONG BOX

(COLUMBIA) Producer-Director, Bryan Forbes; Co-Produced and Written by Larry Gelbart and Burt Shevelove; Suggested by novel by Robert Louis Stevenson; and Lloyd Osborne; Music, John Barry; Director of Photography, Gerry Turpin; Associate Producer, Jack Rik; Costumes, Julie Harris; Assistant Director, Christopher Dryhurst; A Salamander Film Production in Pathe Color. August release.

CAST

Masterman	John Mills
Joseph	Ralph Richardson
Michael	Michael Caine
Morris	Peter Cook
John	Dudley Moore
Julia	Nanette Newman
The Detective	Tony Hancock
Doctor Pratt	Peter Sellers
Major Martha	Cicely Courtneidge
Peacock	Wilfrid Lawson
Patience	Thorley Walters
First Undertaker	Gerald Sim
Military Officer	Peter Graves
Mrs. Hackett	Irene Handl
Clergyman	Norman Bird
Dr. Slattery	John Le Mesurier
First Rough	Norman Rossington
Lawyer	Hilton Edwards
Mercy	Diane Clare
Strangler	Tutte Lemkow

and Jeremy Lloyd, James Villiers, Graham Stark, Dick Gregory, Nicholas Parsons, Willoughby Goddard, Valentine Dyall, Leonard Rossiter, Hamilton Dyce, Timothy Bateson, Donald Oliver, Totti Truman Taylor, Jeremy Roughton, Frank Singuineau, Michael Lees, Andre Morell, Avis Bunnage, Gwendolyn Watts, Vanda Godsell, Marianne Stone, John Junkin, Roy Murray, Donald Tandy, Lionel Gamlin, Martin Terry, Michael Bird, George Selway, Joseph Behrmann, Thomas Gallagher, Charles Bird, Tony Thawnton, The Temperance Seven, Reg Lye, George Spence

John Mills, Michael Caine, Nanette Newman
Above: Peter Cook, Nanette Newman, John Mills,
Dudley Moore, Irene Handl, Ralph Richardson,
Michael Caine

Peter Sellers. Top Left: Ralph Richardson,
John Mills

IT HAPPENED HERE

(LOPERT) Produced, Directed and Written by
Kevin Brownlow, Andrew Mollo; Original Idea,
Kevin Brownlow; Director of Photography, Peter
Suschitzky; A Rath Film. August release.

CAST

Pauline	Pauline Murray
Dr. Fletcher	Sebastian Shaw
Helen Fletcher	Fiona Leland
Honor	Honor Fehrson
IA Commandant	Col. Percy Binns
IA Political Leader	Frank Bennett
IA Group Leader	Bill Thomas
IA Medical Officer	Reginald Marsh
IA NCO	Rex Collett
IA Woman Commandant	Nicolette Bernard
IA Group Leader Noorfiled	Nicholas Moore
SS Officers	Peter Urbe, Graham Adam
American Officer	Brewster Cross
British Partisan Officer	Colonel Pickering
British Medical Officer	Jeremy Dacon
Skipworth	Bart Allison
Dr. Walton	Ralph Wilson
Dr. Westerman	John Herrington
Matron	Bertha Russell
Nurse Drayton	Stella Kembell

and Alfred Zieman, Peter Dineley, Peter Elkins,
Hans-Joachim Schmittel, Klaus Umjo, Frank
Gardner, Ronald Phillips, Christopher Bell,
Norbert Dingeldein, Bob Parker, Tony Oliver,
Jim Joslyn, Pat Sullivan, Derek Milburn,
Barrie Pattison, Rose Paddon, H. G. White,
Rae Wills

Pauline Murray (L)

MADEMOISELLE

(LOPERT) Producer, Oscar Lewenstein; Director, Tony Richardson; Screenplay, Jean Genet; August release.

CAST

Mademoiselle	Jeanne Moreau
Manou	Ettore Manni
Bruno	Keith Skinner
Anton	Umberto Orsini

and Jane Berretta, Mony Reh, Georges Douking, Rosine Liguet, Gabriel Gobin, Pierre Collet

Left: Jeanne Moreau

YOLANTA

(ARTKINO) Director, Vladimir Gorikker; Director of Photography, V. Mass; Orchestra and Chorus of Bolshoi Opera conducted by B. Khaikin; In MagiColor. September release.

CAST

Yolanta	Natalya Rudnaya
	Sung by Galina Oleinichenko
King Rene	Fyodor Nikitin
	Sung by Ivan Petrov
Vaudemont	Yuri Perov
	Sung by Z. Andjaparidze
Duke Robert	Alexander Belyavsky
	Sung by Pavel Lisitsian
Eon-Hakkia	Pyotor Glebov
	Sung by V. Valaitis
Martha	Valentina Ushakova
	Sung by Y. Verhitskaya
Bertrand	Valdis Sandberg
	Sung by V. Yaroslavtsev

Left: Natalya Rudnaya (L)

Mary Peach, Ray Charles

BLUES FOR LOVERS

(20th CENTURY-FOX) Producer, Herman Blaser; Director, Paul Henreid; Screenplay, Burton Wohl; Based on story by Paul Henreid, Burton Wohl; Assistant Directors, Stuart Freeman, Alex Carver-Hill, Nigel Watts; Music, Stanley Black; An Alexander Salkind Production. September release.

CAST

Ray Charles	Ray Charles
Steve Collins	Tom Bell
Peggy Harrison	Mary Peach
Gina Graham	Dawn Addams
David	Piers Bishop
Mrs. Babbidge	Betty McDowall
Margaret	Lucy Appleby
Fred	Joe Adams
Duke Wade	Robert Lee Ross
Bus Conductress	Anne Padwick
Antonia	Monika Henreid

and The Ray Charles Orchestra, and The Raelets

BOLSHOI BALLET '67

(PARAMOUNT) A Mosfilm Production; Directors, Leonid Lavrovsky, Alexander Shelenkov; Screenplay, Leonid Lavrovsky, Alexander Shelenkov, Leo Arnshtam; Directors of Photography, Alexander Shelenkov, Iolanda Chen; Music, Rachmaninoff, Ravel, Tchaikovsky, Prokofiev, Adan, Minkus, Krein; Costumes, V. Ryndina; English commentary by Sidney Carroll; Narrated by Ariane; In Technicolor. September release.

PROGRAM

"Paganini" with Yaroslav Sekh and Ekterina Maximova, "Bolero" with Elena Kholina, Alexander Lavrenjuk, S. Radchenko, "The Stone Flower" with Raissa Struchkova, "The Dying Swan" with A. Osipenko, "Waltzes," "Giselle," "Laurancis," "Don Quixote" performed by members of the Bolshoi Ballet.

Anthony Quinn, Horst Buchholz

MARCO THE MAGNIFICENT

(MGM) Directors, Denys De La Patelliere, Noel Howard; Original Story, Denys De La Patelliere, Raoul J. Levy; Director of Photography, Armand Thirard; Music, Georges Garvarentz; Costumes, Jacques Fonteray; Assistant Directors, Serge Vallin, J. M. Lacor; Produced by ITTAC/Paris, SNC/Paris, Prodi Cinematografica/Roma in association with Avala Film/Belgrade; A Walter Manley Enterprises release; In Eastmancolor. September release.

CAST

Marco Polo	Horst Buchholz
Achmed	Gregoire Aslan
Nayam	Robert Hossein
Girl with whip	Elsa Martinelli
Old Man	Akim Tamiroff
Emir Alaou	Omar Sharif
Ackerman	Orson Welles
Kublai Khan	Anthony Quinn
Marco's Father	Massimo Girotti
Spinello	Folco Lulli
Gogatine	Lee Sue Moon
Guillaume de Tripolis	Bruno Cremer
Nicolo de Vicenza	Jacques Monod
Marco's Uncle	Nica Orlovic
Taha	Mansoureh Rihai

Eduard Isotov, Natasha Sedykh

JACK FROST

(EMBASSY) Director, Alexander Row; Screenplay, Mikhail Volpin, Nikolai Erdman; Director of Photography, Dmitry Surensky; Music, Nikolak Budashkin; A Gorky Central Studios Production in Color. September release.

CAST

Nastenka	Natasha Sedykh
Jack Frost	Alexander Khvylya
Ivan	Eduard Isotov
Witch Baba Yaga	Yuri Millyar
Marfushka	Inna Churikova
Step-mother	Vera Altaiskaya
Old Man	Pavel Pavlenko
Bandit Chieftan	Anatoly Kubatsky

LOVE AND MARRIAGE

(EMBASSY) Producers, Ermanno Donati, Luigi Carpentieri; Directors, Gianni Puccini, Mino Guerrini; Screenplay, Bruno Baratti, Oreste Biancoli; Eliana De Sabata, Jaja Fiastri, Mino Guerrini, Gianni Puccini, Ennio De Concini; Music, Marcello Giombini; Directors of Photography, Luciano Trasatti, Alfio Contini, Riccardo Pallottini; Assistant Director, Ruggero Deodato; Costumes, Luciana Marinucci. September release.

CAST

The First Night:

Concetto	Lando Buzzanca
Enea	Maria Grazia Buccella
Roro	Umberto D'Orsi
Lady on yacht	Luciana Angelillo
Baron	Gianni Del Balzo
Hotel Clerk	Amedeo Girard

One Moment Is Enough:

Marina	Ingeborg Schoener
Giancarlo	Renato Tagliani
Barman	Sandro Moretti
Young man in cinema	Steve Forsyth
Andrea	Enzo Carra
Fisherman	Marino Mase
Don Eugenio	Armando Tarallo
Amelia	Flora Volpe

The Last Card:

Elsa	Eleonora Rossi Drago
Antonio	Aldo Giuffre
Gladys	April Hennessy
Ann	June Weaver
Linda	Ethel Levin
Manicurist	Gioia Durell
First Man	Carlo Loffredo
Second Man	Bruno Scipioni

Saturday, July 18:

Diana	Sylva Koscina
Mario	Philippe Leroy

Sylva Koscina, Philippe Leroy

John Huston as Noah
in
"THE BIBLE"

THE BIBLE
. . . in the beginning

(20th CENTURY-FOX) Producer, Dino De Laurentiis; Director, John Huston; Music, Toshiro Mayuzumi; Associate Producer, Luigi Luraschi; Screenplay, Christopher Fry; Assisted by Jonathan Griffin, Ivo Perilli, Vittorio Bonicell; Director of Photography, Giuseppe Rotunno; Costumes, Maria De Matteis; Choreography, Katherine Dunham; Assistant Directors, Vana Caruso, Ottavio Oppo; Narration by John Huston; Filmed in D-150 and DeLuxe Color. September release.

CAST

Adam .... Michael Parks
Eve .... Ulla Bergryd
Cain .... Richard Harris
Noah .... John Huston
Nimrod .... Stephen Boyd
Abraham .... George C. Scott
Sarah .... Ava Gardner
The Three Angels .... Peter O'Toole
Hagar .... Zoe Sallis
Lot .... Gabriele Ferzetti
Lot's Wife .... Eleonora Rossi Drago
and Franco Nero, Robert Rietty, Grazia Maria Spina, Claudie Lange, Adriana Ambesi, Alberto Lucantoni, Luciano Conversi, Pupella Maggio, Peter Heinze, Angelo Boschariol, Anna Maria Orso, Eric Leutzinger, Gabriella Pallotta, Rosanna De Rocco

Franco Nero, Richard Harris. Above: Ulla Bergryd, Michael Parks (also at top)

John Huston as Noah with his family leaving the Above: Noah leading animals into the ark

tephen Boyd (C). Above: Ava Gardner, Alberto
Lucantoni. Top: Ava Gardner, George C. Scott

Gabriele Ferzetti, Peter O'Toole, Eleonora Rossi Drago
Above: George C. Scott, Alberto Lucantoni
Top: George C. Scott, Zoe Sallis, Luciano Conversi

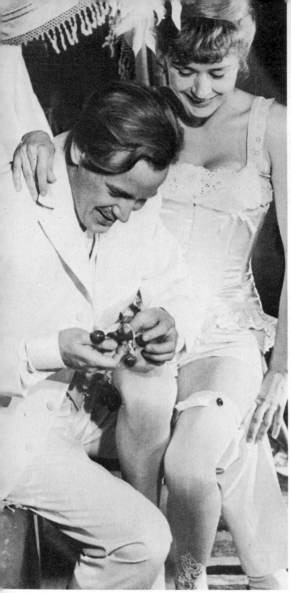

LOVING COUPLES

(PROMINENT) Director, Mai Zetterling; Screenplay, Mai Zetterling. David Hughes; Director of Photography; Sven Nykvist. September release.

CAST

Agda	Harriet Andersson
Adele	Gunnel Lindblom
Angela	Gio Petre
Petra	Anita Gjork
Dr. Jacob Lewin	Gunnar Bjornstrand
Mrs. Lewin	Inga Landgre
Stellan	Jan Malmsjo

and Frank Sundstrom, Eva Dahlbeck, Heinz Hopf, Hans Straat

Top (L): Jan Malmsjo, Harriet Andersson, (R) Heinz Hopf, Eva Dahlbeck, Harriet Andersson, Jan Malmsjo. Below: Harriet Andersson, Heinz Hopf

Jan Malmsjo, Harriet Andersson, also above with Heinz Hopf (L)

BORN FREE

(COLUMBIA) Producers, Sam Jaffe, Paul Radin; Director, James Hill; Screenplay, Gerald L. C. Copley; Based on book by Joy Adamson; Director of Photography, Kenneth Talbot; Music, John Barry; Assistant Director, William P. Cartlidge; Animal Supervisor, Peter Whitehead; In Panavision and ColumbiaColor; An Open Road-High Road-Atlas Co-Production; Presented by Carl Foreman. September release.

CAST

Joy Adamson	Virginia McKenna
George Adamson	Bill Travers
Kendall	Geoffrey Keen
Nuru	Peter Lukoye
Makkede	Omar Chambati
Sam	Bill Godden
Baker	Bryan Epsom
Ken	Robert Cheetham
James	Robert Young
Watson	Geoffrey Best
Indian Doctor	Surya Patel

and Ugas, Henrietta, Mara and the cubs

Bill Travers, Virginia McKenna, also in pictures
left and right above and top with Henrietta,
Mara and the cubs

181

Sylvie

THE SHAMELESS OLD LADY
(CONTINENTAL) Producer, Claude Nedj
Direction and Screenplay, Rene Allio; Ba
on novel by Bertolt Brecht. September relea
CAST
Madame Berthe _____ Syl
Rosalie _____ Malka Ribov
Pierre _____ Victor Lan
Resentful Son _____ Etienne Bie

Malka Ribovska, Sylvie, also above with
Jean Bouise. Top: Berthe (Sylvie) with
her husband (L) and family (R)

Sylvie (R), Malka Ribovska (L) both also above

KALEIDOSCOPE

(WARNER BROS.) Producer, Elliott Kastner; Director, Jack Smight; Screenplay, Robert and Jane-Howard Carrington; Director of Photography, Christopher Challis; Associate Producer, Peter Medak; Music, Stanley Myers; Costumes, Sally Tuffin, Marion Foale; Assistant Director, Kip Gowans; A Winkast Film Production; A Jerry Gershwin-Elliott Kastner Presentation in Technicolor. October release.

CAST

Barney	Warren Beatty
Angel	Susannah York
Manny	Clive Revill
Dominion	Eric Porter
Aimes	Murray Melvin
Billy	George Sewell
Dominion Captain	Stanley Meadows
Dominion Porter	John Junkin
Dominion Chauffeur	Larry Taylor
Museum Receptionist	Yootha Joyce
Exquisite Thing	Jane Birkin
Johnny	George Murcell
Leeds	Anthony Newlands

Susannah York, Warren Beatty
Above: Clive Revill, Warren Beatty

Eric Porter, Clive Revill, Warren Beatty, Susannah Yo
Above and Top: Susannah York, Warren Beatty

184

ROMEO AND JULIET

(EMBASSY) Producer-Director, Paul Czinner; Music, Serge Prokofiev; Choreography, Kenneth Mac Millan; Costumes, Nicholas Georgiadis; Director of Photography, S. D. Onions; Assistant Directors, A. Pearl, Peter Baynham-Honri; Orchestra of Royal Opera House conducted by John Lanchbery; A Paul Czinner Production for Poetic Films Limited in Pathe Color; Presented by Joseph E. Levine. October release.

CAST

Juliet	Margot Fonteyn
Romeo	Rudolf Nureyev
Mercutio	David Blair
Tybalt	Desmond Doyle
Lady Capulet	Julia Farron
Lord Capulet	Michael Somes
Benvolio	Anthony Dowell
Paris	Derek Rencher
Escalus	Leslie Edwards
Rosaline	Georgina Parkinson
Nurse	Gerd Larsen
Friar Laurence	Ronald Hynd
Lord Montague	Christopher Newton
Lady Montague	Betty Kavanagh

Juliet's friends .... Ann Jenner, Ann Howard, Carol Hill, Margaret Lyons, Jennifer Penney, Dianne Horsham
Three Harlots .... Deanne Bergsma, Monica Mason, Carole Needham
Mandolin Dancers .... Keith Rosson, Robert Mead, Lambert Cox, Ian Hamilton, Kenneth Mason, Laurence Ruffell
Guests and Townspeople .... Artists of the Royal Ballet

Rudolf Nureyev, Margot Fonteyn, and above with Derek Rencher

ALFIE

(PARAMOUNT) Producer-Director, Lewis Gilbert; Associate Producer, John Gilbert; Screenplay based on play "Alfie" by Bill Naughton; Director of Photography, Otto Heller; Music, Sonny Rollins; Title Song by Hal David and Burt Bacharach; Sung by Cher; In Techniscope and Technicolor. October release.

CAST

Alfie	Michael Caine
Ruby	Shelley Winters
Siddie	Millicent Martin
Gilda	Julia Foster
Annie	Jane Asher
Carla	Shirley Anne Field
Lily	Vivien Merchant
Woman Doctor	Eleanor Bron
Mr. Smith	Denholm Elliott
Harry	Alfie Bass
Humphrey	Graham Stark
Nat	Murray Melvin
Lofty	Sydney Tafler

Michael Caine (R) also above and top with Julia Foster

Michael Caine, Eleanor Bron
Above: Vivien Merchant, Michael Caine

hael Caine (R). Above: Michael Caine, Shelley
inters. Top: Michael Caine, Denholm Elliott

Millicent Martin, Michael Caine. Above: Jane
Asher, Michael Caine. Top: Murray Melvin,
Michael Caine

EL GRECO

(20th CENTURY-FOX) Producer, Mel Ferrer; Director, Luciano Salce; Screenplay and Story, Guy Elmes; Director of Photography, Leonida Barboni; Costumes, Danilo Donati; Assistant Director, Emilio Miraglia; Produced in DeLuxe Color for Produzioni Artistiche Internazionale-Arco Film and Les Films Du Siecle. October release.

CAST

El Greco	Mel Ferrer
Jeronima de las Cuevas	Rosanna Schiaffino
Francisco	Franco Giacobini
Fra Felix	Renzo Giovampietro
Cardinal Nino de Guevara	Mario Feliciani
Don Diego of Castile	Nino Crisman
Don Miguel de las Cuevas	Adolfo Celi
Don Luis	Angel Aranda
Maria	Gabriella Giorgelli
Isabel	Rosy Di Pietro
Zaida	Rossana Martini
Pignatelli	Giulio Donnini
The Prosecutor	Andrea Bosic
Master of Arms	Giuliana Farnese
Leoni	Ontanoni
King Philip II	Ferdinando Rey

Left: Rosanna Schiaffino, Mel Ferrer

RUN FOR YOUR WIFE

(ALLIED ARTISTS) Producers, Henry Chroscicki, Alfonso Sansome; Associate Producer, Gray Frederickson; Screenplay, Rafael Azlona, Ennio Flaiano, G. L. Polidoro; Story, Rudolfo Sonego; Music, Nino Oliviero; A Sancro Film-Les Film Borderie Production in Technicolor and Techniscope. October release.

CAST

Riccardo Vanzi	Ugo Tognazzi
Nicole	Marina Vlady
Nita	Rhonda Fleming
Jenny	Juliet Prowse
Louise	Graziella Granata
Carlo	Carlo Mazzoni
Teenager	Ruth Laney
Mary	Sharon Obeck
Call Girl	Cherie Latimer

Left: Ugo Tognazzi, Rhonda Fleming

Peter McEnery, Susan Hampshire

THE FIGHTING PRINCE OF DONEGAL

(BUENA VISTA) Producer, Walt Disney; Co-Producer, Bill Anderson; Director, Michael O'Herlihy; Screenplay, Robert Westerby; Based on book "Red Hugh, Prince of Donegal" by Robert T. Reilly; Director of Photography, Arthur Ibbetson; Music, George Bruns; Costumes, Anthony Mendleson; Associate Producer, Hugh Attwooll; Assistant Director, David Bracknell; In Technicolor. October release.

CAST

Hugh O'Donnell	Peter McEnery
Kathleen MacSweeney	Susan Hampshire
Henry O'Neill	Tom Adams
Captain Leeds	Gordon Jackson
Lord MacSweeney	Andrew Keir
Sean O'Toole	Donal McCann
Martin	Maurice Roeves

and Norman Wooland, Richard Leech, Peter Jeffrey, Marie Kean, Bill Owen, Peggy Marshall, Fidelma Murphy, John Forbes Robertson, Patrick Holt, Robert Cawdron, Maire O'Neill, Maire Ni Ghrainne, Roger Croucher, Keith McConnell, Inigo Jackson, Peter Cranwell

10:30 P.M. SUMMER

(LOPERT) Producers, Jules Dassin, Anatole Litvak; Director, Jules Dassin; Screenplay, Jules Dassin, Marguerite Duras; Music Cristobal Halffter; Director of Photography, Gabor Podgany; In Technicolor. October release.

CAST

Maria	Melina Mercouri
Claire	Romy Schneider
Paul	Peter Finch
Rodrigo Palestra	Julian Mateos
Judith	Isabel Maria Perez
Rodrigo's Wife	Beatriz Savon

Julian Mateos, Melina Mercouri. Above: Romy Schneider, Peter Finch. Top: Melina Mercouri

Peter Finch, Melina Mercouri (also above), Romy Schneider

Lynn Redgrave, Charlotte Rampling. Above: Lynn
Redgrave, Charlotte Rampling, Alan Bates
Top: Lynn Redgrave (C)

Lynn Redgrave, Alan Bates. Above: James Ma
Rachel Kempson. Top: Alan Bates,
Charlotte Rampling

GEORGY GIRL

(COLUMBIA) Producers, Robert A. Goldston, Otto Plaschkes; Director, Silvio Narizzano; Screenplay, Margaret Forster, Peter Nichols; Based on novel by Margaret Forster; Music, Alexander Faris; Title Song, Tom Springfield, Jim Dale; Sung by The Seekers; Children's Dance Music, Brian Hunter; Director of Photography, Ken Higgins; Associate Producer, George Pitcher; Assistant Director, Carl Mannin; Clothes, Mary Quant. October release.

CAST

James	James Mason
Jos	Alan Bates
Georgy	Lynn Redgrave
Meredith	Charlotte Rampling
Ted	Bill Owen
Doris	Clare Kelly
Ellen	Rachel Kempson
Peg	Denise Coffey
Health Visitor	Dorothy Alison
Hospital Sister	Peggy Thorpe-Bates
Hospital Nurse	Dandy Nichols
Salesman	Terence Soall
Registry Office Clerk	Jolyan Booth

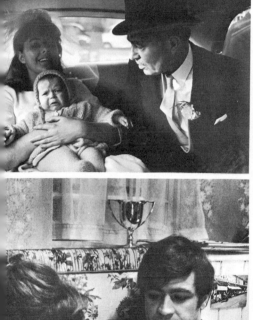

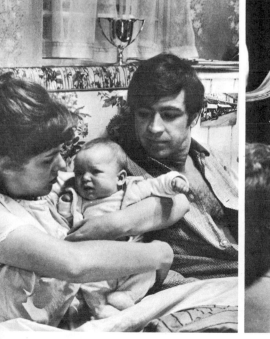

Lynn Redgrave, Alan Bates
Above: Lynn Redgrave, James Mason

Lynn Redgrave. Above: James Mason, Lynn Redgrave, Bill Owen, Clare Kelly

THE LIQUIDATOR

(MGM) Producer, Leslie Elliot; Associate Producer, Harry Fine; Director, Jack Cardiff; Screenplay, Peter Yeldham; Based on novel by John Gardner; Director of Photography, Ted Scaife; Music, Lalo Schifrin; Costumes, Elizabeth Haffenden, Jean Bridges; In Panavision and Metrocolor. November release.

CAST

Boysie Oakes	Rod Taylor
Mostyn	Trevor Howard
Iris	Jill St. John
The Chief	Wilfrid Hyde White
Sheriek	Akim Tamiroff
Coral	Gabriella Licudi
Griffen	Eric Sykes
Quadrant	David Tomlinson

Rod Taylor, Gabriella Licudi. Above: Rod Tay[lor,] Jill St. John. Top: Betty McDowell, Rod Tayl[or.] Left: Rod Taylor, Jo Rawbettom. Top: Ken[...] Wayne, Rod Taylor, Gal Galili

Oskar Werner, Julie Christie, Alex Scott. Above:
Oskar Werner, Julie Christie (also Right Top and
Center). Top: Oskar Werner, Cyril Cusack

FAHRENHEIT 451

(UNIVERSAL) Executive Producer, Lewis M.
Allen; Associate Producer, Mickey Delamar;
Director, Francois Truffaut, Jean-Louis Rich-
ard; Based on novel by Ray Bradbury; Director
of Photography, Nick Roeg; Costumes, Tony
Walton; Assistant Director, Bryan Coates; A
Vineyard Films Limited Production in Techni-
color. November release.

CAST

Linda and Clarisse	Julie Christie
Montag	Oskar Werner
Captain	Cyril Cusack
Fabian	Anton Diffring
Man in flat/Book Man	Jeremy Spenser
Henri Brulard	Alex Scott

IS PARIS BURNING?

(PARAMOUNT) Producer, Paul Graetz; Director, Rene Clement; Screenplay, Gore Vidal, Francis Ford Coppola, Jean Aurenche, Pierre Bost, Claude Brule; From the book by Larry Collins, Dominique LaPierre; Director of Photography, Marcel Grignon; Costumes, Jean Zay, Pierre Nourry; A Transcontinental-Marianne Production in Panavision; A Paramount-Seven Arts Presentation. November release.

CAST

Morandat	Jean-Paul Belmondo
Monod	Charles Boyer
Francoise Labe	Leslie Caron
Henri Karcher	Jean-Pierre Cassel
G. I. in tank	George Chakiris
Lebel	Claude Dauphin
Jacques Chaban-Delmas	Alain Delon
Patton	Kirk Douglas
Bradley	Glenn Ford
Von Choltitz	Gert Frobe
Powell	E. G. Marshall
Bizien	Yves Montand
Warren	Anthony Perkins
Leclerc	Claude Rich
Cafe Proprietress	Simone Signoret
Sibert	Robert Stack
Gallois	Pierre Vaneck
Claire	Marie Versini
G. I. with Warren	Skip Ward
Nordling	Orson Welles
Colonel Rol	Bruno Cremer
A Parisienne	Suzy Delair
Parodi	Pierre Dux
Hitler	Billy Frick
Bayet	Daniel Gelin
Von Arnim	Harry Meyen
Pisani	Michel Piccoli
Serge	Jean-Louis Trintignant

and Sacha Pitoeff, Wolfgang Preiss, Michel Berger, Gehrard Borman, Georges Claisse, Germaine De France, Doc Ericson, Michel Etcheverry, Pascal Fardoulis, Bernard Fresson, Ernst Furbringer, Clara Gansard, Rol Gauffin, Georges Geret, Michel Gonzales, Konrad Georg, Klaus Holm, Jean-Pierre Honore, Peter Jakob, Catherine Kamenka, Billy Kearns, Joelle Latour, Michael Lonsdale, Rober Lumont, Maria Machado, Aime De March, Felix Marten, Paloma Matta, Hannes Messemer, Pierre Mirat, Harald Momm, Georges Montant, Russ Moro, Del Negro, Jean Negroni, Alain Pommier, Georges Poujouley, Michel Puterflam, Christian Rode, Serge Rousseau, Michel Sales, Wolfgang Saure, Georges Staquet, Otto Stern, Henia Suchar, Toni Taffin, Pierre Tamin, Jean Valmont, Jo Warfield, Joachim Westhoss, Jean-Pierre Zola

Jean-Paul Belmondo, Marie Versini, Daniel Gelin

Leslie Caron, Alain Delon

Glenn Ford, Robert Stack. Above: Anthony Perkins, Skip Ward. Top: Gert Frobe, Orson Welles

Gina Lollobrigida, Douglas Byng, Peggy Mount, Alec Guinness, Robert Morley, Derek Fowldes, Leonard Rossiter

HOTEL PARADISO

(MGM) Producer-Director, Peter Glenville; Screenplay, Peter Glenville, Jean-Claude Carriere; Adapted from play "L'Hotel du Libre Echange" by Georges Feydeau and Maurice Desvallieres; Director of Photography, Henri Decae; Music, Laurence Rosenthal; Associate Producer, Pierre Jourdan; Costumes, Jacques Dupont; Assistant Director, Georges Pellegrin; In Panavision and Metrocolor. November release.

CAST

Benedict Boniface	Alec Guinness
Marcelle Cot	Gina Lollobrigida
Henri Cot	Robert Morley
Angelique	Peggy Mount
Anniello	Akim Tamiroff
La Grand Antoinette	Marie Bell
Maxime	Derek Fowldes
Mr. Martin	Douglas Byng
Duke	Robertson Hare
Victoire	Ann Beach
Inspector	Leonard Rossiter
George	David Battley
Turk	Dario Moreno
Georges Feydeau	Peter Glenville

Gina Lollobrigida, Alec Guinness, also above and left with Peggy Mount, Robert Morley. Upper Left: Akim Tamiroff, Marie Bell, Robertson Hare, Dario Moreno

THE DEFECTOR

(SEVEN ARTS) Producer-Director, Raoul Levy;
Screenplay, Raoul Levy, Robert Guenette; Based
on novel "The Spy" by Paul Thomas; In
Color. November release.

CAST

Prof. James Bower .... Montgomery Clift
Counselor Peter Heinzman .... Hardy Kruger
CIA Agent Adam .... Roddy McDowall
Frieda Hoffman .... Macha Meril
Orlovsky .... David Opatoshu
Ingrid .... Christine Delaroche
Dr. Saltzer .... Hannes Messemer
The Major .... Karl Lieffen

**Left: Montgomery Clift, Roddy McDowall,
Hardy Kruger**

Montgomery Clift, Christine Delaroche
196 Above: Macha Meril, Hardy Kruger, Montgomery Clift

Montgomery Clift, Hardy Kruger
Above: Hardy Kruger, David Opatoshu

DR. GOLDFOOT AND THE GIRL BOMBS

(AMERICAN INTERNATIONAL) Producer, Fulvio Lucisano; Director, Mario Bava; Screenplay, Louis M. Heyward, Robert Kaufman; Story, James Hartford; Music, Les Baxter; Title Song, Guy Hemrick, Jerry Styner; In Technicolor. November release.

CAST

Dr. Goldfoot	Vincent Price
Bill Dexter	Fabian
Amateur Sleuths	Franco and Ciccio
Rosanna	Laura Antonelli

Right: Laura Antonelli, Fabian

Francoise Dorleac, Lionel Stander. Above: Francoise Dorleac. Right: Donald Pleasence

CUL-DE-SAC

(SIGMA III) Producer, Gene Gutowski; Direction and Screenplay, Roman Polanski; A Michael Klinger-Tony Tensor Production; A Filmways Presentation. November release.

CAST

George	Donald Pleasence
Teresa	Francoise Dorleac
Richard	Lionel Stander
Albert	Jack MacGowran
Christopher	Iain Quarrier
His Father	Geoffrey Sumner
His Mother	Renee Houston
Cecil	William Franklyn
Nicholas	Trevor Delaney
Mrs. Fairweather	Marie Kean
Mr. Fairweather	Robert Dorning
Jacqueline	Jackie Bissett

Vladimir Pucholt, Hana Brejchova (also top right)

LOVES OF A BLONDE

(PROMINENT) Directed and Written by Mil
Forman; A C.B.K. Production. Decemb
release.

CAST

Andula	Hana Brejchov
Milda	Vladimir Puch
Vacovsky	Vladimir Mens
Milda's Mother	Milda Jezkov
Milda's Father	Josef Seban

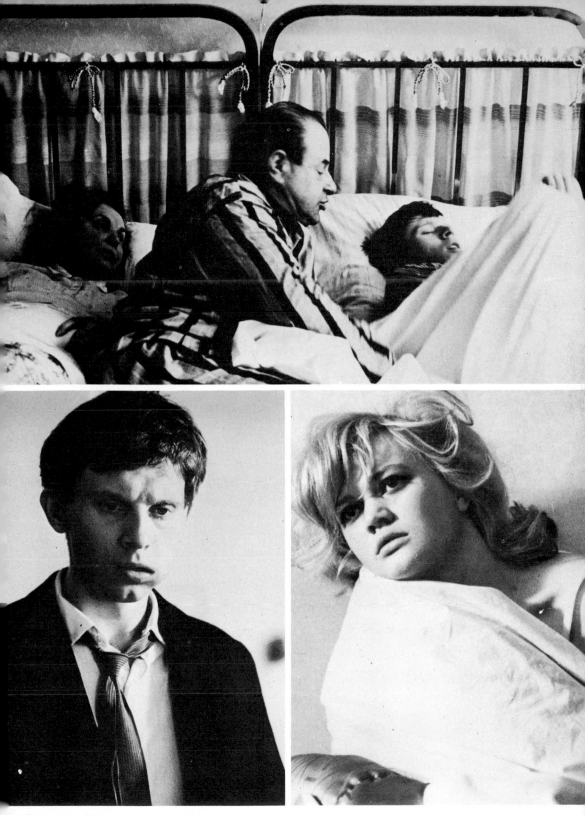

Vladimir Pucholt, and top with Milda Jezkova,
Josef Sebanek

Hana Brejchova

FUNERAL IN BERLIN

(PARAMOUNT) Producer, Charles Kasher; Director, Guy Hamilton; Screenplay, Evan Jones; Based on novel by Len Deighton; Assistant Director, David Bracknell; Presented by Harry Saltzman; A Lowndes Production in Panavision and Technicolor. December release.

CAST

Harry Palmer	Michael Caine
Samantha Steel	Eva Renzi
Johnny Vulkan	Paul Hubschmid
Colonel Stok	Oscar Homolka
Ross	Guy Doleman
Mrs. Ross	Rachel Gurney
Hallam	Hugh Burden
Reinhart	Thomas Holtzmann
Kreutzmann	Gunter Meisner
Aaron Levine	Heinz Schubert
Werner	Wolfgang Volz
Otto Rukel	Klaus Jepsen
Artur	Herbert Fux
Benjamin	Rainer Brandt
Monika	Ira Hagen
Brigit	Marte Keller

Uschi Heyer, Paul Hubschmid,
Michael Caine, Eva Renzi

Rainer Brandt, Heinz Schubert, Eva Renzi
Above: Michael Caine, Oscar Homolka

Paul Hubschmid, Michael Caine, Wolfgang Volz,
Herbert Fux, Gunter Meisner (in coffin)

Lionel Jeffries, Eric Portman, Laurence Harvey   Daliah Lavi, Laurence Harvey, Lionel Jeffries

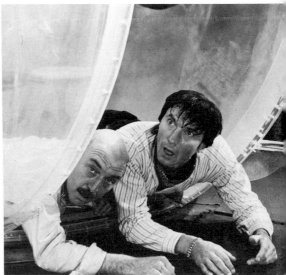

Lionel Jeffries, Eric Sykes. Above: Paul Ford,
Daliah Lavi. Right: Lionel Jeffries, Laurence Harvey

THE SPY WITH A COLD NOSE

(EMBASSY) Executive Producer, Joseph E. Levine; Producer, Leonard Lightstone; Director, Daniel Petrie; Story and Screenplay, Ray Galton, Alan Simpson; Associate Producer, Robert Porter; Music, Riz Ortolani; Assistant Director, Colin Brewer; An Associated London Films Production in Color. December release.

CAST

Dr. Francis Travellyan	Laurence Harvey
Princess Natasha Romanova	Daliah Lavi
Stanley Farquhar	Lionel Jeffries
Wrigley	Eric Sykes
British Ambassador	Eric Portman
Pond-Jones	Denholm Elliott
Russian Premier	Colin Blakely
Elsie Farquhar	June Whitfield
Belly Dancer	Nai Bonet
Disraeli	Disraeli
American General	Paul Ford
Professor	Peter Bayliss
Chief of M. I. 5	Robert Flemyng
M. I. 5 Commander	Robin Bailey
Night Club Hostess	Geneveve
Nurse	Norma Foster
Lady Blanchflower	Renee Houston
Braithwaite	Michael Trubshawe
Miss Marchbanks	Amy Dalby

AFTER THE FOX

(UNITED ARTISTS) Producer, John Bryan; Director, Vittorio De Sica; Screenplay, Neil Simon; Music, Burt Bacharach; Title Song, Hal David, Burt Bacharach; Sung by The Hollies and Peter Sellers; Director of Photography, Leonida Barboni; Costumes, Piero Tosi; Associate Producer, Maurizio Lodi-Fe; Assistant Director, Franco Cirino; Produced by Delegate Productions and Nancy Enterprises in Panavision and DeLuxe Color. December release.

CAST

Aldo Vanucci	Peter Sellers
Tony Powell	Victor Mature
Gina Romantica	Britt Ekland
Harry	Martin Balsam
Okra	Akim Tamiroff
Pollo	Paolo Stoppa
Siepi	Tino Buazzelli
Carlo	Mac Ronay
Mama Vanucci	Lidia Brazzi
Police Chief	Lando Buzzanca
Bikini Girl	Maria Grazia Buccella
Chief of Interpol	Maurice Denham
Detectives	Tiberio Murgia, Francesco De Leone
Cafe Owner	Carlo Croccolo
Mayor	Nino Musco
Doctor	Pier Luigi Pizzi
Singer	Lino Mattera
Prosecuting Counsel	Daniele Vargas
Judge	Franco Sportelli

and Piero Gerlini, Giustino Durano, Mimmo Poli, Enzo Fiermonte, Roberto De Simoni, Angelo Spaggiari, Timothy Bateson, David Lodge

Peter Sellers, Martin Balsam, Victor Mature
Above: Peter Sellers, Lidia Brazzi, Britt Ekland
Top: Peter Sellers

Britt Ekland, Victor Mature, Peter Sellers
Above: Maria Grazia Buccella, Akim Tamiroff
(back), Peter Sellers

Britt Ekland, Peter Sellers, Lidia Brazzi, Maria Grazia Buccella, Victor Mature, Martin Balsam
Top (L): Tino Buazzelli, Peter Sellers, Mac Ronay, Paolo Stoppa
(R) Victor Mature, Martin Balsam

SHOOT LOUD, LOUDER . . . I DON'T UNDERSTAND

(EMBASSY) Producer, Pietro Notarianni; Executive Producer, Joseph E. Levine; Director, Eduardo De Filippo; Screenplay, Eduardo De Filippo, Suso Cecchi D'Amico; Based on play "Le Voci di Dentro" by Eduardo De Filippo; Music, Nino Rota; Director of Photography, Aiace Parolin; Assistant Director, Francesco Massaro; Costumes, Enrico Job; A Master Film Production in Color. December release.

CAST

Alberto Saporito	Marcello Mastroianni
Tania Mottini	Raquel Welch
Pasquale Cimmaruta	Guido Alberti
Carlo Saporito	Leopoldo Trieste
Aunt Rosa Cimmaruta	Tecla Scarano
Uncle Nicola	Eduardo De Filippo
Elvira Cimmaruta	Rosalba Grottesi
Aniello Amitrano	Paolo Ricci
Mrs. Amitrano	Regina Bianchi
Chief Police Inspector	Franco Parenti
Beautiful Woman	Angela Luce
Lt. Bertolucci	Silvano Tranquilli
Matilde Cimmaruta	Pina D'Amato
Marshal Bagnacavallo	Carlo Bagno
Maid	Pia Morra
Luigi Cimmaruta	Gino Minopoli
Deputy Police Inspector	Alberto Bugli
Carmelo Vitiello	Ignazio Spalla

Raquel Welch, Marcello Mastroianni (also above)

204

Raquel Welch, Marcello Mastroianni
Top: Marcello Mastroianni, Paolo Ricci

ARRIVEDERCI, BABY!

(PARAMOUNT) Direction and Screenplay, Ken Hughes; Story, Ken Hughes, Ronald Harwood; Suggested by "The Careful Man" by Richard Deming; Music, Dennis Farnom; Additional Music, Tibor Kunstler and His Gypsy Orchestra, and The Plainsmen; Director of Photography, Denys Coop; Assistant Director, Colin Brewer; Costumes, Elizabeth Haffenden, Joan Bridge; A Seven Arts-Ray Stark Presentation; In Panavision and Technicolor. December release.

CAST

Nick Johnson	Tony Curtis
Francesca	Rosanna Schiaffino
Parker	Lionel Jeffries
Gigi	Zsa Zsa Gabor
Baby	Nancy Kwan
Fenella	Fenella Fielding
Aunt Miriam	Anna Quayle
Conte de Rienzi and Maximilian	Warren Mitchell
Romeo	Mischa Auer
Capt. O'Flannery	Noel Purcell
American Brasshat	Alan Gifford
German Brasshat	Joseph Furst
Butler	Monti De Lyle
French Inspector	Bernard Spear
Italian Dressmaker	Eileen Way
Head Waiter	Bruno Barnabe
Gypsy Baron	Gabor Baraker
Ruby's Boyfriend	Tony Baron
Matron	Eunice Black
Radio Engineers	John Brandon, Windsor Davies
Romano	Franco DeRosa
Maids	Iole Marinelli, Miki Iveria
Priest	Henri Vidon
Photographer	Raymond Young

Fenella Fielding, Tony Curtis. Above: Tony Curtis, Nancy Kwan. Top: Anna Quayle Below: Tony Curtis, Zsa Zsa Gabor

Tony Curtis, Rosanna Schiaffino (also above)

BLOW-UP

(PREMIER) Producer, Carlo Ponti; Director, Michelangelo Antonioni; Screenplay, Antonioni, Tonino Guerra, in collaboration with Edward Bond; Story, Antonioni; Director of Photography, Carlo di Palma; Music, Herbert Hancock; Assistant Director, Claude Watson; In Metro-Color. December release.

CAST

Jane	Vanessa Redgrave
Thomas	David Hemmings
Patricia	Sarah Miles

Models: Verushka, Jill Kennington, Peggy Moffit, Rosaleen Murray, Ann Norman, Melanie Hampshire

Vanessa Redgrave, Ronan O'Casey, David Hemmings
Above: Vanessa Redgrave, David Hemmings

206

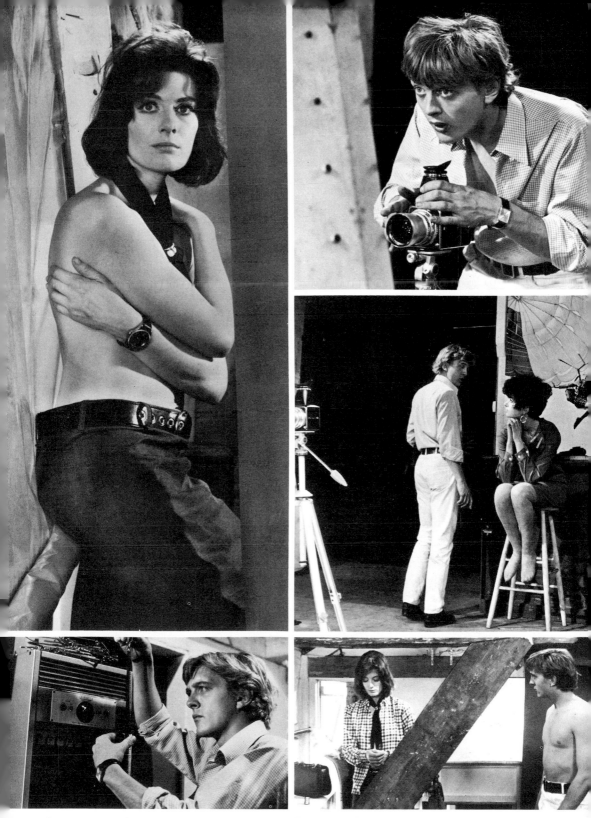

David Hemmings. Above: Vanessa Redgrave　　　　Vanessa Redgrave, David Hemmings. Above:
David Hemmings, Mary Khal. Top: David Hemmings

KISS THE GIRLS AND MAKE THEM DIE

(COLUMBIA) Producer, Dino De Laurentiis; Executive Producers, Salvatore Argento, Dino Maiuri; Director, Henry Levin; Screenplay, Jack Pulman, Dino Maiuri; Story, Dino Maiuri; Music, Mario Nascimbene; Harmonica Soloist, John Sebastian; Title Song sung by Lydia MacDonald; Lyrics, Howard Greenfield; Director of Photography, Aldo Tonti; Costumes, Maria Dematteis, Piero Gherardi; Assistant Directors, Giorgio Gentili, Gianni Cozzo; In Technicolor. December release.

CAST

Kelly	Michael Connors
Susan	Dorothy Provine
James	Terry-Thomas
Lord Aldric	Terry-Thomas
Ardonian	Raf Vallone
Ringo	Oliver McGreevy
Omar	Sandro Dori
Karin	Beverly Adams
Sylvia	Nicoletta Machiavelli
Grace	Margaret Lee
Gioia	Marilu Tolo
Wilma Soong	Seyna Seyn

Dorothy Provine, Raf Vallone, Terry-Thomas

Michael Connors, Dorothy Provine. Above: Oliver McGreevy, Raf Vallone, Seyna Seyn, Andy Ho (R)

Michael Connors, Oliver McGreevy, Raf Vallone Above: Sandro Dori, Dorothy Provine

George Segal, Senta Berger

Max von Sydow, George Segal

nta Berger, Max von Sydow. Above: George Segal,
Alec Guinness. Right: George Segal (on floor)

THE QUILLER
MEMORANDUM

(20th CENTURY-FOX) Producer, Ivan Foxwell;
Director, Michael Anderson; Screenplay, Harold
Pinter; Based on novel by Adam Hall; Director
of Photography, Erwin Hiller; Music, John
Barry; Song "Wednesday's Child" by John
Barry, Mack David; Sung by Matt Monro;
Assistant Director, Clive Reed; In Panavision
and DeLuxe Color. December release.

CAST
Quiller	George Segal
Pol	Alec Guinness
Oktober	Max von Sydow
Inge	Senta Berger
Gibbs	George Sanders
Weng	Robert Helpmann
Gibb's Associate	Robert Flemyng
Hengel	Peter Carsten
Headmistress	Edith Schneider
Hassler	Gunter Meisner
Jones	Robert Stass

Paul Scofield, Wendy Hiller   Susannah York, Wendy Hiller, Paul Scofield

Robert Shaw, Nigel Davenport, Susannah York,
Paul Scofield, Wendy Hiller. Above: Robert Shaw,
Vanessa Redgrave

Colin Redgrave, Susannah York
Above: Robert Shaw, Paul Scofield

A MAN FOR ALL SEASONS

(COLUMBIA) Producer-Director, Fred Zinnemann; Executive Producer, William N. Graf; Screenplay, Robert Bolt; Based on his play; Music, Georges Delerue; Director of Photography, Ted Moore; Costumes, Elizabeth Haffenden, Joan Bridge; Assistant Directors, Peter Bolton, Al Burgess, Bill Graf, Jr.; In Technicolor. December release.

CAST

Thomas More	Paul Scofield
Alice More	Wendy Hiller
Thomas Cromwell	Leo McKern
King Henry VIII	Robert Shaw
Cardinal Wolsey	Orson Welles
Margaret More	Susannah York
Duke of Norfolk	Nigel Davenport
Rich	John Hurt
William Roper	Corin Redgrave
Matthew	Colin Blakely
Averil Machin	Yootha Joyce
King's Representative	Anthony Nichols
Jailer	John Nettleton
Matthew's Wife	Eira Heath
Maid	Molly Urquhart
Courtier	Paul Hardwick
Norfolk's Aide	Michael Latimer
Captain of Guard	Philip Brack
Governor of Tower	Martin Boddey
Executioner	Eric Mason
Messenger	Matt Zinnerman
Anne Boleyn	Vanessa Redgrave

Paul Scofield, Nigel Davenport

Paul Scofield (R) Above: Orson Welles, Paul Scofield

Paul Scofield. Above: Paul Scofield, John Hurt, Leo McKern

Paul Scofield
in
"A MAN FOR ALL SEASONS"

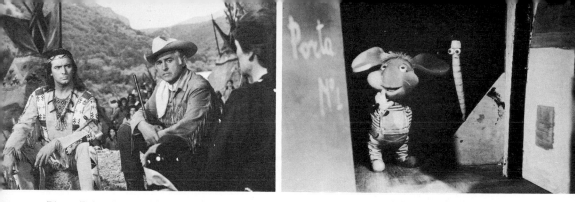

Pierre Brice, Stewart Granger
in "Rampage At Apache Wells"

"The Magic World Of Topo Gigio"

RAMPAGE AT APACHE WELLS (Columbia) Producer, Horst Wendlandt; Director, Harald Philipp; Based on novel by Karl May; In Cinemascope and ColumbiaColor. January release. CAST: Stewart Granger, Pierre Brice, Harald Leipnitz, Macha Meril.

MONDO PAZZO (Rizzoli) Producers, Mario Maffei, Giorgio Cecchini; Director of Photography, Benito Frattari; Music, Nino Oliviero; Directed by Gualtiero Jacopetti, Franco Prosperi; Commentary written by Gualtiero Jacopetti; In Technicolor. January release. A sequel to "Mondo Cane," presenting more bizarre, cruel, and exotic customs of people around the world.

THE MAGIC WORLD OF TOPO GIGIO (Columbia) Directors, Franco Serino, Luca De Rico; Screenplay, Perego, Mario Faustinelli, Guido Stagnaro; Director of Photography, Giorgio Battilana; Music, Armando Trovaioli; A Richard David-Jolly Film Presentation in Color. January release. Animated film featuring the Italian mouse Topo.

SANDRA (Royal) Producer, Franco Cristaldi; Director, Luchino Visconti; Screenplay, Suso Cecchi d'Amico, Enrico Medioli, Luchino Visconti. January release. CAST: Claudia Cardinale, Michael Craig, Jean Sorel, Marie Bell, Renzo Ricci, Fred Williams, Amalia Troiani.

MAEDCHEN IN UNIFORM (7 Arts) A CCO-Farbfilm Production. January release. CAST: Lilli Palmer, Romy Schneider, Christine Kaufmann, Therese Giehse.

GHIDRA, THE THREE-HEADED MONSTER (Continental) A Toho Production; Director, Inoshiro Honda; Screenplay, Shinichi Sekizawa; Director of Photography, Hajime Koizumi; In Color. January release. CAST: Yosuke Natsuki, Yuriko Hoshi, Kiroshi Koizumi, Takashi Shimura, Em Ito, Yumi Ito.

UNDERWORLD INFORMERS (Continental) Producer, William MacQuitty; Director, Ken Annakin; Screenplay, Alun Falcuner. January release. CAST: Nigel Patrick, Catherine Woodville, Margaret Whiting, Colin Blakely, Darren Nesbitt.

AGENT 8¾ (Continental) Producers, Ralph Thomas-Betty E. Box; Director, Betty E. Box; Screenplay, Lukas Heller; In Color. January release. CAST: Dirk Bogarde, Sylva Koscina, Robert Morley, Leo McKern, Roger Delgado, John Le Mesurier, Richard Pasco, Eric Pohlmann, Alan Tilvern.

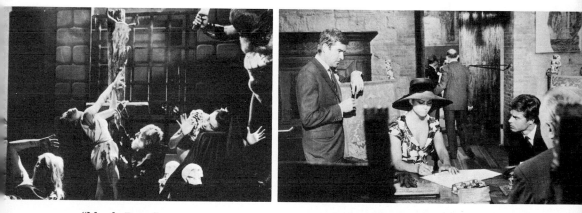

"Mondo Pazzo"

Michael Craig, Claudia Cardinale, Jean Sorel
in "Sandra"

THE GREAT WALL (Magna) Producer, Masaichi Nagata; Director, Shigeo Tanaka; Screenplay, Fuji Yahiro; Director of Photography, Machio Takahashi; Music, Akira Ifukube; A Daiei Production in Technicolor. January release. CAST: Shintaro Katsu, Fujiko Yamamoto, Ken Utsui, Hiroshi Kawaguchi, Ayako Wakao, Kohiro Hongo, Raizo Ichikawa, Ganjiro Makamura.

RESURRECTION (Artkino) A Mosfilm Production; Based on novel by Leo Tolstoy. January release. CAST: Tamara Syomia, Yevgeni Matveyev, Nina Samsonova.

**Virginia Field, Dennis Price
in "The Earth Dies Screaming"**

**Sylva Koscina, Dirk Bogarde
in "Agent 8¾"**

THE EARTH DIED SCREAMING (20th Century-Fox) Executive Producer, Robert L. Lippert; Director, Terence Fisher; Director of Photography, Arthur Lavis; Screenplay, Henry Cross. January release. CAST: Willard Parker, Virginia Field, Dennis Price, Vanda Godsell, Thorley Walters, David Spenser, Anna Falk.

THE LOST WORLD OF SINBAD (American International) Executive Producer, Yuko Tanaka; Director, Senkichi Taniguchi; Screenplay, Takeshi Kimura; Director of Photography, Shinichi Sekizawa; Music, Masaru Satoh; A Toho Production in Colorscope. January release. CAST: Toshiro Mifune, Makoto Satoh, Jun Funado, Ichiro Arishima, Miye Hama, Kumi Mizuno, Eiko Wakabayashi, Mitsuko Kusabue, Tadao Nakamura, Jun Tazaki, Takashi Shimura.

FIVE GENTS' TRICK BOOK (Toho) Producer, Masumi Fujimoto; Director, Sayo Marubayashi; Screenplay, Ryozo Kasahara; Director of Photography, Takeshi Suzuki; Music, Yosijuki Kozu; In Eastman Color. January release. CAST: Hisaya Morishige, Asami Kuji, Yoko Tsukasa, Daisuko Kaio, Norihei Miki, Franky Sakal, Junko Ikeuchi, Michiyo Aratama, Reiko Dan.

THE PLAGUE OF THE ZOMBIES (20th Century-Fox) Producer, Anthony Nelson Keys; Director, John Gilling; Screenplay, John Elder; Music, James Bernard; Director of Photography, Arthur Grant; Assistant Director, Martyn Green; A Seven Arts-Hammer Production in DeLuxe Color. January release. CAST: Andre Morell, Diane Clare, Book Williams, Jacqueline Pearce, John Carson, Alexander Davion, Michael Ripper, Dennis Chinnery, Louis Mahoney, Roy Royston, Marcus Hammond, Ben Aris, Tim Condroy, Bernard Egan, Norman Mann, Francis Willey, Jerry Verno, Jolyan Booth.

THE WAR OF THE ZOMBIES (American International) Director, Giuseppe Vari; A Galatea Production in Colorscope. January release. CAST: John Drew Barrymore, Susi Andersen, Ettore Manni, Ida Galli, Philippe Hersent, Mino Doro, Ivano Staccioli, Matilde Calnan, Giulio Maculani.

DRACULA—PRINCE OF DARKNESS (20th Century-Fox) Producer, Anthony Nelson Keys; Director, Terence Fisher; Screenplay, John Sansom; Music, James Bernard; Director of Photography, Michael Reed; Assistant Director, Bert Batt; A Seven Arts-Hammer Production in DeLuxe Color. January release. CAST: Christopher Lee, Barbara Shelley, Andrew Keir, Francis Matthews, Suzan Farmer, Charles Tingwell, Thorley Walters, Philip Latham, Walter Brown, George Woodbridge, Jack Lambert, Philip Ray, Joyce Hemson, John Maxim.

**Richard Harrison (R)
in "Secret Agent Fireball"**

**Fraser MacIntosh, Tim Barrett
in "The Boy Cried Murder"**

SECRET AGENT FIREBALL (American International) Director, Martin Donan; In WideScope and Color. January release. CAST: Richard Harrison, Dominique Boschero, Wandisa Guida.

THE BOY CRIED MURDER (Universal) Producer, Philip N. Krasne; Director, George Breakston; Screenplay, Robin Estridge; A Carlos-Avala Production in association with Bernard Luber in Color. CAST: Veronica Hurst, Phil Brown, Fraser MacIntosh, Tim Barrett, Beba Loncar, Edward Steel, Anita Sharpe-Bolster.

"The Plague Of The Zombies"

Toshiro Mifune (L)
in "The Lost World Of Sinbad"

IMPOSSIBLE ON SATURDAY (Magna) Director, Alex Joffe; Story and Screenplay, Jean Ferry, Pierre Levy-Corti, Shabatai-Tevet, Alex Joffe. February release. CAST: Robert Hirsch, Dahlia Friedland, Mischa Asherov, Teddy Bilis, Geula Nuni, Yoni Levi.

FLAME AND THE FIRE (Continental) Producers, Vernon P. Becker, Mitchell R. Leiser; Director, Pierre Dominique Gaisseau; Commentary, Charles Romine; Narrated by Gaisseau; Music, Michael Colicchio; In Eastman Color. February release. A documentary on vanishing tribes in Brazil, Australia, Africa and New Guinea.

MAKE LIKE A THIEF (Emerson) Produced and Written by Palmer Thompson; Directors, Thompson, Richard Long; Director of Photography, Kalle Peronkoski; Music, Erkki Meloski; In Eastman Color. February release. CAST: Richard Long, Ake Lindman, Pirkko Mannola, Rosemary Precht, Juhani Kumpalinen, Aulekki Tarnanen, Esko Salamen.

THE MERMAID (Lee) Producer, Runme Shaw; Director, Kao Li; Screenplay, Chang Chien; Assistant Director, Yueh Cheng-chun; Director of Photography, Tung Shao-yung; Music, Wang Fu-ling; In Color. February release. CAST: Ching Miao, Au-yang Sha-fei, Yang Tse-ching, Chiang Kuang-chao, Yeh Ching, Chen Yuen-hua, Tung Di, Li Yuen-chung.

ESCAPE BY NIGHT (Allied Artists) Producer, Maurice J. Wilson; Director, Montgomery Tully; Music, John Veale; Screenplay, Maurice J. Wilson, Montgomery Tully; Based on Novel "Clash By Night" by Rupert Croft-Cooke. March release. CAST: Terence Longdon, Jennifer Jayne, Harry Fowler, Peter Sallis, Alan Wheatley, Vanda Godsell, Arthur Lovegrove, Hilda Fenemore, Mark Dignam, John Arnatt, Richard Carpenter, Stanley Meadows, Robert Brown, Tom Bowman, Ray Amsten.

THE MERRY WIVES OF WINDSOR (Sigma III) Producer, Norman Foster; Director, George Tressler; Screenplay adapted from Otto Nicolai's opera by Norman Foster; Music played by Zagreb Symphony; In Color. March release. CAST: Norman Foster, Colette Boky, Mildred Miller, Igor Gorin, Lucia Popp, Ernst Schutz.

THE REDEEMER (Empire) Producer, Rev. Patrick Peyton; Director, Joseph Breen; Screenplay, Tom Blackburn, Robert Hugh O'Sullivan, John T. Kelly, James O'Hanlon; Music, David Raksin; Narrated by Sebastian Cabot; In Todd-AO and Eastman Color. March release. CAST: Luis Alvarez, Maruchi Fresno, Virgilio Texeira, Manuel Monroy, Jose Marco Davo, Carlos Casaraville, Antonio Vilar, Felix Acaso, Heve Donay, Jacinto San Emeterio, Macdonald Carey (voice of Christ).

"The House With An Attic"

Norman Foster
in "The Merry Wives Of Windsor"

THE HOUSE WITH AN ATTIC (Artkino) Produced in Russia in color. February release. CAST: Nellie Mychkova, Sergei Yakovlev.

EROICA (Amerpol) Producer-Director, Andrez Munk. March release. CAST: Edward Dziewonski, Barbara Polomska, Ignacy Machowski, Kazimierz Rudski, Josef Nowak, Roman Klosowski, Wojciech Siemion, Josef Kostecki, Tadeusz Lominicki.

"Ghidrah, The Three-Headed Monster"

Jennifer Daniels
in "The Reptile"

OHAYO (Shochiku) Produced, Directed and Written by Yasujiro Ozu. March release. CAST: Kuniko Mayake, Chisu Ryu, Koji Shidara, Masahiko Shimazu, Yoshiko Kuga, Keiji Sada.

RUSSIAN ADVENTURE (United Roadshow) Directors, Leonid Kristy, Roman Karmen, Boris Dolin, Oleg Lebedev, Solomon Kogan, Vassily Katanian; Narration and Prologue, Homer McCoy; Narrated by Bing Crosby; Music, Aleksandr Lokshin, Ilya Schweitzer, Yuri Effimov; A Soveportfilm in Cinerama. Released under the auspices of the Cultural Exchange Program. March release.

W.I.A. (WOUNDED IN ACTION) (Myriad) Producers, Irving Sunasky, Samuel Zerinsky; Directed and Written by Irving Sunasky; Director of Photography, Enrique Rogales; Music, Leopold Silos. March release. CAST: Steve Marlo, Maura McGiveney, Leopoldo Salcedo, Mary Humphrey, Albert Quinton, Victor Izay, Bella Flores, John Horn, Peter E. Deuel, Joe Sison, Brennan Wood, Romy Brion.

ILLUSION OF BLOOD (Toho) Producer, Ichiro Sato; Director, Shiro Toyoda; Screenplay, Toshio Yazumi; Story, Nanboku Tsuruya; Director of Photography, Hiroshi Murai; Music, Toru Takemitsu; In Tohoscope and Eastman Color. March release. CAST: Tatsuya Nakadai, Mariko Okada, Junko Ikeuchi, Kanzaburo Nakamura, Mayumi Ozora, Keiko Awaji, Eitaro Izawa, Masao Mishima.

THE REPTILE (20th Century-Fox) Producer, Anthony Nelson Keys; Director, John Gilling; Screenplay, John Elder; Music, Don Banks; Assistant Director, Bill Cartlidge; A Seven Arts-Hammer Production in DeLuxe Color. April release. CAST: Noel Willman, Jennifer Daniels, Ray Barrett, Jacqueline Pearce, Michael Ripper, John Laurie, Marne Maitland, David Baron, Charles Lloyd Pack, Harold Goldblatt, George Woodbridge.

THE MURDER GAME (20th Century-Fox) Producers, Robert L. Lippert, Jack Parsons; Director, Sidney Salkow; Screenplay, Harry Spalding; Based on story by Irving Yergin; Director of Photography, Geoffrey Faithful; Assistant Director, Gordon Gilbert; Music, Carlo Martelli. April release. CAST: Ken Scott, Marla Landi, Trader Faulkner, Conrad Phillips, Gerald Sim, Duncan Lamont, Rosamund Greenwood, Victor Brooks, Ballard Berkeley, Jimmy Gardner, Peter Bathurst, Jennifer White, Frank Thornton, Gretchen Franklyn, John Dunbar, Clement Freud, Derek Partridge.

MAN FROM COCODY (American International) Director, Christian-Jaque; Screenplay, Claude Rank; A Euro-France Films-Gaumont International Production in Franscope and Eastmancolor. CAST: Jean Marais, Liselotte Pulver, Philippe Clay, Nancy Holloway, Maria Bracia Buccela, Jacques Morel, Robert Dalban.

Margaret Whiting
in "Underworld Informers"

Massimo Serato, Tony Russel
in "The Secret Seven"

JUDEX (Continental) Director, Georges Franju; Original Screenplay by Louis Feuillade and Arthur Bernede adapted by Francis Lacassin and Jacques Champreux; A French-Italian Co-Production. April release. CAST: Michel Vitold, Channing Pollock, Jacques Jouanneau, Edith Scob, Francine Berge, Theo Sarapo, Philippe Mareuil, Rene Genin, Sylva Koscina.

THE SECRET SEVEN (MGM) Film Columbus-Roma, Atenea Films-Madrid Production; Director, Alberto De Martino; In Techniscope and Eastmancolor. CAST. Tony Russel, Helga Line, Massimo Serato, Gerard Tichy, Renato Baldini, Livio Lorenzon, Barta Barry, Joseph Marco, Kriss Huerta, Gianni Solaro, Francesco Sormano, Emma Baron, Pedro Mari, Tomas Blanco, Renato Montalbano.

Olivier, Sandrine, Claire, and Jean-Claude Drouot
in "Le Bonheur"

Tom Bell, Diane Baker, David Opatoshu
in "Sands Of Beersheba"

CONTEST GIRL (Continental) Producer-Director, Val Guest; Screenplay, Val Guest, Robert Muller; In Cinemascope and Color. May release. CAST: Ian Hendry, Janette Scott, Ronald Fraser, Edmund Purdom, Jean Claudio, Kay Walsh, Norman Bird, Janina Faye, Tommy Trinder, David Weston, Francis Matthews, Linda Christian.

LE BONHEUR (Clover) Directed and Written by Agnes Varda; Music by Mozart; In Color. May release. CAST: Jean-Claude Drouot, Sandrine Drouot, Olivier Drouot, Marie France Boyer.

CLOUDS OVER ISRAEL (Israel) Producers, Mati Raz, Harold Cornsweet; Director, Ivan Lengyel; Screenplay, Moshe Hadar; A Harold Cornsweet-Israel Co-Production. May release. CAST: Yiftach Spector, Ehud Banai, Dina Doronne, Shimon Israeli, Hadara Azulai, Shaike Levi, Itzhak Benyamini, Itzhak Barzilai, Ygal Alon.

SECRET AGENT SUPER DRAGON (United Screen Arts) Producer, Robert Amoros; Director, Calvin J. Padgett; A Co-Production of Ramofilm-Fono Roma, Film Borderie, and Gloria Film; In Color. CAST: Ray Danton, Marisa Mell, Margaret Lee, Jess Hahn, Carlo D'Angelo.

SANDS OF BEERSHEBA (Landau/Unger) Produced, Directed and Written by Alexander Ramati. May release. CAST: Diane Baker, David Opatoshu, Tom Bell, Paul Stassino, Didi Ramati.

THE MYSTERY OF THUG ISLAND (Columbia) Producer, Nino Battiferri; Director, Luigi Capuano; A Liber-Echberg Film in Color. May release. CAST: Guy Madison, Peter Van Eyck, Inge Schoner, Giacomo Risso Stuart.

A YOUNG WORLD (Lopert) Producer, Raymond Froment; Director, Vittorio De Sica; Screenplay, Cesare Zavattini; Director of Photography, Jean Boffety; Presented by Harry Saltzman; June release. CAST: Christine DeLaRoche, Nino Castelnuovo, Tanya Lopert, Nadiege Ragoo, Madeleine Robinson, Pierre Brasseur, Jeanne Aubert, Jean-Pierre Darras, George Wilson, Isa Miranda, Francoise Brion.

GULLIVER'S TRAVELS BEYOND THE MOON (Continental) Producer, Tiroshi Okawa; Director, Yoshio Kuroda; Screenplay, Shinichi Sekizawa, Director of Animation, Hideo Furusawa; Music, Milton and Anne DeLugg; A Toei Production in Color. A Full-length animated film.

Trader Faulkner (L), Ken Scott (in door),
Marla Landi in "The Murder Game"

Guy Madison (C)
in "The Mystery Of Thug Island"

DESTINATION INNER SPACE (Magna) Executive Producer, Fred Jordan; Producer, Earle Lyon; Associate Producer, Wendell E. Niles, Jr.; Director, Francis Lyon; Screenplay, Arthur C. Pierce; A Harold Goldman-United Pictures Presentation in Color. May release. CAST: Scott Brady, Sheree North, Gary Merrill, Mike Road, Wende Wagner, James Hong.

SWEET LIGHT IN A DARK ROOM (Promenade) Director, Jiri Weiss; Screenplay, Jiri Weiss, Jan Otcenasek; A Barandov Studio Production. June release. CAST: Dana Smutna, Ivan Mistrik, Jirina Sejbalova, Frantisek Smolik, Blanka Bohdanova, Jiri Kodet, Eva Mrazova, Karla Chadimova, Milos Nedbal, Anna Meliskova.

Nino Castelnuovo, Christine DeLaRoche
in "A Young World"

Marianne Koch, Lex Barker
in "A Place Called Glory"

MANDRAGOLA (Europix) Producer, Alfred Bini; Director, Alberto Lattuado; Screenplay, Alberto Lattuado, Luigi Magni, Stefano Strucchi. June release. CAST: Rosanna Schiaffino, Philippe Leroy, Jean Claude Brialy, Toto, Romolo Valli, Armando Bandini, Nilla Pizzi.

THE MAGNIFICENT CONCUBINE (Frank Lee) Executive Producer, Doven Chow; Producer, Runme Shaw; Director, Li Han-hsiang; Screenplay, Wang Chih-po; Shaw Brothers Production in Color. June release. CAST: Li Li-hua, Yen Chuan, Chao Lei, Li Hsiang-chun, Yang Chih-ching, Ku Wen-tsung, Ho Pin, Lin Ching, Weng Mu-lan, Lily Mo Chau.

THE WINNER (Gillmor-Kingsley) Formerly "A Heart As Big As That." Producer, Pierre Braunberger; Direction and Photography by Francois Reichenbach. June release. CAST: Abdoulaye Faye, Marcel Bruchard, Milou Pladner, Luce Vidi, Yasumiko, Michele Morgan, Jean-Paul Belmondo.

A PLACE CALLED GLORY (Embassy) Executive Producers, Fred Wallach, Michael Echarry; Producers, Bruce Balaban, Danilo Sabatini; Director, Ralph Gideon; Screenplay, Edward Di Lorenzo, Jerold Hayden Boyd, Fernando Lamas; Story, Jerold Hayden Boyd; Director of Photography, Federico G. Larraya; Music, Angel Arteaga; Assistant Director, Enrique Bergier, Costumes, Itala Scandariato; A Midega Film-CCC Film Co-Production in Techniscope and Pathecolor. July release. CAST: Lex Barker, Pierre Brice, Marianne Koch, Jorge Rigaud, Gerard Tichy, Angel Del Pozo, Santiago Ontanon, Hans Nielsen.

THE UNCLE (Lenart) Producer, Robert Goldston; Director, Desmond Davis; Screenplay, Desmond Davis, Margaret Abrams; Based on Miss Abrams' book; A British Lion Production. July release. CAST: Rupert Davies, Brenda Bruce, Robert Duncan, William Marlowe, Ann Lynn, Christopher Ariss, Maurice Denham.

ENGAGEMENT ITALIANO (Sedgeway) Producer, Pietro Notarianni; Directed and Written by Alfredo Giannetti; A Co-Production of Archimede Films and France Cinema. July release. CAST: Rossano Brazzi, Annie Girardot, Tony Anthony, Merisa Merlini.

DR. WHO AND THE DALEKS (Continental) Executive Producer, Joe Vegoda; Producers, Milton Subotsky, Max J. Rosenberg; Director, Gordon Flemyng; Based on BBC TV serial by Terry Nation; In Technicolor and Techniscope. July release. CAST: Peter Cushing, Roy Castle, Jennie Linden, Roberta Tovey, Barrie Ingham, Geoffrey Toone, Mark Petersen, John Brown, Michael Coles, Yvonne Antrobus.

MACABRO (Trans American) Producer, Guido Giambarolomei; Director, Romolo Marcellini; Narrated by Marvin Miller; In Color. July release. A "shock" documentary of grotesque and bloody practices throughout the world.

Nick Adams (LC)
in "Frankenstein Conquers The World"

"Macabro"

FRANKENSTEIN CONQUERS THE WORLD (American International) A Toho Company Ltd.-Henry G. Saperstein Production in Colorscope. July release. CAST: Nick Adams.

SALTO (Kanawha) Directed and Written by Tadeusz Konwicki; A Polish State Film Co. production. August release. CAST: Zbigniew Cybulski, Gustaw Holoubek, Marta Lippinska, Irena Laskowska, Wojciech Liemion, Wlodzimierz Borunski, Zdzislaw Maklakiewicz, Andrzej Lapicki.

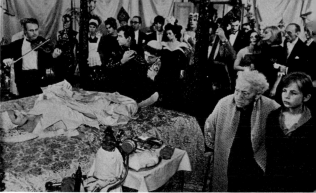

Mylene Demongeot, Frederick Stafford
in "OSS 117—Mission For A Killer"

Ingrid Thulin, Naima Wifstrand, Jorgen Lindstrom
in "Night Games"

KANCHENJUNGHA (Harrison) Produced, Directed, Written, and Music Composed by Satyajit Ray;
In Color. August release. CAST: Chhabi Biswas,
Karuna Banerji, Anil Chatterjee, Anubhe Gupta,
Subrata Sen, Indrani Singh, Nilima Roy Chowdhury,
N. Viswanathan, Pahari Sanyal, Arun Mukherjee,
Vidya Singh.

GOOD TIMES, WONDERFUL TIMES (Rogosin)
Producer-Director, Lionel Rogosin; Associate Producer, James Vaughan; Screenplay, Lionel Rogosin,
James Vaughan, Tadeusz Makarczynski. August
release. An Anti-War Documentary with "in
people" but no professional actors, with dramatic
footage from the past wars.

LA VISTA (Promenade) Producer, Moris Ergas;
Director, Antonio Pietrangeli; An Italian-French
Co-Production. August release. CAST: Sandra
Milo, Francois Perier, Mario Adorf, Angela Minervini, Gaston Moschin, Didi Perego.

TIME LOST AND TIME REMEMBERED (Continental) Formerly titled "I Was Happy Here";
Producer, Roy Millichip; Director, Desmond Davis;
Screenplay, Desmond Davis, Edna O'Brien; Based
on Miss O'Brien's book; A Rank Production. August release. CAST: Sarah Miles, Cyril Cusack,
Julian Glover, Sean Caffrey, Marie Kean, Eve
Belton, Cardew Robinson.

NIGHT GAMES (Sandrews) Director, Mai Zetterling; Screenplay, Mai Zetterling, David Hughes;
Based on novel by Mai Zetterling; Director of
Photography, Rune Ericson, George Riedel; Music, Jan Johansson,
George Riedel; A Sandrews Production. September
release. CAST: Ingrid Thulin, Keve Hjelm, Jorgen
Lindstrom, Lena Brundin, Naima Wifstrand, Rune
Lindstrom.

OSS 117—MISSION FOR A KILLER (Embassy)
Producer, Paul Cadeac; Director, Andre Hunebelle;
Screenplay, Jean Halain, Pierre Foucaud, Andre
Hunebelle; Based on novel by Jean Bruce; Director
of Photography, Marcel Grignon; Music, Michel
Magne; Costumes, Jo Ranzato; In Color and Franscope. September release. CAST: Frederick Stafford, Mylene Demongeot, Raymond Pellegrin, Perette Pradier, Annie Andersson, Francois Maistre,
Jacques Riberolles, Yves Furet, Guy Delorme,
Jean-Pierre Janic, Claude Carliez.

MASCULINE FEMININE (Royal) Directed and
Written by Jean Luc Godard. October release.
CAST: Jean-Pierre Leaud, Chantal Goya, Marlene
Jobert, Michel Debord, Catherine-Isabelle Duport,
Eva-Britt Strandber, Antoine Bourseiller, Brigitte
Bardot.

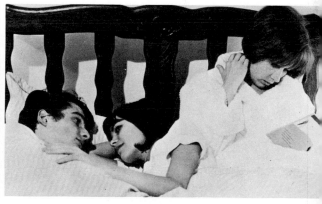

Stathis Giallelis, Janet Margolin
in "The Eavesdropper"

"Masculine Feminine"

THE EAVESDROPPER (Royal) Producer, Paul
M. Heller; Director, Leopoldo Torre Nilsson;
Screenplay, Beatriz Guido, Joe Goldberg, Mabel
Itzcovich, Edmundo Eidhelbaum, and Nilsson;
Story, Beatriz Guido and Nilsson; Director of
Photography, Alberto Etchebehere; Music, Lopez
Furst. September release. CAST: Janet Margolin,
Stathis Giallelis, Lautaro Murua, Leonardo Favio,
Nelly Meden, Ignacio de Soroa, Elena Tortesina.

THE CHRISTMAS THAT ALMOST WASN'T
(Childhood) Producer, Barry B. Yellen; Director,
Rossano Brazzi; Screenplay, Lyrics, and Story, Paul
Tripp; Songs, Ray Carter; Music, Bruno Nicolai; In
Color. November release. CAST: Rossano Brazzi,
Paul Tripp, Lidia Brazzi, Alberto Rabagliati,
Mischa Auer, Sonny Fox.

**Tom Adams, Dawn Addams
in "Where The Bullets Fly"**

**Marie Versini, Christopher Lee
in "The Brides Of Fu Manchu"**

**Ugo Tognazzi
in "A Very Handy Man"**

90 DEGREES IN THE SHADE (Landau/Unger) Producer, Raymond Stross; Director, Jiri Weiss; Screenplay, David Mercer; Music, Ludek Hulan. November release. CAST: Anne Heywood, James Booth, Rudolf Hrusinski.

TOKYO OLYMPIAD (American International) Produced by The Organizing Committee for the Games of the XVIII Olympiad in Tokyo; Director, Kon Ichikawa; Written by Natto Wada, Yoshio Shiraskawa, Shuntaro Tanikawa, Kon Ichikawa; Music, Toshiro Mayuzumi; A Jack Douglas Presentation in Cinemascope and Eastmancolor. November release. CAST: Participants in the Olympic Games.

WHERE THE BULLETS FLY (Embassy) Producer, James Ward; Director, John Gilling; Story and Screenplay, Michael Pittock; Associate Producer, George Fowler; Director of Photography, David Holmes; Music, Kenny Graham; Title Song, Bob Kingston and Ronald Bridges; Sung by Susan Maughan; Assistant Director, Ray Frift; Costumes, Joanna Wright; A Puck Films Production in Color; Presented by Joseph E. Levine. November release. CAST: Tom Adams, Dawn Addams, Tim Barrett, Michael Ripper, Sidney James, Wilfrid Brambell, Joe Baker, Ronald Leigh-Hunt, Bryan Mosley, Michael Ward, Heidi Erich, Suzan Farmer.

A PISTOL FOR RINGO (Embassy) Producers, Luciano Ercoli, Alberto Pugliese; Direction and Screenplay, Duccio Tessari; Director of Photography, Francisco Marin; Music, Ennio Morricone; Costumes, Carlo Gentili; In Color. November release. CAST: Montgomery Wood, Fernando Sancho, Hally Hammond, Nieves Navarro, Antonio Casas, George Martin.

THE TEXICAN (Columbia) Producers, John C. Champion, Bruce Balaban; Director, Lesley Selander; Executive Producers, Paul C. Ross, Julian Ludwig; Screenplay, John C. Champion; Director of Photography, Francis Marin; Music, Nico Fidenco; Assistant Director, Joseph Espinosa; Costumes, Ralph Borque; In Techniscope and Technicolor. December release. CAST: Audie Murphy, Broderick Crawford, Diana Lorys, Aldo Sambrel, Anthony Casas, Gerard Tichy, Anthony Molino, John Peral, Helga Genth, Luz Marquez.

YOUNG APHRODITES (Janus) Producers, George Zervos, Nikos Koundouros; Director, Nikos Koundouros; Screenplay, Vassilis Vassilikos, Costas Sphikas; A Protelco Production. December release. CAST: Takis Emmanouel, Elen Prokopiou, Vangelis Joannides, Cleopatra Rota, Anestis Vlachos, Yannis Jeannino, C. Papaconstantinou.

THE BRIDES OF FU MANCHU (7 Arts) Producers, Oliver A Unger, Harry Alan Towers; Director, Don Sharp; Screenplay, Peter Welbeck; Based on characters created by Sax Rohmer; Director of Photography, Ernest Stewart; Music, Bruce Montgomery; Assistant Director, Barrie Melrose; A Hallam Production in Technicolor. December release. CAST: Christopher Lee, Douglas Wilmer, Marie Versini, Tsai Chin, Henrich Wilhelm Drache.

A VERY HANDY MAN (Rizzoli) Producer Nino Krisman; Director, Alessandro Blasetti; Screenplay, Sergio Amidei, Elio Bartolini, Carlo Romano; Based on Luigi Pirandello play; Director of Photography, Leonida Barboni; Music, Carlo Savina; A Federiz-Film Napoleon-Cinecitta Production. December release. CAST: Ugo Tognazzi, Giovanna Ralli, Pierre Brasseur, Anouk Aimee.

DO YOU KEEP A LION AT HOME? (Brandon) Director, Pavel Hobl; Director of Photography, Jiri Vojta; A CeskoslovenskyFilm-Export Production December release. CAST: Ladislaw Ocenasek Josef Filip, Olga Machoninova, Jan Brychta.

GALIA (Zenith) Director, Georges Lautner; Screenplay, Vahe Katcha; Music, Johann Sebastian Bach A French-Italian Co-Production. December release CAST: Mireille Darc, Venantino Venantini, Francoise Prevost, Jacques Riberolles, Francois Chaumette.

dith Anderson   Lew Ayres   Carroll Baker   Richard Basehart   Anne Baxter

BIOGRAPHICAL DATA

(Name, real name, place and date of birth, and school attended)

ADAMS, EDIE: (Edith) Kingston, Pa., Apr. 16, 1931. Juilliard School of Music, Columbia.

ADAMS, JULIE: (Betty May) Waterloo, Iowa, Oct. 17, 1928. Little Rock Jr. College.

ADDAMS, DAWN: Felixstowe, Suffolk, Eng., Sept. 21, 1930. Royal Academy.

ADRIAN, IRIS: (Iris Adrian Hostetter) Los Angeles, May 29, 1913.

AGAR, JOHN: Chicago, Jan. 31, 1921.

AHERNE, BRIAN: Worcestershire, Eng., May 2, 1902. Malvern College, U. of London.

AHN, PHILIP: Los Angeles, Mar. 29, 1911. U. of Calif.

ALBERGHETTI, ANNA MARIA: Pesaro, Italy, May 15, 1936.

ALBERT, EDDIE: (Eddie Albert Heimberger) Rock Island, Ill., Apr. 22, 1908. U. of Minn.

ALBRIGHT, LOLA: Akron, Ohio, July 20, 1925.

ALDA, ROBERT: (Alphonso D'Abruzzo) New York City, Feb. 26, 1914. NYU.

ALEXANDER, BEN: Goldfield, Nev., May 26, 1911. U. of Calif., Stanford.

ALLBRITTON, LOUISE: Oklahoma City, July 3, 1920. U. of Okla.

ALLEN, STEVE: New York City, Dec. 26, 1921.

ALLYSON, JUNE: (Ella Geisman) Westchester, N.Y., Oct. 7, 1923.

AMES, LEON: (Leon Wycoff) Portland, Ind., Jan. 20, 1903.

ANDERSON, JUDITH: Adelaide, Australia, Feb. 10, 1898.

ANDERSON, MICHAEL, JR.: London, Eng., 1943.

ANDES, KEITH: Ocean City, N.J., July 12, 1920. Temple U., Oxford.

ANDREWS, DANA: Collins, Miss., Jan. 1, 1912. Sam Houston College.

ANDREWS, HARRY: Tonbridge, Kent, Eng., 1911.

ANGEL, HEATHER: Oxford, Eng., Feb. 9, 1909. Wycombe Abbey School.

ANGELI, PIER: (Anna Maria Pierangeli) Sardinia, June 19, 1932.

ANN-MARGRET: Stockholm, Sweden, Apr. 28, 1941. Northwestern U.

ANSARA, MICHAEL: Lowell, Mass., Apr. 15, 1922. Pasadena Playhouse.

ANTHONY, TONY: Clarksburg, W. Va., Oct. 16, 1937. Carnegie Tech.

ARCHER, JOHN: (Ralph Bowman) Osceola, Neb., May 8, 1915. U. of S. Calif.

ARDEN, EVE: (Eunice Quedens) Mill Valley, Calif.

ARLEN, RICHARD: Charlottesville, Va., Sept. 1, 1900. St. Thomas College.

ARNAZ, DESI: Santiago, Cuba, Mar. 2, 1917. Colegio de Dolores.

ARNESS, JAMES: Minneapolis, Minn., May 26, 1923. Beloit College.

ARTHUR, JEAN: NYC, Oct. 17, 1908.

ARTHUR, ROBERT: (Robert Arthaud) Aberdeen, Wash., June 18. U. of Wash.

ASTAIRE, FRED: Omaha, Neb., May 10, 1900.

ASTOR, MARY: (Lucile V. Langhanke) Quincy, Ill., May 3, 1906. Kenwood-Loring School.

ATTENBOROUGH, RICHARD: Cambridge, Eng., Aug. 29, 1923. Royal Academy of Dramatic Art.

AUMONT, JEAN PIERRE: Paris, Jan. 5, 1913. French Nat'l School of Drama.

AUTRY, GENE: Tioga, Texas, Sept. 29, 1907.

AVALON, FRANKIE: (Francis Thomas Avallone) Philadelphia, Sept. 18, 1940.

AYLMER, FELIX: Corsham, Eng., Feb. 21, 1889. Oxford.

AYRES, LEW: Minneapolis, Minn., Dec. 28, 1908.

BACALL, LAUREN: (Betty Perske) NYC, Sept. 16, 1924. American Academy of Dramatic Art.

BACKUS, JIM: Cleveland, Ohio, Feb. 25, 1913. American Academy of Dramatic Art.

BADDELEY, HERMIONE: Shropshire, Eng., Nov. 13, 1908. Margaret Morris School.

BAILEY, PEARL: Newport News, Va., March 29.

BAINTER, FAY: Los Angeles, Dec. 7, 1892. Girls' Collegiate School.

BAKER, CARROLL: Johnstown, Pa., May 28, 1931. St. Petersburg Jr. College.

BAKER, STANLEY: Glamorgan, Wales, Feb. 28, 1928.

BALIN, INA: Brooklyn, Nov. 12, 1937. NYU.

BALL, LUCILLE: Jamestown, N.Y., Aug. 6, 1911. Chatauqua Musical Inst.

BANCROFT, ANNE: (Anne Italiano) NYC, Sept. 17, 1931. American Academy of Dramatic Art.

BANKHEAD, TALLULAH: Huntsville, Ala., Jan. 31, 1903. Mary Baldwin School.

BANNEN, IAN: Airdrie, Scot., June 29, 1928.

BARDOT, BRIGITTE: Paris, 1934.

BARKER, LEX: (Alexander Crichlow Barker) Rye, N.Y., May 8, 1919.

BARRY, DONALD: (Donald Barry de Acosta) Houston, Tex. Texas School of Mines.

BARRY, GENE: (Eugene Klass) NYC, June 14, 1921.

BARRYMORE, JOHN DREW: Beverly Hills, Calif., June 4, 1932. St. John's Military Academy.

BARTHOLOMEW, FREDDIE: London, Mar. 28, 1924.

BARTON, JAMES: Gloucester, N.J., Nov. 1, 1890.

BASEHART, RICHARD: Zanesville, Ohio, Aug. 31.

BATES, ALAN: Allestree, Derbyshire, Eng., Feb. 17, 1934. Royal Academy of Dramatic Art.

BATES, BARBARA: Denver, Colo., Aug. 6.

BAXTER, ALAN: East Cleveland, Ohio, Nov. 19, 1911. Williams U.

BAXTER, ANNE: Michigan City, Ind., May 7, 1923. Ervine School of Drama.

BEAL, JOHN: (J. Alexander Bliedung) Joplin, Mo., Aug. 13, 1909. Pa. U.

BEATTY, ROBERT: Hamilton, Ont., Can., Oct. 19, 1909. U. of Toronto.

BEATTY, WARREN: Richmond, Virginia, March 30, 1937.

BEAUMONT, HUGH: Lawrence, Kan., Feb. 16, 1909. U. of Chattanooga, USC.

Barbara Bel Geddes   Harry Belafonte   Ingrid Bergman   Ernest Borgnine   Capucine

BECKETT, SCOTTY: Oakland, Calif., Oct. 4, 1920.

BEERY, NOAH, JR.: NYC, Aug. 10, 1916. Harvard Military Academy.

BEGLEY, ED: Hartford, Conn., Mar. 25, 1901. Conn. School for Boys.

BELAFONTE, HARRY: NYC, Mar. 1, 1927.

BEL GEDDES, BARBARA: NYC, Oct. 31, 1922.

BELLAMY, RALPH: Chicago, June 17, 1905.

BENNETT, BRUCE: (Herman Brix) Tacoma, Wash., U. of Wash.

BENNETT, JOAN: Palisades, N.J., Feb. 27, 1910. St. Margaret's School.

BENNY, JACK: (Jack Kubelsky) Waukegan, Ill.

BERGEN, EDGAR: Chicago, Feb. 16, 1903. Northwestern U.

BERGEN, POLLY: Knoxville, Tenn., July 14, 1930. Compton Jr. College.

BERGERAC, JACQUES: Biarritz, France, May 26, 1927. Paris U. of Law.

BERGMAN, INGRID: Stockholm, Sweden, Aug. 29, 1917. Royal Dramatic Theatre School.

BERLE, MILTON: (Milton Berlinger) NYC, July 12, 1908. Professional Children's School.

BERLINGER, WARREN: Brooklyn, Aug. 31, 1937. Columbia University.

BEST, JAMES: Corydon, Ind., July 26, 1926.

BETTGER, LYLE: Philadelphia, Feb. 13, 1915. American Academy of Dramatic Art.

BEYMER, RICHARD: Avoca, Iowa, Feb. 21, 1939.

BISHOP, JULIE: (formerly Jacqueline Wells) Denver, Colo., Aug. 30, 1917. Westlake School.

BLACKMER, SIDNEY: Salisbury, N.C., July 13, 1898. U. of N.C.

BLAINE, VIVIAN: (Vivian Stapleton) Newark, N.J., Nov. 21, 1924.

BLAIR, BETSY: (Betsy Boger) NYC, Dec. 11.

BLAKE, AMANDA: (Beverly Louise Neill) Buffalo, N.Y., Feb. 20.

BLONDELL, JOAN: NYC, Aug. 30, 1909.

BLOOM, CLAIRE: London, Feb. 15, 1931. Badminton School.

BLUE, BEN: Montreal, Can., Sept. 12, 1901.

BLUE, MONTE: Indianapolis, Jan. 11, 1890.

BLYTH, ANN: Mt. Kisco, N.Y., Aug. 16, 1928. New Wayburn Dramatic School.

BOGARDE, DIRK: London, Mar. 28, 1921. Glasgow & Univ. College.

BOLGER, RAY: Dorchester, Mass., Jan. 10, 1906.

BOND, DEREK: Glasgow, Scot., Jan. 26, 1920. Askes School.

BONDI, BEULAH: Chicago, May 3, 1892.

BOONE, PAT: Jacksonville, Fla., June 1, 1934. Columbia U.

BOONE, RICHARD: Los Angeles. Stanford U.

BOOTH, SHIRLEY: NYC, Aug. 30, 1907.

BORGNINE, ERNEST: Hamden, Conn., Jan. 24, 1918. Randall School of Dramatic Art.

BOWMAN, LEE: Cincinnati, Dec. 28, 1914. American Academy of Dramatic Art.

BOYD, STEPHEN: (William Millar) Belfast, Ire., 1928.

BOYER, CHARLES: Figeac, France, Aug. 28, 1899. Sorbonne U.

BRACKEN, EDDIE: NYC, Feb. 7, 1920. Professional Children's School.

BRADY, SCOTT: (Jerry Tierney) Brooklyn, Sept. 13, 1924. Bliss-Hayden Dramatic School.

BRAND, NEVILLE: Kewanee, Ill., Aug. 13, 1921.

BRANDO, JOCELYN: San Francisco, Nov. 18, 1919. Lake Forest College, American Academy.

BRANDO, MARLON: Omaha, Neb., Apr. 3, 1924. New School of Social Research.

BRASSELLE, KEEFE: Elyria, Ohio, Feb. 7.

BRAZZI, ROSSANO: Bologna, Italy, 1916. U. of Florence.

BRENT, GEORGE: Dublin, Ire., Mar. 15, 1904. Dublin U.

BRENT, ROMNEY: (Romulo Larralde) Saltillo, Mex., Jan. 26, 1902.

BRIAN, DAVID: NYC, Aug. 5, 1914. CCNY.

BRIDGES, LLOYD: San Leandro, Calif., Jan. 15, 1913.

BRODIE, STEVE: (Johnny Stevens) Eldorado, Kan., Nov. 25, 1919.

BROMFIELD, JOHN: (Farron Bromfield) South Bend, Ind., June 11, 1922. St. Mary's College.

BROOKS, GERALDINE: (Geraldine Stroock) NYC, Oct. 29, 1925. American Academy of Dramatic Art.

BROWN, JAMES: Desdemona, Tex., Mar. 22, 1920. Baylor U.

BROWN, JOE E.: Helgate, Ohio, July 28, 1892.

BROWN, TOM: NYC, Jan. 6, 1913. Professional Children's School.

BRUCE, VIRGINIA: Minneapolis, Sept. 29, 1910.

BRYNNER, YUL: Sakhalin Island, Japan, June 15, 1915.

BUCHANAN, EDGAR: Humansville, Mo. U. of Oregon.

BUCHHOLZ, HORST: Berlin, Ger., Dec. 4, 1933. Ludwig Dramatic School.

BUETEL, JACK: Dallas, Tex., Sept. 5, 1917.

BURKE, BILLIE: Washington, D.C., Aug. 7, 1885.

BURNET, CAROL: San Antonio, Tex., Apr. 26, 1935. UCLA.

BURNS, GEORGE: (Nathan Birnbaum) NYC.

BURR, RAYMOND: New Westminster, B.C., Can., May 21, 1917. Stanford, U. of Cal., Columbia.

BURTON, RICHARD: (Richard Jenkins) Pontrhydyfen, S. Wales, Nov. 10, 1925. Oxford.

BYGRAVES, MAX: London, Oct. 16, 1922. St. Joseph's School.

BYINGTON, SPRING: Colorado Springs, Oct. 17, 1898.

BYRNES, EDD: NYC, July 30, 1933. Haaren High.

CABOT, BRUCE: (Jacques de Bujac) Carlsbad, N.Mex. U. of South.

CABOT, SUSAN: Boston, July 9, 1927.

CAESAR, SID: Yonkers, N.Y., Sept. 8, 1922.

CAGNEY, JAMES: NYC, July 1, 1904. Columbia.

CAGNEY, JEANNE: NYC, Mar. 25, 1919. Hunter College.

CALHOUN, RORY: (Francis Timothy Durgin) Los Angeles, Aug. 8, 1923.

CALLAN, MICHAEL: (Martin Calininff) Philadelphia, Nov. 22, 1935.

CALVERT, PHYLLIS: London, Feb. 18, 1917. Margaret Morris School.

CALVET, CORINNE: (Corinne Dibos) Paris, Apr. 30. U. of Paris.

CAMERON, ROD: (Rod Cox) Calgary, Alberta, Can., Dec. 7, 1912.

CANALE, GIANNA MARIA: Reggio Calabria, Italy, Sept. 12.

CANOVA, JUDY: Jacksonville, Fla., Nov. 20, 1916.

CAPUCINE: (Germaine Lefebvre) Toulon, France, Jan. 6.

CAREY, HARRY, JR.: Saugus, Calif., May 16. Black Fox Military Academy.

CAREY, MACDONALD: Sioux City, Iowa, Mar. 15, 1913. U. of Wisc., U. of Iowa.

ck Connors   Ellen Corby   Noel Coward   Joan Crawford   James Darren

CAREY, PHILIP: Hackensack, N.J., July 15, 1925. U. of Miami.

CARMICHAEL, HOAGY: Bloomington, Ind., Nov. 22, 1899. Ind. U.

CARMICHAEL, IAN: Hull, Eng., June 18, 1920. Scarborough College.

CARNEY, ART: Mt. Vernon, N. Y., Nov. 4, 1918.

CARON, LESLIE: Paris, July 1, 1931. Nat'l Conservatory, Paris.

CARRADINE, JOHN: NYC, Feb. 5, 1906.

CARROLL, JOHN: (Julian La-Faye) New Orleans.

CARROLL, MADELEINE: West Bromwich, Eng., Feb. 26, 1906. Birmingham U.

CARROLL, PAT: Shreveport, La., May 5, 1927. Catholic U.

CARSON, JOHNNY: Corning, Iowa, Oct. 23, 1925. U. of Neb.

CASSAVETES, JOHN: NYC, 1929. Colgate College, Academy of Dramatic Arts.

CASTLE, PEGGIE: Appalachia, Va., Dec. 22, 1927. Mills College.

CAULFIELD, JOAN: Orange, N.J., June 1. Columbia U.

CERVI, GINO: Bologna, Italy, May 3, 1901.

CHAMPION, GOWER: Geneva, Ill., June 22.

CHAMPION, MARGE: Los Angeles, Sept. 2.

CHANDLER, LANE: (Lane Oakes) Culbertson, Mont., June 4, 1899. Ill. U.

CHANEY, LON, JR.: (Creighton Chaney) Oklahoma City, 1915.

CHAPLIN, CHARLES: London, Apr. 16, 1889.

CHARISSE, CYD: (Tula Ellice Finklea) Amarillo, Tex., Mar. 8, 1923. Hollywood Professional School.

CHASE, ILKA: NYC, Apr. 8, 1905.

CHRISTIAN, LINDA: (Blanca Rosa Welter) Tampico, Mex., Nov. 13, 1924.

CHURCHILL, SARAH: London, Oct. 7, 1916.

CILENTO, DIANE: Queensland, Australia, Oct. 5, 1933. American Academy of Dramatic Arts.

CLARK, DANE: NYC, Feb. 18, 1915. Cornell and Johns Hopkins U.

CLARK, DICK: Mt. Vernon, N. Y., Nov. 30, 1929. Syracuse University.

CLARK, FRED: Lincoln, Calif., Mar. 9, 1914. Stanford U.

CLARKE, MAE: Philadelphia, Aug. 16, 1910.

CLEMENTS, STANLEY: Long Island, N.Y., July 16, 1926.

CLOONEY, ROSEMARY: Maysville, Ky., May 23, 1928.

COCA, IMOGENE: Philadelphia, Nov. 18, 1908.

COLBERT, CLAUDETTE: (Claudette Chauchoin) Paris, Sept. 13, 1907. Art Students League.

COLE, GEORGE: London, Apr. 22, 1925.

COLLINS, JOAN: London, May 23. Francis Holland School.

CONNERY, SEAN: Edinburgh, Scot., Aug. 25, 1930.

CONNORS, CHUCK: (Kevin Joseph Connors) Brooklyn, Apr. 10, 1924. Seton Hall College.

CONTE, RICHARD: (Nicholas Conte) NYC, Mar. 24, 1914. Neighborhood Playhouse.

COOGAN, JACKIE: Los Angeles, Oct. 26, 1914. Villanova College.

COOK, ELISHA, JR.: San Francisco, Dec. 26, 1907. St. Albans.

COOPER, BEN: Hartford, Conn., Sept. 30. Columbia U.

COOPER, GLADYS: Lewisham, Eng., Dec. 18, 1891.

COOPER, JACKIE: Los Angeles, Sept. 15, 1921.

COOPER, MELVILLE: Birmingham, Eng., Oct. 15, 1896. King Edward's School.

COOTE, ROBERT: London, Feb. 4, 1909. Hurstpierpont College.

CORCORAN, DONNA: Quincy, Mass., Sept. 29.

CORDAY, MARA: (Marilyn Watts) Santa Monica, Calif., Jan. 3, 1932.

COREY, JEFF: NYC, Aug. 10, 1914. Fagin School.

COREY, WENDELL: Dracut, Mass., Mar. 20, 1914.

CORRI, ADRIENNE: Glasgow, Scot., Nov. 13, 1933. Royal Academy of Dramatic Art.

CORTESA, VALENTINA: Milan, Italy, Jan. 1, 1925.

COTTEN, JOSEPH: Petersburg, Va., May 15, 1905.

COURTENAY, TOM: Hull, Eng., 1937. Royal Academy of Dramatic Arts.

COURTLAND, JEROME: Knoxville, Tenn., Dec. 27, 1926.

COWARD, NOEL: Teddington-on-the-Thames, Eng., Dec. 16, 1899.

COX, WALLY: Detroit, Dec. 6, 1924. CCNY.

CRABBE, BUSTER (LARRY): (Clarence Linden) Oakland, Calif., U. of S. Cal.

CRAIG, JAMES: (James H. Meador) Nashville, Tenn., Feb. 4, 1912. Rice Inst.

CRAIG, MICHAEL: India in 1929.

CRAIN, JEANNE: Barstow, Cal., May 25, 1925.

CRAWFORD, JOAN: (Lucille LeSueur) San Antonio, Tex., Mar. 23, 1908.

CROSBY, BING: (Harry Lillith Crosby) Tacoma, Wash., May 2, 1904. Gonzaga College.

CROWLEY, PAT: Olyphant, Pa., Sept. 17, 1933.

CUMMINGS, CONSTANCE: Seattle, Wash., May 15, 1910.

CUMMINGS, ROBERT: Joplin, Mo., June 9, 1910. Carnegie Tech.

CUMMINS, PEGGY: Prestatyn, N. Wales, Dec. 18, 1926. Alexandra School.

CURRIE, FINLAY: Edinburgh, Scot., Jan. 20, 1878. Watson School.

CURTIS, TONY: (Bernard Schwartz) NYC, June 3, 1925.

CUSHING, PETER: Kenley, Surrey, Eng., May 26, 1913.

CUTTS, PATRICIA: London, July 20, 1927. Royal Academy of Dramatic Arts.

DAHL, ARLENE: Minneapolis, Aug. 11. U. of Minn.

DAMONE, VIC: (Vito Farinola) Brooklyn, June 12.

DANTINE, HELMUT: Vienna, Oct. 7, 1918. U. of Calif.

DANTON, RAY: NYC, Sept. 19, 1931. Carnegie Tech.

DARCEL, DENISE: (Denise Billecard) Paris, Sept. 8, 1925. U. of Dijon.

DARIN, BOBBY: (Robert Walden Cassotto) NYC, May 14, 1936. Hunter College.

DARREN, JAMES: Philadelphia, June 8, 1936. Stella Adler School.

DARRIEUX, DANIELLE: Bordeaux, France, May 1, 1917. Lycée LaTour.

DARVI, BELLA: (Bella Wegier) Sosnoviec, Poland, Oct. 23, 1928.

DA SILVA, HOWARD: Cleveland, Ohio, May 4, 1909. Carnegie Tech.

DAUPHIN, CLAUDE: Corbeil, France, Aug. 19, 1903. Beaux Arts School.

DAVIS, BETTE: Lowell, Mass., Apr. 5, 1908. John Murray Anderson Dramatic School.

DAVIS, SAMMY, JR.: NYC, Dec. 8, 1925.

223

Olivia De Havilland   Richard Egan   Virginia Field   John Forsythe   Judy Garla

DAY, DENNIS: (Eugene Dennis McNulty) NYC, May 21, 1917. Manhattan College.

DAY, DORIS: (Doris Kappelhoff) Cincinnati, Apr. 3, 1924.

DAY, LARAINE: (Laraine Johnson) Roosevelt, Utah, Oct. 13, 1920.

DEAN, JIMMY: Plainview, Tex., Aug. 10, 1928.

DE CARLO, YVONNE: Vancouver, B.C., Can., Sept. 1, 1924. Vancouver School of Drama.

DE CORDOVA, ARTURO: Merida, Yucatan, May 8, 1908. Cavin Inst.

DEE, FRANCES: Los Angeles, Nov. 26, 1907. Chicago U.

DEE, JOEY: (Joseph Di Nicola) Passaic, N.J., June 11, 1940. Patterson State College.

DEE, SANDRA: Bayonne, N.J., Apr. 23, 1942.

DE FORE, DON: Cedar Rapids, Iowa, Aug. 25, 1917. U. of Iowa.

DE HAVEN, GLORIA: Los Angeles, July 23, 1926.

DE HAVILLAND, OLIVIA: Tokyo, Japan, July 1, 1916. Notre Dame Convent School.

DEL RIO, DOLORES: (Dolores Ansunsolo) Durango, Mex., Aug. 3, 1905. St. Joseph's Convent.

DENISON, MICHAEL: Doncaster, York, Eng., Nov. 1, 1915. Oxford.

DENNY, REGINALD: Richmond, Surrey, Eng., Nov. 21, 1891. St. Francis Xavier College.

DEREK, JOHN: Hollywood, Aug. 12, 1926.

DE SICA, VITTORIO: Sora, Caserta, Italy, July 7, 1902.

DEVINE, ANDY: Flagstaff, Ariz., Oct. 7, 1905. Ariz. State College.

DE WILDE, BRANDON: Brooklyn, Apr. 9, 1942.

DE WOLFE, BILLY: (William Andrew Jones) Wollaston, Mass., Feb. 18.

DEXTER, ANTHONY: (Walter Reinhold Alfred Fleischmann) Talmadge, Neb., Jan. 19, 1919. U. of Iowa.

DICKINSON, ANGIE: Kulm, N. Dak., Sept. 30. Glendale College.

DIETRICH, MARLENE: (Maria Magdalene von Losch) Berlin, Ger., Dec. 27, 1904. Berlin Music Academy.

DILLMAN, BRADFORD: San Francisco, Apr. 14, 1930. Yale.

DOMERGUE, FAITH: New Orleans, June 16, 1925.

DONAHUE, TROY: (Merle Johnson) NYC, Jan. 27. Columbia University.

DONNELL, JEFF: (Jean Donnell) South Windham, Me., July 10, 1921. Yale Drama School.

DONNELLY, RUTH: Trenton, N.J., May 17, 1896.

DORS, DIANA: Swindon, Wilshire, Eng., Oct. 23, 1931. London Academy of Music.

DOUGLAS, KIRK: Amsterdam, N.Y., Dec. 9, 1916. St. Lawrence U.

DOUGLAS, MELVYN: (Melvyn Hesselberg) Macon, Ga., Apr. 5, 1901.

DRAKE, BETSY: Paris, Sept. 11, 1923.

DRAKE, CHARLES: (Charles Ruppert) NYC, Oct. 2, 1914. Nichols College.

DREW, ELLEN: (formerly Terry Ray) Kansas City, Mo., Nov. 23, 1915.

DRISCOLL, BOBBY: Cedar Rapids, Iowa, Mar. 3, 1937.

DRU, JOANNE: (Joanne LaCock) Logan, W. Va., Jan. 31, 1923. John Robert Powers School.

DUFF, HOWARD: Bremerton, Wash., Nov. 24, 1917.

DUNNE, IRENE: Louisville, Ky., Dec. 20, 1904. Chicago College of Music.

DUNNOCK, MILDRED: Baltimore, Jan. 25. Johns Hopkins and Columbia U.

DURANTE, JIMMY: NYC, Feb. 10, 1893.

DURYEA, DAN: White Plains, N.Y., Jan. 23, 1907. Cornell.

DVORAK, ANN: (Ann McKim) NYC, Aug. 2, 1912.

EASTON, ROBERT: Milwaukee, Nov. 23, 1930. U. of Texas.

EATON, SHIRLEY: London, 1937. Aida Foster School.

EDDY, NELSON: Providence, R.I., June 29, 1901.

EDWARDS, VINCE: NYC, July 9, 1928. American Academy of Dramatic Art.

EGAN, RICHARD: San Francisco, July 29, 1923. Stanford U.

EGGAR, SAMANTHA: London, 1940.

ELLIOTT, DENHOLM: London, May 31, 1922. Malvern College.

ELSOM, ISOBEL: Cambridge, Eng., Mar. 16, 1894.

EMERSON, FAYE: Elizabeth, La., July 8, 1917. San Diego State College.

ERICKSON, LEIF: Alameda, Calif., Oct. 27, 1914. U. of Calif.

ERICSON, JOHN: Dusseldorf, Ger., Sept. 25, 1926. American Academy of Dramatic Art.

ESMOND, CARL: Vienna, June 14, 1906. U. of Vienna.

EVANS, DALE: (Frances Smith) Uvalde, Texas, Oct. 31, 1912.

EVANS, GENE: Holbrook, Ariz., July 11, 1922.

EVANS, MAURICE: Dorchester, Eng., June 3, 1901.

EWELL, TOM: (Yewell Tompkins) Owensboro, Ky., Apr. 29, 1909. U. of Wisc.

FABIAN: (Fabian Forte) Philadelphia, 1940.

FAIRBANKS, DOUGLAS, JR.: NYC, Dec. 9, 1909. Collegiate School.

FARR, FELICIA: Westchester, N.Y., Oct. 4, 1932. Penn State College.

FARRELL, CHARLES: Onset Bay, Mass., Aug. 9, 1901. Boston U.

FARRELL, GLENDA: Enid, Okla., June 30, 1904.

FELLOWS, EDITH: Boston, May 20, 1923.

FERNANDEL: (Fernand Joseph Desire Constandin) Marseilles, France, 1903.

FERRER, JOSE: Santurce, P.R., Jan. 8, 1912. Princeton U.

FERRER, MEL: Elberon, N.J., Aug. 25, 1917. Princeton U.

FIELD, BETTY: Boston, Feb. 8, 1918. American Academy of Dramatic Art.

FINCH, PETER: London, Sept. 28, 1916.

FINNEY, ALBERT: Salford, Lancashire, Eng., May 9, 1936. Royal Academy of Dramatic Arts.

FISHER, EDDIE: Philadelphia, Aug. 10, 1928.

FITZGERALD, GERALDINE: Dublin, Ire., Nov. 24, 1914. Dublin Art School.

FLEMING, RHONDA: (Marilyn Louis) Los Angeles, Aug. 10.

FLEMYNG, ROBERT: Liverpool, Eng., Jan. 3, 1912. Haileybury College.

FOCH, NINA: Leyden, Holland, Apr. 20, 1924.

FONDA, HENRY: Grand Island, Neb., May 16, 1905. Minn. U.

FONDA, JANE: NYC, Dec. 21, 1937. Vassar.

FONDA, PETER: NYC, Feb. 23, 1939. U. of Omaha.

FONTAINE, JOAN: Tokyo, Japan, Oct. 22, 1917.

FORD, GLENN: (Gwylln Ford) Quebec, Can., May 1.

FORD, PAUL: Baltimore, Nov. 2, 1901. Dartmouth.

FOREST, MARK: (Lou Degni) Brooklyn, Jan. 1933.

FORREST, STEVE: Huntsville, Tex., Sept. 29. UCLA.

FORSYTHE, JOHN: Penn's Grove, N.J., Jan. 29, 1918.

FOSTER, PRESTON: Ocean City, N.J., Aug. 24, 1904.

FRANCES, CONNIE: (Constance Franconero) Newark, N.J., Dec. 12, 1938.

| Robert Goulet | Gloria Grahame | Rex Harrison | Susan Hayward | Charlton Heston |

FRANCIOSA, ANTHONY: NYC, Oct. 25.

FRANCIS, ANNE: Ossining, N. Y., Sept. 16.

FRANCIS, ARLENE: (Arlene Kazanjian) Boston, 1908. Finch School.

FRANCIS, KAY: (Katherine Gibbs) Oklahoma City, Jan. 13, 1899. Cathedral School.

FRANZ, ARTHUR: Perth Amboy, N. J., Feb. 29, 1920. Blue Ridge College.

FRANZ, EDUARD: Milwaukee, Wisc., Oct. 31, 1902.

FREEMAN, MONA: Baltimore, June 9, 1926.

FURNEAUX, YVONNE: Lille, France, 1928. Oxford U.

GABIN, JEAN: Villette, France, May 17, 1904.

GABOR, EVA: Budapest, Hungary, Feb. 11, 1925.

GABOR, ZSA ZSA: (Sari Gabor) Budapest, Hungary, Feb. 6, 1923.

GAM, RITA: Pittsburgh, Apr. 2, 1928.

GARBO, GRETA: (Greta Gustafson) Stockholm, Sweden, Sept. 18, 1906.

GARDINER, REGINALD: Wimbledon, Eng., Feb. 1903. Royal Academy of Dramatic Arts.

GARDNER, AVA: Smithfield, N.C., Dec. 24, 1922. Atlantic Christian College.

GARLAND, JUDY: (Frances Gumm) Grand Rapids, Minn., June 10, 1922.

GARNER, JAMES: (James Baumgarner) Norman, Okla., Apr. 7, 1928. Berghof School.

GARNER, PEGGY ANN: Canton, Ohio, Feb. 3, 1932.

GARRETT, BETTY: St. Joseph, Mo., May 23, 1919. Annie Wright Seminary.

GASSMAN, VITTORIO: Genoa, Italy, Sept. 1, 1922. Rome Academy of Dramatic Art.

GAVIN, JOHN: Los Angeles, Apr. 8. Stanford U.

GAYNOR, JANET: Philadelphia, Oct. 6, 1906.

GAYNOR, MITZI: Chicago, Sept. 4, 1931.

GENN, LEO: London, Aug. 9, 1905. Cambridge.

GIELGUD, JOHN: London, Apr. 14, 1904. Royal Academy of Dramatic Arts.

GILLMORE, MARCOLO: London, May 31, 1897. American Academy of Dramatic Art.

GILMORE, VIRGINIA: (Sherman Poole) Del Monte, Calif., July 26, 1919. U. of Calif.

GISH, DOROTHY: Massillon, Ohio, Mar. 11, 1898.

GISH, LILLIAN: Springfield, Ohio, Oct. 14, 1896.

GLEASON, JACKIE: Brooklyn, Feb. 26, 1916.

GODDARD, PAULETTE: Great Neck, N.Y., June 3, 1911.

GOMEZ, THOMAS: NYC, July 10, 1905.

GORDON, RUTH: Wollaston, Mass., Oct. 30, 1896. American Academy of Dramatic Art.

GOULET, ROBERT: Lawrence, Mass., Nov. 26, 1933. Edmonton School.

GRABLE, BETTY: St. Louis, Mo., Dec. 18, 1916. Hollywood Professional School.

GRAHAME, GLORIA: (Gloria Grahame Hallward) Los Angeles, Nov. 28, 1929.

GRANGER, FARLEY: San Jose, Calif., July 1, 1925.

GRANGER, STEWART: (James Stewart) London, May 6, 1913. Webber-Douglas School of Acting.

GRANT, CARY: (Archibald Alexander Leach) Bristol, Eng., Jan. 18, 1904.

GRANT, KATHRYN: (Olive Grandstaff) Houston, Tex., Nov. 25, 1933. UCLA.

GRAVES, PETER: Minneapolis, Mar. 18. U. of Minn.

GRAY, COLEEN: (Doris Jensen) Staplehurst, Neb., Oct. 23, 1922. Hamline U.

GRAYSON, KATHRYN: (Zelma Hedrick) Winston-Salem, N.C., Feb. 9, 1923.

GREENE, RICHARD: Plymouth, Eng., Aug. 25, 1918. Cardinal Vaughn School.

GREENWOOD, JOAN: London, 1919. Royal Academy of Dramatic Arts.

GREER, JANE: Washington, D.C., Sept. 9, 1924.

GREY, VIRGINIA: Los Angeles, Mar. 22, 1923.

GRIFFITH, ANDY: Mt. Airy, N.C., June 1, 1926. U. of N.C.

GRIFFITH, HUGH: Marian Glas, Anglesey, N. Wales, May 30, 1912.

GRIZZARD, GEORGE: Roanoke Rapids, N.C., Apr. 1, 1928. U. of N.C.

GUINNESS, ALEC: London, Apr. 2, 1914. Pembroke Lodge School.

HAAS, HUGO: Czechoslovakia, Feb. 19, 1902. Conservatory of Drama and Music.

HACKETT, BUDDY: Brooklyn, Aug. 31, 1924.

HALE, BARBARA: DeKalb, Ill., Apr. 18, 1922. Chicago Academy of Fine Arts.

HAMILTON, GEORGE: Memphis, Tenn., Aug. 12, 1939. Hackley School.

HAMILTON, MARGARET: Cleveland, Ohio, Dec. 9, 1902. Hathaway-Brown School.

HAMILTON, NEIL: Lynn, Mass., Sept. 9, 1899.

HARDING, ANN: (Dorothy Walton Gatley) Fort Sam Houston, Texas, Aug. 17, 1904.

HARRIS, JULIE: Grosse Pointe, Mich., Dec. 2, 1925. Yale Drama School.

HARRISON, NOEL: London, Jan. 29, 1936.

HARRISON, REX: Huyton, Cheshire, Eng., Mar. 5, 1908.

HARTMAN, ELIZABETH: Youngstown, O., Dec. 23, 1941. Carnegie Tech.

HARVEY, LAURENCE: Yonishkis, Lithuania, Oct. 1, 1928. Meyerton College.

HATTON, RAYMOND: Red Oak, Iowa, July 7, 1892.

HAVER, JUNE: Rock Island, Ill., June 10, 1926.

HAVOC, JUNE: (June Hovick) Seattle, Wash., Nov. 1916.

HAWKINS, JACK: London, Sept. 14, 1910. Trinity School.

HAYES, HELEN: (Helen Brown) Washington, D.C., Oct. 10, 1900. Sacred Heart Convent.

HAYES, MARGARET: (Maggie) Baltimore, Dec. 5, 1925.

HAYWARD, SUSAN: (Edythe Marrener) Brooklyn, June 30, 1919.

HAYWORTH, RITA: (Margarita Cansino) NYC, Oct. 17, 1919.

HECKART, EILEEN: Columbus, Ohio, Mar. 29. Ohio State U.

HEDISON, DAVID: Providence, R.I., May 20, 1929. Brown U.

HEFLIN, VAN: Walters, Okla., Dec. 13, 1910.

HENDERSON, MARCIA: Andover, Mass., July 22, 1932. American Academy of Dramatic Art.

HENDRIX, WANDA: Jacksonville, Fla., Nov. 3, 1928.

HENREID, PAUL: Trieste, Jan. 10, 1908.

HEPBURN, AUDREY: Brussels, Belgium, May 4, 1929.

HEPBURN, KATHARINE: Hartford, Conn., Nov. 8, 1909. Bryn Mawr.

HESTON, CHARLTON: Evanston, Ill., Oct. 4, 1924. Northwestern U.

HICKMAN, DARRYL: Hollywood, Calif., July 28, 1933. Loyola U.

HILLER, WENDY: Bramhall, Cheshire, Eng., Aug. 15, 1912. Winceby House School.

HOLLIMAN, EARL: Tennasas Swamp, Delhi, La., Sept. 11. UCLA.

HOLLOWAY, STANLEY: London, Oct. 1, 1890.

HOLM, CELESTE: NYC, Apr. 29, 1919.

HOMEIER, SKIP: (George Vincent Homeier) Chicago, Oct. 5, 1930. UCLA.

Van Johnson   Glynis Johns   Hardy Kruger   Jessie Royce Landis   Perry Lope

HOMOLKA, OSCAR: Vienna, Aug. 12, 1898. Vienna Dramatic Academy.

HOPE, BOB: London, May 26, 1904.

HOPKINS, MIRIAM: Bainbridge, Ga., Oct. 18, 1902. Syracuse U.

HOPPER, DENNIS: Dodge City, Kan., May 17, 1936.

HORNE, LENA: Brooklyn, June 30, 1917.

HORTON, EDWARD EVERETT: Brooklyn, Mar. 18, 1888. Columbia U.

HORTON, ROBERT: Los Angeles, July 29, 1924. UCLA.

HOWARD, RONALD: Norwood, Eng., Apr. 7, 1918. Jesus College.

HOWARD, TREVOR: Kent Eng., Sept. 29, 1916. Royal Academy of Dramatic Arts.

HUDSON, ROCK: (Roy Fitzgerald) Winnetka, Ill., Nov. 17, 1925.

HUNT, MARSHA: Chicago, Oct. 17, 1917.

HUNTER, IAN: Cape Town, S.A., June 13, 1900. St. Andrew's College.

HUNTER, JEFFREY: (Henry H. McKinnies) New Orleans, Nov. 25. Northwestern U.

HUNTER, KIM: (Janet Cole) Detroit, Nov. 12, 1922.

HUNTER, TAB: NYC, July 11, 1931.

HUSSEY, RUTH: Providence, R.I., Oct. 30, 1917. U. of Mich.

HUTTON, BETTY: (Betty Thornberg) Battle Creek, Mich., Feb. 26, 1921.

HUTTON, ROBERT: (Robert Winne) Kingston, N.Y., June 11, 1920. Blair Academy.

HYER, MARTHA: Fort Worth, Tex., Aug. 10, 1930. Northwestern U.

IRELAND, JOHN: Vancouver, B.C., Can., Jan. 30, 1915.

IVES, BURL: Hunt Township, Ill., June 14, 1909. Charleston Ill. Teachers College.

JAECKEL, RICHARD: Long Beach, N.Y., Oct. 10, 1926.

JAFFE, SAM: NYC, Mar. 8, 1898.

JAGGER, DEAN: Lima, Ohio, Nov. 7, 1903. Wabash College.

JANSSEN, DAVID: Naponee, Neb., Mar. 27, 1930.

JARMAN, CLAUDE, JR.: Nashville, Tenn., Sept. 27, 1934.

JASON, RICK: NYC, May 21, 1926. American Academy of Dramatic Art.

JEAN, GLORIA: (Gloria Jean Schoonover) Buffalo, N.Y., Apr. 14, 1928.

JEFFREYS, ANNE: Goldsboro, N.C., Jan. 26, 1923. Anderson College.

JERGENS, ADELE: Brooklyn, Nov. 26, 1922.

JOHNS, GLYNIS: Durban, S. Africa, Oct. 5, 1923.

JOHNSON, CELIA: Richmond, Surrey, Eng., Dec. 18, 1908. Royal Academy of Dramatic Arts.

JOHNSON, VAN: Newport, R.I., Aug. 28, 1916.

JONES, CAROLYN: Amarillo, Tex., 1933.

JONES, DEAN: Morgan County, Ala., Jan. 25, 1936. Asbury College.

JONES, JENNIFER: (Phyllis Isley) Tulsa, Okla., Mar. 2, 1919. American Academy of Dramatic Art.

JONES, SHIRLEY: Smithton, Pa., March 31.

JOURDAN, LOUIS: Marseilles, France, June 18, 1921.

JURADO, KATY: (Maria Christina Jurado Garcia) Guadalajara, Mex., 1927.

KARLOFF, BORIS: (William Henry Pratt) London, Nov. 23, 1887. Uppingham School.

KASZNAR, KURT: Vienna, Aug. 12, 1913. Gymnasium, Vienna.

KAUFMANN, CHRISTINE: Lansdorf, Graz, Austria, Jan. 11, 1945.

KAYE, DANNY: (David Daniel Kominski) Brooklyn, Jan. 18, 1913.

KAYE, STUBBY: NYC, Nov. 11, 1918.

KEEL, HOWARD: (Harold Keel) Gillespie, Ill., Apr. 13, 1919.

KEITH, BRIAN: Bayonne, N.J., Nov. 14, 1921.

KEITH, IAN: Boston, Feb. 27, 1899. American Academy of Dramatic Art.

KEITH, ROBERT: Fowler, Ind., Feb. 10, 1898.

KELLY, GENE: Pittsburgh, Aug. 23, 1912. U. of Pittsburgh.

KELLY, GRACE: Philadelphia, Nov. 12, 1929. American Academy of Dramatic Art.

KELLY, JACK: Astoria, N.Y., Sept. 16, 1927. UCLA.

KELLY, NANCY: Lowell, Mass., Mar. 25, 1921. Bentley School.

KENNEDY, ARTHUR: Worcester, Mass., Feb. 17, 1914. Carnegie Tech.

KERR, DEBORAH: Helensburgh, Scot., Sept. 30, 1921. Smale Ballet School.

KERR, JOHN: NYC, Nov. 15, 1931. Harvard and Columbia.

KITT, EARTHA: North, S.C., Jan. 26, 1928.

KNOWLES, PATRIC: (Reginald Lawrence Knowles) Horsforth, Eng., Nov. 11, 1911.

KNOX, ALEXANDER: Strathroy, Ont., Can., Jan. 16, 1907. Western Ontario U.

KNOX, ELYSE: Hartford, Conn., Dec. 14, 1917. Traphagen School.

KOHNER, SUSAN: Los Angeles, Nov. 11, 1936. U. of Calif.

KORVIN, CHARLES: (Geza Korvin Karpathi) Czechoslovakia, Nov. 21. Sorbonne.

KOSLECK, MARTIN: Barkotzen, Ger., Mar. 24, 1914. Max Reinhardt School.

KREUGER, KURT: St. Moritz, Switz., July 23, 1917. U. of London.

KRUGER, HARDY: Berlin, Ger., Apr. 12, 1928.

KRUGER, OTTO: Toledo, Ohio, Sept. 6, 1885. Michigan and Columbia U.

LAHR, BERT: (Irving Lashrheim) NYC, Aug. 13, 1895.

LAKE, VERONICA: (Constance Keane) Lake Placid, N.Y., Nov. 14, 1919. McGill U.

LAMARR, HEDY: Vienna, 1915.

LAMAS, FERNANDO: Buenos Aires, Jan. 9, 1920.

LAMB, GIL: Minneapolis, June 14, 1906. U. of Minn.

LAMOUR, DOROTHY: Dec. 10, 1914. Spence's School.

LANCASTER, BURT: NYC, Nov. 2, 1913. NYU.

LANCHESTER, ELSA: (Elsa Sullivan) London, Oct. 28, 1902.

LANDIS, JESSIE ROYCE: Chicago, Nov. 25, 1904. Chicago Conservatory.

LANGAN, GLENN: Denver, Colo., July 8, 1917.

LANGE, HOPE: Redding Ridge, Conn., Nov. 28. Reed College.

LANGTON, PAUL: Salt Lake City, Apr. 17, 1913. Travers School of Theatre.

LANSBURY, ANGELA: London, Oct. 16, 1925. London Academy of Music.

LAURIE, PIPER: (Rosetta Jacobs) Detroit, Jan. 22, 1932.

LAWFORD, PETER: London, Sept. 7, 1923.

LAWRENCE, BARBARA: Carnegie, Okla., Feb. 24, 1930. UCLA.

LAWRENCE, CAROL: Melrose Park, Ill., Sept. 5, 1935.

LEDERER, FRANCIS: Karlin, Prague, Czechoslovakia, Nov. 6, 1906.

LEE, CHRISTOPHER: London, May 27, 1922. Wellington College.

LEE, GYPSY ROSE: (Rose Hovick) Seattle, Wash., Feb. 9, 1914.

LEIGH, JANET: (Jeanette Helen Morrison) Merced, Calif., July 6, 1927. College of Pacific.

LEIGH, VIVIEN: (Vivien Mary Hartley) Darjeeling, India, Nov. 5, 1913. Royal Academy of Dramatic Arts.

226

| Ida Lupino | Fred MacMurray | Dorothy Malone | Roddy McDowall | Yvette Mimieux |

LEIGHTON, MARGARET: Barnt Green, Worcestershire, Eng., Feb. 26, 1922. Church of England College.

LEMBECK, HARVEY: Brooklyn, Apr. 15, 1923. U. of Ala.

LEMMON, JACK: Boston, Feb. 8, 1925. Harvard.

LESLIE, BETHEL: NYC, Aug. 3, 1929. Breaney School.

LESLIE, JOAN: (Joan Brodell) Detroit, Jan. 26, 1925. St. Benedict's.

LEVENE, SAM: NYC, 1907.

LEWIS, JERRY: Newark, N.J., Mar. 16, 1926.

LINDFORS, VIVECA: Uppsala, Sweden, Dec. 29, 1920. Stockholm Royal Dramatic School.

LIVESEY, ROGER: Barry, Wales, June 25, 1906. Westminster School.

LLOYD, HAROLD: Burchard, Neb., July 28, 1904.

LOCKHART, JUNE: NYC, June 25, 1925. Westlake School.

LOCKWOOD, MARGARET: Karachi, Pakistan, Sept. 15, 1916. Royal Academy of Dramatic Arts.

LOLLOBRIGIDA, GINA: Subiaco, Italy, 1928. Rome Academy of Fine Arts.

LOM, HERBERT: Prague, Czechoslovakia, 1917. Prague U.

LONDON, JULIE: (Julie Peck) Santa Rosa, Calif., Sept. 26, 1926.

LONG, RICHARD: Chicago, Dec. 17, 1927.

LOPEZ, PERRY: NYC, July 22, 1931. NYU.

LORD, JACK: (Ryan) NYC, Dec. 30, 1930. NYU.

LOREN, SOPHIA: (Sofia Scicolone) Rome, Italy, Sept. 20, 1934.

LOUISE, ANITA: (Anita Louise Fremault) NYC, 1917. Professional Children's School.

LOY, MYRNA: (Myrna Williams) Helena, Mont., Aug. 2, 1905. Westlake School.

LUKAS, PAUL: Budapest, Hungary, May 26, 1895. Actors Academy of Hungary.

LUND, JOHN: Rochester, N.Y., Feb. 6, 1913.

LUNDIGAN, WILLIAM: Syracuse, N.Y., June 12, 1914. Syracuse U.

LUPINO, IDA: London, Feb. 4, 1918. Royal Academy of Dramatic Arts.

LYNDE, PAUL: Mt. Vernon, Ohio, June 13, 1926. Northwestern U.

LYNLEY, CAROL: NYC, Feb. 13, 1942.

LYNN, DIANA: (Dolly Loehr) Los Angeles, Oct. 7, 1926.

LYNN, JEFFREY: Auburn, Mass., 1910. Bates College.

MacARTHUR, JAMES: Los Angeles, Dec. 8, 1937. Harvard.

MacGINNIS, NIALL: Dublin, Ire., Mar. 29, 1913. Dublin U.

MacLAINE, SHIRLEY: (Beaty) Richmond, Va., Apr. 24, 1934.

MacLANE, BARTON: Columbia, S.C., Dec. 25, 1902. Wesleyan University.

MacMAHON, ALINE: McKeesport, Pa., May 8, 1899. Barnard College.

MacMURRAY, FRED: Kankakee, Ill., Aug. 30, 1908. Carroll College.

MacRAE, GORDON: East Orange, N.J., Mar. 12, 1921.

MADISON, GUY: (Robert Moseley) Bakersfield, Calif., Jan. 19, 1922. Bakersfield Jr. College.

MAGNANI, ANNA: Alexandria, Egypt, Mar. 7, 1908. Rome Academy of Dramatic Art.

MAHARIS, GEORGE: Astoria, L.I., N.Y., Sept. 1, 1928. Actors Studio.

MAHONEY, JOCK: (Jacques O'Mahoney) Chicago, Feb. 7, 1919. U. of Iowa.

MALDEN, KARL: (Malden Sekulovich) Gary, Ind., Mar. 22, 1914.

MALONE, DOROTHY: Chicago, Jan. 30, 1930. S. Methodist U.

MANSFIELD, JAYNE: (Vera Jane Palmeri) Bryn Mawr, Pa., Apr. 19, 1933. UCLA.

MARCH, FREDRIC: (Frederick McIntyre Bickel) Racine, Wisc., Aug. 31, 1897. U. of Wisc.

MARGO: (Maria Marguerita Guadalupe Boldao y Castilla) Mexico City, May 10, 1918.

MARGOLIN, JANET: NYC, July 25, 1943. Walden School.

MARLOWE, HUGH: (Hugh Hipple) Philadelphia, Jan. 30, 1914.

MARSHALL, BRENDA: (Ardis Anderson Gaines) Isle of Negros, P.I., Sept. 29, 1915. Texas State College.

MARSHALL, E. G.: Owatonna, Minn., June 18, 1910. U. of Minn.

MARTIN, DEAN: (Dino Crocetti) Steubenville, Ohio, June 17, 1917.

MARTIN, MARY: Wetherford, Tex., Dec. 1, 1914. Ward-Belmont School.

MARTIN, TONY: Oakland, Cal., Dec. 25, 1913. St. Mary's College.

MARVIN, LEE: NYC, Feb. 19, 1924.

MARX, GROUCHO: (Julius Marx) NYC, Oct. 2, 1895.

MASON, JAMES: Huddersfield, Yorkshire, Eng., May 15, 1909. Cambridge.

MASON, PAMELA: (Pamela Kellino) Westgate, Eng., Mar. 10, 1918.

MASSEN, OSA: Copenhagen, Den., Jan. 13, 1916.

MASSEY, RAYMOND: Toronto, Can., Aug. 30, 1896. Oxford.

MATTHAU, WALTER: NYC, Oct. 1, 1923.

MATURE, VICTOR: Louisville, Ky., Jan. 29, 1916.

MAXWELL, MARILYN: Clarinda, Iowa, Aug. 3, 1922.

MAYEHOFF, EDDIE: Baltimore, July 7. Yale.

McCAMBRIDGE, MERCEDES: Joliet, Ill., March 17. Mundelein College.

McCARTHY, KEVIN: Seattle, Wash., Feb. 15, 1914. Minn. U.

McCLORY, SEAN: Dublin, Ire., March 8, 1924. U. of Galway.

McCREA, JOEL: Los Angeles, Nov. 5, 1905. Pomona College.

McDERMOTT, HUGH: Edinburgh, Scot., Mar. 20, 1908.

McDOWALL, RODDY: London, Sept. 17, 1928. St. Joseph's.

McGAVIN, DARREN: Spokane, Wash., May 7, 1922. College of Pacific.

McGIVER, JOHN: NYC, Nov. 5, 1915. Fordham, Columbia U.

McGUIRE, DOROTHY: Omaha, Neb., June 14, 1919. Wellesley.

McNALLY, STEPHEN: (Horace McNally) NYC, July 29, Fordham U.

McNAMARA, MAGGIE: NYC, June 18. St. Catherine.

McQUEEN, STEVE: Indianapolis, Mar. 24.

MEADOWS, AUDREY: Wuchang, China, 1924. St. Margaret's.

MEADOWS, JAYNE: (formerly, Jayne Cotter) Wuchang, China, Sept. 27, 1923. St. Margaret's.

MEDWIN, MICHAEL: London, 1925. Instut Fischer.

MEEKER, RALPH: (Ralph Rathgeber) Minneapolis, Nov. 21, 1920. Northwestern U.

MERCOURI, MELINA: Athens, Greece, 1925.

MEREDITH, BURGESS: Cleveland, Ohio, Nov. 16, 1909. Amherst.

MERKEL, UNA: Covington, Ky., Dec. 10, 1903.

MERMAN, ETHEL: (Ethel Zimmerman) Astoria, N.Y., Jan. 16, 1912.

MIFUNE, TOSHIRO: Tsingtao, China, Apr. 1, 1920.

MILES, VERA: Boise City, Okla., Aug. 23.

MILLAND, RAY: (Reginald Truscott-Jones) Neath, Wales, Jan. 3, 1908. King's College.

MILLER, ANN: (Lucille Ann Collier) Houston, Tex., Apr. 12, 1923. Lawler Professional School.

227

| Agnes Moorehead | Ramon Novarro | Maureen O'Hara | Lilli Palmer | Anthony Perk |

MILLER, MARVIN: St. Louis, July 18, 1913. Washington U.

MILLS, HAYLEY: London, Apr. 18, 1946. Elmhurst School.

MILLS, JOHN: Suffolk, Eng., Feb. 22, 1908.

MIMIEUX, YVETTE: Los Angeles, Jan. 8. Hollywood High.

MINEO, SAL: NYC, Jan. 10, 1939. Lodge School.

MIRANDA, ISA: (Ines Sampietro) Milan, Italy, July 5, 1917.

MITCHELL, CAMERON: Dallastown, Pa., Nov. 1918. NY Theatre School.

MITCHELL, JAMES: Sacramento, Calif., Feb. 29, 1920. LACC.

MITCHUM, ROBERT: Bridgeport, Conn., Aug. 6, 1917.

MONTALBAN, RICARDO: Mexico City, Nov. 25, 1920.

MONTAND, YVES: (Yves Montand Livi) Mansummano, Tuscany, Oct. 13, 1921.

MONTGOMERY, ELIZABETH: Los Angeles, Apr. 15, 1933. American Academy of Dramatic Art.

MONTGOMERY, GEORGE: (George Letz) Brady, Mont., Aug. 29, 1916. U. of Mont.

MONTGOMERY, ROBERT: (Henry, Jr.) Beacon, N.Y., May 21, 1904.

MOORE, CONSTANCE: Sioux City, Iowa, Jan. 18, 1922.

MOORE, DICK: Los Angeles, Sept. 12, 1925.

MOORE, KIERON: County Cork, Ire., 1925. St. Mary's College.

MOORE, ROGER: London, Oct. 14. Royal Academy of Dramatic Arts.

MOORE, TERRY: (Helen Koford) Los Angeles, Jan. 7, 1929.

MOOREHEAD, AGNES: Clinton, Mass., Dec. 6, 1906. American Academy of Dramatic Art.

MORE, KENNETH: Gerrards Cross, Eng., Sept. 20, 1914. Victoria College.

MORENO, RITA: Humacao, P.R., Dec. 11, 1931.

MORGAN, DENNIS: (Stanley Morner) Prentice, Wisc., Dec. 10, 1920. Carroll College.

MORGAN, HARRY (HENRY): (Harry Bratsburg) Detroit, Apr. 10, 1915. U. of Chicago.

MORGAN, MICHELE: (Simone Roussel) Paris, Feb. 29, 1920. Paris Dramatic School.

MORISON, PATRICIA: NYC, 1919.

MORLEY, ROBERT: Wiltshire, Eng., May 26, 1908. Royal Academy of Dramatic Arts.

MORRIS, CHESTER: NYC, Feb. 16, 1901. Art Students League.

MORRIS, HOWARD: NYC, Sept. 4, 1919. NYU.

MORROW, VIC: Bronx, N.Y., Feb. 14, 1932. Fla. Southern College.

MORSE, ROBERT: Newton, Mass., May 18, 1931.

MOSTEL, ZERO: Brooklyn, Feb. 28, 1915. CCNY.

MUNI, PAUL: (Muni Weisenfreund) Lemberg, Austria, Sept. 22, 1895.

MURPHY, AUDIE: Kingston, Tex., June 20, 1924.

MURPHY, GEORGE: New Haven, Conn., July 4, 1904. Yale.

MURRAY, DON: Hollywood, July 31, 1929. American Academy of Dramatic Art.

MURRAY, KEN: (Don Court) NYC, July 14, 1903.

NADER, GEORGE: Pasadena, Calif., Oct. 19, 1921. Occidental College.

NAGEL, CONRAD: Keokuk, Iowa, Mar. 16, 1897. Highland Park College.

NAPIER, ALAN: Birmingham, Eng., Jan. 7, 1903. Birmingham University.

NATWICK, MILDRED: Baltimore, June 19, 1908. Bryn Mawr.

NEAL, PATRICIA: Packard, Ky., Jan. 20, 1926. Northwestern U.

NEFF, HILDEGARDE: (Hildegard Knef) Ulm, Ger., Dec. 28, 1925. Berlin Art Academy.

NELSON, DAVID: NYC, Oct. 24, 1936. USC.

NELSON, GENE: (Gene Berg) Seattle, Wash., Mar. 24, 1920.

NELSON, HARRIET HILLIARD: (Peggy Lou Snyder) Des Moines, Iowa, July 18.

NELSON, LORI: (Dixie Kay Nelson) Sante Fe, N.M., Aug. 15, 1933.

NELSON, OZZIE: (Oswald) Jersey City, N.J., Mar. 20, 1907. Rutgers U.

NELSON, RICK: (Eric Hilliard Nelson) Teaneck, N.J., May 8, 1940.

NESBITT, CATHLEEN: Cheshire, Eng., Nov. 24, 1889. Victoria College.

NEWLEY, ANTHONY: Hackney, London, Sept. 21, 1931.

NEWMAN, PAUL: Cleveland, Ohio, Jan. 26, 1925. Yale.

NICOL, ALEX: Ossining, N.Y., Jan. 20, 1919. Actors Studio.

NIELSEN, LESLIE: Regina, Saskatchewan, Can., Feb. 11, 1926. Neighborhood Playhouse.

NIVEN, DAVID: Kirriemuir, Scot., Mar. 1, 1910. Sandhurst College.

NOLAN, LLOYD: San Francisco, Aug. 11, 1902. Stanford U.

NOONAN, TOMMY: Bellingham, Wash., Apr. 29, 1922. NYU.

NORTH, SHEREE: (Dawn Bethel) Los Angeles, Jan. 17, 1933. Hollywood High.

NOVAK, KIM: (Marilyn Novak) Chicago, Feb. 13, 1933. LACC.

NOVARRO, RAMON: (Ramon Samaniegoes) Durango, Mex., Feb. 6, 1905.

NUGENT, ELLIOTT: Dover, Ohio, Sept. 20, 1900. Ohio State U.

NUYEN, FRANCE: Marseilles, France, 1939. Beaux Arts School.

OBERON, MERLE: (Estelle Merle O'Brien Thompson) Tasmania, Feb. 19, 1911.

O'BRIAN, HUGH: (Hugh J. Krampe) Rochester, N.Y., Apr. 19, 1928. Cincinnati U.

O'BRIEN, EDMOND: NYC, Sept. 10, 1915. Fordham, Neighborhood Playhouse.

O'BRIEN, MARGARET: (Angela Maxine O'Brien) Los Angeles, Jan. 15, 1937.

O'BRIEN, PAT: Milwaukee, Nov. 11, 1899. Marquette U.

O'CONNELL, ARTHUR: NYC, Mar. 29, 1908. St. John's.

O'CONNOR, DONALD: Chicago, Aug. 28, 1925.

O'DONNELL, CATHY: (Ann Steely) Siluria, Ala., July 6, 1925. Oklahoma City U.

O'HARA, MAUREEN: (Maureen FitzSimons) Dublin, Ire., Aug. 17, 1921. Abbey School.

O'HERLIHY, DAN: Wexford, Ire., May 1, 1919. National U.

OLIVIER, LAURENCE: Dorking, Eng., May 22, 1907. St. Edward's, Oxford.

O'NEAL, PATRICK: Ocala, Fla., Sept. 26, 1927. U. of Fla.

O'SHEA, MICHAEL: NYC, Mar. 17, 1906.

O'SULLIVAN, MAUREEN: Byle, Ire., May 17, 1911. Sacred Heart Convent.

OWEN, REGINALD: Wheathampstead, Eng., Aug. 5, 1887. Tree's Academy.

PAGE, GERALDINE: Kirksville, Mo., Nov. 22, 1924. Goodman School.

PAGET, DEBRA: (Debralee Griffin) Denver, Aug. 19, 1933.

PAIGE, JANIS: (Donna Mae Jaden) Tacoma, Wash., Sept. 16, 1922.

PALANCE, JACK: Lattimer, Pa., Feb. 18, 1920. U. of N.C.

PALMER, BETSY: East Chicago, Ind., Nov. 1, 1929. DePaul U.

PALMER, GREGG: (Palmer Lee) San Francisco, Jan. 25, 1927. U. of Utah.

PALMER, LILLI: Posen, Austria, May 24, 1914. Ilka Gruning School.

PALMER, MARIA: Vienna, Sept. 5, 1924. College de Bouffement.

PARKER, CECIL: Hastings, Sussex, Eng., Sept. 3, 1897. St. Francis Xavier College.

PARKER, ELEANOR: Cedarville, Ohio, June 26, 1922. Pasadena Playhouse.

PARKER, FESS: Fort Worth, Tex., Aug. 16. USC.

orothy Provine   Sidney Poitier   Lee Remick   Cliff Robertson   Maria Schell

PARKER, JEAN: (Mae Green) Deer Lodge, Mont., Aug. 11, 1918.

PARKER, SUZY: (Cecelia Parker) San Antonio, Tex., Oct. 28.

PARKER, WILLARD: (Worster Van Eps) NYC, Feb. 5, 1912.

PARSONS, LOUELLA: Freeport, Ill., Aug. 6, 1893. Dixon College.

PATRICK, NIGEL: London, May ?, 1913.

PATTERSON, LEE: Vancouver, Can., 1929. Ontario College of Art.

PAVAN, MARISA: (Marisa Pierangeli) Cagliari, Sardinia, June 19, 1932. Torquado Tasso College.

PAYTON, BARBARA: Cloquet, Minn., Nov. 16, 1927.

PEACH, MARY: Durban, S. Africa, 1934.

PEARSON, BEATRICE: Denison, Tex., July 27, 1920.

PECK, GREGORY: La Jolla, Calif., Apr. 5, 1916. U. of Calif.

PEPPARD, GEORGE: Detroit, Oct. 1. Carnegie Tech.

PERKINS, ANTHONY: NYC, Apr. 14, 1932. Rollins College.

PERREAU, GIGI: (Ghislaine) Los Angeles, Feb. 6, 1941.

PETERS, JEAN: (Elizabeth) Canton, Ohio, Oct. 15, 1926. Ohio State U.

PICERNI, PAUL: NYC, Dec. 1, 1922. Loyola U.

PICKENS, SLIM: (Louis Bert Lindley, Jr.) Kingsberg, Calif., June 29, 1919.

PICKFORD, MARY: (Gladys Mary Smith) Toronto, Can., Apr. 8, 1893.

PIDGEON, WALTER: East St. John, N.B., Can., Sept. 23, 1898.

PINE, PHILLIP: Hanford, Calif., July 16, 1925. Actors' Lab.

PLEASENCE, DONALD: Workshop, Eng., Oct. 5, 1919. Sheffield School.

PLESHETTE, SUZANNE: NYC, Jan. 31. Syracuse U.

PLUMMER, CHRISTOPHER: Toronto, Can., 1927.

PODESTA, ROSANA: Tripoli, June 20, 1934.

POITIER, SIDNEY: Miami, Fla., Feb. 20, 1924.

PORTMAN, ERIC: Yorkshire, Eng., July 13, 1903. Rishworth School.

POWELL, JANE: (Suzanne Burce) Portland, Ore., Apr. 1.

POWELL, WILLIAM: Pittsburgh, July 29, 1892. American Academy of Dramatic Art.

POWERS, MALA: (Mary Ellen) San Francisco, Dec. 29, 1921. UCLA.

PRENTISS, PAULA: (Paula Ragusa) San Antonio, Tex., Mar. 4. Northwestern U.

PRESLE, MICHELINE: (Micheline Chassagne) Paris, Aug. 22, 1922. Rouleau Drama School.

PRESLEY, ELVIS: Tupelo, Miss., Jan. 8, 1935.

PRESNELL, HARVE: Modesto, Calif., Sept. 14, 1933. USC.

PRESTON, ROBERT: (Robert Preston Meservey) Newton Highlands, Mass., June 8, 1918. Pasadena Playhouse.

PRICE, DENNIS: Twyford, Eng., 1915. Oxford.

PRICE, VINCENT: St. Louis, May 27, 1911. Yale.

PRINCE, WILLIAM: Nicholas, N.Y., Jan. 26, 1913. Cornell U.

PROVINE, DOROTHY: Deadwood, S.D., Jan. 20, 1937. U. of Wash.

PURCELL, NOEL: Dublin, Ire., Dec. 23, 1900. Irish Christian Brothers.

PURDOM, EDMUND: Welwyn Garden City, Eng., Dec. 19. St. Ignatius College.

QUAYLE, ANTHONY: Lancashire, Eng., 1913. Old Vic School.

QUINN, ANTHONY: Chihuahua, Mex., Apr. 21, 1915.

RAFFERTY, FRANCES: Sioux City, Iowa, June 26, 1922. UCLA.

RAINES, ELLA: (Ella Wallace Rains Olds) Snoqualmie Falls, Wash., Aug. 6, 1921. U. of Washington.

RAINS, CLAUDE: London, Nov. 10, 1889.

RANDALL, TONY: Tulsa, Okla., Feb. 26, 1920. Northwestern U.

RANDELL, RON: Sydney, Australia, Oct. 8, 1920. St. Mary's College.

RATHBONE, BASIL: Johannesburg, S. Africa, June 13, 1892. Repton College.

RAY, ALDO: (Aldo DaRe) Pen Argyl, Pa., Sept. 25, 1926. UCLA.

RAYE, MARTHA: (Margie Yvonne Reed) Butte, Mont., Aug. 27, 1916.

RAYMOND, GENE: (Raymond Guion) NYC, Aug. 13, 1908.

REAGAN, RONALD: Tampico, Ill., Feb. 6, 1911. Eureka College.

REASON, REX: Berlin, Ger., Nov. 30, 1928. Pasadena Playhouse.

REDFORD, ROBERT: Santa Monica, Calif., Aug. 18, 1937. American Academy of Dramatic Art.

REDGRAVE, MICHAEL: Bristol, Eng., Mar. 20, 1908. Cambridge.

REDMAN, JOYCE: County Mayo, Ire., 1919. Royal Academy of Dramatic Arts.

REED, DONNA: (Donna Mullenger) Denison, Iowa, Jan. 27, 1921. LACC.

REEVES, STEVE: Glasgow, Mont., Jan. 21, 1926.

REINER, CARL: NYC, Mar. 20, 1923.

REMICK, LEE: Quincy, Mass., Dec. 14, 1935. Barnard College.

RENNIE, MICHAEL: Bradford, Eng., Aug. 25, 1909. Cambridge.

RETTIG, TOMMY: Jackson Heights, N.Y., Dec. 10, 1941.

REYNOLDS, DEBBIE: (Mary Frances Reynolds) El Paso, Tex., Apr. 1, 1932.

REYNOLDS, MARJORIE: Buhl, Idaho, Aug. 12, 1921.

RICH, IRENE: Buffalo, N.Y., Oct. 13, 1897. St. Margaret's School.

RICHARDS, JEFF: (Richard Mansfield Taylor) Portland, Ore., Nov. 1. USC.

RICHARDSON, RALPH: Cheltenham, Eng., Dec. 19, 1902.

RITTER, THELMA: Brooklyn, Feb. 14, 1905. American Academy of Dramatic Art.

ROBARDS, JASON: Chicago, July 26, 1922. American Academy of Dramatic Art.

ROBERTSON, CLIFF: La Jolla, Calif., Sept. 9, 1925. Antioch College.

ROBINSON, EDWARD G.: (Emanuel Goldenberg) Bucharest, Rum., Dec. 12, 1893. Columbia U.

ROBSON, FLORA: South Shields, Eng., Mar. 28, 1902. Royal Academy of Dramatic Arts.

ROCHESTER: (Eddie Anderson) Oakland, Calif., Sept. 18, 1905.

ROGERS, CHARLES "BUDDY": Olathe, Kan., Aug. 13, 1904. U. of Kan.

ROGERS, GINGER: (Virginia Katherine McMath) Independence, Mo., July 16, 1911.

ROGERS, ROY: (Leonard Slye) Cincinnati, Nov. 5, 1912.

ROLAND, GILBERT: (Luis Antonio Damasco De Alonso) Juarez, Mex., Dec. 11, 1905.

ROMAN, RUTH: Boston, Dec. 23. Bishop Lee Dramatic School.

ROMERO, CESAR: NYC, Feb. 15, 1907. Collegiate School.

ROONEY, MICKEY: (Joe Yule, Jr.) Brooklyn, Sept. 23, 1922.

ROTH, LILLIAN: Boston, Dec. 13, 1910.

RUGGLES, CHARLES: Los Angeles, Feb. 8, 1892.

RULE, JANICE: Cincinnati, Aug. 15, 1931.

RUSH, BARBARA: Denver, Colo., Jan. 4. U. of Calif.

RUSSELL, JANE: Bemidji, Minn., June 21, 1921. Max Reinhardt School.

RUSSELL, JOHN: Los Angeles, Jan. 3, 1921. U. of Calif.

RUSSELL, ROSALIND: Waterbury, Conn., June 4, 1912. American Academy of Dramatic Arts.

Romy Schneider

Dick Shawn

Jean Seberg

Russ Tamblyn

Shirley Temp

RUTHERFORD, ANN: Toronto, Can., 1924.

RUTHERFORD, MARGARET: London, May 11, 1892. Wimbledon Hill School.

RYAN, ROBERT: Chicago, Nov. 11, 1913. Dartmouth.

SAINT, EVA MARIE: Newark, N.J., July 4, 1924. Bowling Green State U.

ST. JOHN, BETTA: Hawthorne, Calif., Nov. 26, 1929.

SANDERS, GEORGE: St. Petersburg, Russia, 1906. Brighton College.

SANDS, TOMMY: Chicago, Aug. 27, 1937.

SAN JUAN, OLGA: NYC, Mar. 16, 1927.

SAXON, JOHN: (Carmen Orrico) Brooklyn, Aug. 5, 1935.

SCALA, GIA: Liverpool, Eng., Mar. 3, 1936. Stella Adler School.

SCHELL, MARIA: Vienna, Jan. 15, 1926.

SCHELL, MAXIMILIAN: Vienna, Dec. 8, 1930.

SCHNEIDER, ROMY: Vienna, Sept. 23, 1938.

SCOFIELD, PAUL: Hurstpierpont, Eng., Jan. 21, 1922. London Mask Theatre School.

SCOTT, GEORGE C.: Wise, Va., Oct. 18, 1927. U. of Mo.

SCOTT, GORDON: (Gordon M. Werschkul) Portland, Ore., Aug. 3, 1927. Oregon U.

SCOTT, MARTHA: Jamesport, Mo., Sept. 22, 1914. U. of Mich.

SCOTT, RANDOLPH: Orange County, Va., Jan. 23, 1903. U. of N.C.

SEARS, HEATHER: London, 1935.

SEBERG, JEAN: Marshalltown, Iowa, Nov. 13, 1938. Iowa U.

SELLERS, PETER: Southsea, Eng., Sept. 8, 1925. Aloysius College.

SELWART, TONIO: Wartenberg, Ger., June 9, 1906. Munich U.

SEYLER, ATHENE: (Athene Hannen) London, May 31, 1889.

SEYMOUR, ANNE: NYC, Sept. 11, 1909. American Laboratory Theatre.

SHATNER, WILLIAM: Montreal, Can., Mar. 22, 1931. McGill U.

SHAW, SEBASTIAN: Holt, Eng., May 29, 1905. Gresham School.

SHAWLEE, JOAN: Forest Hills, N.Y., Mar. 5, 1929.

SHAWN, DICK: (Richard Schulefand) Buffalo, N.Y., Dec. 1. U. of Miami.

SHEARER, MOIRA: Dunfermline, Scot., Jan 17, 1926. London Theatre School.

SHEARER, NORMA: Montreal, Can., Aug. 10, 1904.

SHEFFIELD, JOHN: Pasadena, Calif., Apr. 11, 1931. UCLA.

SHERIDAN, ANN: Denton, Tex., Feb. 21, 1915. N. Tex. State Teachers College.

SHORE, DINAH: (Frances Rose Shore) Winchester, Tenn., Mar. 1, 1917. Vanderbilt U.

SHOWALTER, MAX: (Formerly Casey Adams) Caldwell, Kan., June 2, 1917. Pasadena Playhouse.

SIDNEY, SYLVIA: NYC, Aug. 8, 1910. Theatre Guild School.

SIGNORET, SIMONE: (Simone Kaminker) Wiesbaden, Ger., Mar. 25, 1921. Solange Sicard School.

SILVERS, PHIL: (Philip Silversmith) Brooklyn, May 11, 1912.

SIM, ALASTAIR: Edinburgh, Scot., 1900.

SIMMONS, JEAN: London, Jan. 31, 1929. Aida Foster School.

SIMON, SIMONE: Marseilles, France, Apr. 23, 1914.

SINATRA, FRANK: Hoboken, N.J., Dec. 12, 1915.

SKELTON, RED: (Richard Skelton) Vincennes, Ind., July 18, 1913.

SLEZAK, WALTER: Vienna, Austria, May 3, 1902.

SMITH, ALEXIS: Penticton, Can., June 8, 1921. LACC.

SMITH, JOHN: (Robert E. Van Orden) Los Angeles, Mar. 6, 1931. UCLA.

SMITH, KATE: (Kathryn Elizabeth) Greenville, Va., May 1, 1909.

SMITH, KENT: NYC, Mar. 19, 1907. Harvard U.

SMITH, ROGER: South Gate, Calif., Dec. 18, 1932. U. of Ariz.

SOMMER, ELKE: Germany, 1941.

SOTHERN, ANN: (Harriet Lake) Valley City, N.D., Jan. 22, 1911. Washington U.

STACK, ROBERT: Los Angeles, Jan. 13, 1919. USC.

STANG, ARNOLD: Chelsea, Mass., Sept. 28, 1925.

STANLEY, KIM: (Patricia Reid) Tularosa, N.M., Feb. 11, 1925. U. of Tex.

STANWYCK, BARBARA: (Ruby Stevens) Brooklyn, July 16, 1907.

STAPLETON, MAUREEN: Troy, N.Y., June 21, 1925.

STEEL, ANTHONY: London, May 21, 1920. Cambridge.

STEELE, TOMMY: London, Dec. 17, 1936.

STEIGER, ROD: Westhampton, N.Y., Apr. 14, 1925.

STERLING, JAN: (Jane Sterling Adriance) NYC, Apr. 3, 1923. Fay Compton School.

STERLING, ROBERT: (Robert Sterling Hart) Newcastle, Pa., Nov. 13, 1917. U. of Pittsburgh.

STEVENS, CONNIE: (Concetta Ann Ingolie) Brooklyn, Aug. 8, 1938. Hollywood Professional School.

STEVENS, INGER: (Inger Stensland) Stockholm, Sweden, Oct. 18. Columbia U.

STEVENS, MARK: (Richard) Cleveland, Ohio, Dec. 13, 1922.

STEWART, ELAINE: Montclair, N.J., May 31, 1929.

STEWART, JAMES: Indiana, Pa., May 20, 1908. Princeton.

STEWART, MARTHA: (Martha Haworth) Bardwell, Ky., Oct. 7, 1922.

STORM, GALE: (Josephine Cottle) Bloominton, Tex., Apr. 5, 1922.

STRASBERG, SUSAN: NYC, May 22, 1938.

STRAUSS, ROBERT: NYC, Nov. 8, 1913.

STRUDWICK, SHEPPERD: Hillsboro, N.C., Sept. 22, 1907. U. of N.C.

SULLIVAN, BARRY: (Patrick Barry) NYC, Aug. 29, 1912. NYU.

SULLY, FRANK: (Frank Sullivan) St. Louis, 1910. St. Teresa's College.

SWANSON, GLORIA: (Josephine Swenson) Chicago, Mar. 27, 1898. Chicago Art Inst.

SWINBURNE, NORA: Bath, Eng., July 24, 1902. Royal Academy of Dramatic Arts.

SYLVESTER, WILLIAM: Oakland, Calif., Jan. 31, 1922. Royal Academy of Dramatic Arts.

SYMS, SYLVIA: London, 1934. Convent School.

TALBOT, LYLE: (Lysle Hollywood) Pittsburgh, Feb. 8, 1904.

TALBOT, NITA: NYC, Aug. 8, 1930. Irvine Studio School.

TAMBLYN, RUSS: Los Angeles, Dec. 30.

TANDY, JESSICA: London, June 7, 1909. Dame Owens' School.

TAYLOR, DON: Freeport, Pa., Dec. 13, 1920. Penn State U.

TAYLOR, ELIZABETH: London, Feb. 27, 1932. Byron House School.

TAYLOR, KENT: (Louis Weiss) Nashua, Iowa, May 11, 1907.

TAYLOR, ROBERT: (S. Arlington Brugh) Filley, Neb., Aug. 5, 1911. Pomona College.

TEAL, RAY: Grand Rapids, Mich., Jan. 12, 1902. Pasadena Playhouse.

TEMPLE, SHIRLEY JANE: Santa Monica, Calif., Apr. 23, 1928.

TERRY-THOMAS: (Thomas Terry Hoar Stevens) Finchley, London, July 14, 1911. Ardingly College.

THATCHER, TORIN: Bombay, India, Jan. 15, 1905. Royal Academy of Dramatic Arts.

Peter Ustinov

Shelley Winters

Keenan Wynn

Susannah York

Efrem Zimbalist, Jr.

THAXTER, PHYLLIS: Portland, Me., Nov. 20, 1921. St. Genevieve School.

THOMAS, DANNY: (Amos Jacobs) Deerfield, Mich., Jan. 6, 1914.

THOMPSON, MARSHALL: Peoria, Ill., Nov. 27, 1925. Occidental College.

THORNDIKE, SYBIL: Gainsborough, Eng., Oct. 24, 1882. Guild Hall School of Music.

TIERNEY, GENE: Brooklyn, Nov. 20, 1920. Miss Farmer's School.

TIERNEY, LAWRENCE: Brooklyn, Mar. 15, 1919. Manhattan College.

TODD, RICHARD: Dublin, Ire., June 11, 1919. Shrewsbury School.

TONE, FRANCHOT: Niagara Falls, N.Y., Feb. 27, 1905. Cornell U.

TRACY, LEE: Atlanta, Ga., Apr. 11, 1898. Union College.

TRACY, SPENCER: Milwaukee, Apr. 5, 1900. Marquette U., American Academy of Dramatic Art.

TRACY, WILLIAM: Pittsburgh, Dec. 1, 1917. American Academy of Dramatic Art.

TRAVERS, BILL: Newcastle-on-Tyne, Eng., Jan. 3, 1922.

TRAVIS, RICHARD: (William Justice) Carlsbad, N.M., Apr. 17, 1913.

TREMAYNE, LES: London, Apr. 16, 1913. Northwestern, Columbia, UCLA.

TRUEX, ERNEST: Kansas City, Mo., Sept. 19, 1890.

TRYON, TOM: Hartford, Conn., Jan. 14, 1926. Yale.

TUCKER, FORREST: Plainfield, Ind., Feb. 12, 1919. George Washington U.

TURNER, LANA: (Julia Jean Turner) Wallace, Idaho, Feb. 8, 1920.

TYLER, BEVERLY: (Beverly Jean Saul) Scranton, Pa., July 5, 1928.

ULRIC, LENORE: New Ulm, Minn., July 21, 1894.

USTINOV, PETER: London, Apr. 16, 1921. Westminster School.

VALLEE, RUDY: (Hubert) Island Pond, Vt., July 28, 1901. Yale.

VALLI, ALIDA: Pola, Italy, May 31, 1921. Rome Academy of Drama.

VAN DOREN, MAMIE: (Joan Lucile Olander) Rowena, S.D., Feb. 6, 1933.

VAN ROOTEN, LUIS: Mexico City, Nov. 29, 1906. U. of Pa.

VENUTA, BENAY: San Francisco, Jan. 27, 1911.

VERDON, GWEN: Culver City, Calif., Jan. 13, 1925.

VITALE, MILLY: Rome, Italy, July 16, 1938. Lycée Chateaubriand.

VYE, MURVYN: Quincy, Mass., July 15, 1913. Yale.

WAGNER, ROBERT: Detroit, Feb. 10, 1930.

WALBROOK, ANTON: Vienna, Nov. 19, 1900.

WALBURN, RAYMOND: Plymouth, Ind., Sept. 9, 1887.

WALKER, CLINT: Hartford, Ill., May 30, 1927. USC.

WALKER, NANCY: (Ann Myrtle Swoyer) Philadelphia, May 10, 1921.

WALLACH, ELI: Brooklyn, Dec. 7, 1915. CCNY, U. of Tex.

WALSTON, RAY: New Orleans, Nov. 22, 1918. Cleveland Playhouse.

WARDEN, JACK: Newark, N.J., Sept. 18, 1920.

WASHBOURNE, MONA: Birmingham, Eng., Nov. 27, 1903.

WATERS, ETHEL: Chester, Pa., Oct. 31, 1900.

WATLING, JACK: London, Jan. 13, 1923. Italia Conti School.

WAYNE, DAVID: (Wayne McKeehan) Travers City, Mich., Jan. 30, 1916. Western Michigan State U.

WAYNE, JOHN: (Marion Michael Morrison) Winterset, Iowa, May 26, 1907. USC.

WEAVER, MARJORIE: Crossville, Tenn., Mar. 2, 1913. Indiana U.

WEBB, ALAN: York, Eng., July 2, 1906. Dartmouth.

WEBB, JACK: Santa Monica, Calif., Apr. 2, 1920.

WELD, TUESDAY: (Susan) NYC, Aug. 27, 1943. Hollywood Professional School.

WELDON, JOAN: San Francisco, Aug. 5, 1933. San Francisco Conservatory.

WELLES, ORSON: Kenosha, Wisc., May 6, 1915. Todd School.

WERNER, OSKAR: Vienna, Nov. 13, 1922.

WEST, MAE: Brooklyn, Aug. 17, 1892.

WHITE, JESSE: Buffalo, N.Y., Jan. 3, 1919.

WHITE, WILFRID HYDE: Gloucestershire, Eng., May 12, 1903. Royal Academy of Dramatic Arts.

WHITMAN, STUART: San Francisco, Feb. 1, 1929. CCLA.

WIDMARK, RICHARD: Sunrise, Minn., Dec. 26, 1914. Lake Forest U.

WILCOXON, HENRY: British West Indies, Sept. 8, 1905.

WILDE, CORNELL: NYC, Oct. 13, 1915. CCNY, Columbia.

WILDING, MICHAEL: Westcliff, Eng., July 23, 1912. Christ's Hospital.

WILLIAMS, EMLYN: Mostyn, Wales, Nov. 26, 1905. Oxford.

WILLIAMS, ESTHER: Los Angeles, Aug. 8, 1923.

WILLIAMS, GRANT: NYC, Aug. 18, 1930. Queens College.

WILLIAMS, JOHN: Chalfont, Eng., Apr. 15, 1903. Lancing College.

WILSON, MARIE: Anaheim, Calif., Dec. 30, 1917. Cumnock School.

WINDSOR, MARIE: (Emily Marie Bertelson) Marysvale, Utah, Dec. 11, 1924. Brigham Young University.

WINTERS, JONATHAN: Dayton, Ohio, Nov. 11, 1925. Kenyon College.

WINTERS, ROLAND: Boston, Nov. 22, 1904.

WINTERS, SHELLEY: (Shirley Schrift) St. Louis, Aug. 18, 1922. Wayne U.

WINWOOD, ESTELLE: Kent, Eng., Jan. 24, 1883. Lyric Stage Academy.

WITHERS, GOOGIE: Karachi, India, Mar. 12, 1917. Italia Conti School.

WOLFIT, DONALD: Newark-on-Trent, Eng., Apr. 20, 1902. Magnus School.

WOOD, NATALIE: (Natasha Gurdin) San Francisco, July 20, 1938.

WOOD, PEGGY: Brooklyn, Feb. 9, 1894.

WOODWARD, JOANNE: Thomasville, Ga., Feb. 27, 1931. Neighborhood Playhouse.

WOOLAND, NORMAN: Dusseldorf, Ger., Mar. 16, 1910. Edward VI School.

WRAY, FAY: Alberta, Can., Sept. 10, 1907.

WRIGHT, TERESA: NYC, Oct. 27, 1918.

WYATT, JANE: Campgaw, N.J., Aug. 10, 1912. Barnard College.

WYMAN, JANE: (Sarah Jane Fulks) St. Joseph, Mo., Jan. 4, 1914.

WYMORE, PATRICE: Miltonvale, Kan., Dec. 17, 1927.

WYNN, KEENAN: NYC, July 27, 1916. St. John's.

WYNN, MAY: (Donna Lee Hickey) NYC, Jan. 8, 1930.

YORK, DICK: (Richard Allen York) Fort Wayne, Ind., Sept. 4, 1928. DePaul U.

YORK, SUSANNAH: London, 1942.

YOUNG, ALAN: (Angus) North Shield, Eng., Nov. 19, 1919.

YOUNG, GIG: (Byron Barr) St. Cloud, Minn., Nov. 4, 1917. Pasadena Playhouse.

YOUNG, LORETTA: (Gretchen) Salt Lake City, Jan. 6, 1913. Immaculate Heart College.

YOUNG, ROBERT: Chicago, Feb. 22, 1907.

ZETTERLING, MAI: Sweden, May 27, 1925. Ordtuery Theatre School.

ZIMBALIST, EFREM, JR.: NYC, Nov. 30, 1923. Yale.

OBITUARIES

Gertrude Berg

Ralph Bunker

Francis X. Bushman

BAKALEINIKOFF, CONSTANTIN, 68, music director at RKO for many years before retirement 10 years ago, died in Hollywood, Sept. 3, 1966. Before joining RKO in 1941, he was with Paramount and MGM. A sister survives.

BAKER, ART, 68, actor and former MC for TV's "You Asked For It," died of a heart attack on Aug. 26, 1966 in a Los Angeles bank. A veteran radio and TV actor, he had also appeared in such films as "The Farmer's Daughter," "State Of The Union," and "The Walls Of Jericho."

BARKER, CECIL, 50, film and TV producer, died of a heart attack Nov. 12, 1966 in Beverly Hills. Served as production aide on "Gone With The Wind" and "Portrait Of Jenny" before producing "The Red Skelton Show" and "Branded" for TV. His last film was "Fly From The Hawk." His widow and two daughters survive.

BAUMAN, SCHAMYL, 72, pioneer film producer-director of more than 50 films, died Feb. 28, 1966 in Stockholm. Best known films in The States were "We Two," "We Three," and "Gentle Thief Of Love."

BERG, GERTRUDE, 66, the typical Jewish mother to millions of radio, television, stage, and screen fans, died Sept. 14, 1966 in NY's Doctors Hospital of a heart failure after a brief illness. She wrote as much as she acted in all mediums. Her Goldberg family became history after their first radio appearance in 1929. In 1949 they became TV staples, and in 1951 they were filmed in "Molly." Survivors are her husband of 48 years, Louis Berg, a son and a daughter.

BORBERG, WILLY, winner of two Academy Awards for development in sound technique, died July 14, 1966 at his home in Briarcliff Manor, N. Y. He developed and patented 20 instruments for sound and projection. A wife, daughter, and son survive.

BUNKER, RALPH, 77, film and stage actor, died of a stroke Apr. 28, 1966 in NYC. His best known film role was in "The Ghost Goes West."

BUSHMAN, FRANCIS X., 83, romantic hero of the silent films, and more recently a character actor, died Aug. 23, 1966 in his home in Pacific Palisades as a result of a fall in his kitchen. He was scheduled to report for a film the next day. His classic features made him the screen's first matinee idol, and 18 secretaries were hired to answer his fan mail. His career was shattered in 1918 when he divorced his wife, who had borne him five children, a secret that had been kept from his public. He then began his radio and eventually TV careers. His attempted come-back in 1926 in "Ben-Hur" was not successful, however he continued to appear in bit parts until his death. Of his 424 roles, the best known were "Lost Years," "When Soul Meets Soul," "The Spy's Deceit," "Blood Will Tell," "Social Quicksand," "Under Royal Patronage," "Graustark," "Romeo and Juliet," "The Great Secret," "Wilson," "David and Bathsheba." His fourth wife, and six children survive. Interment was in the Memorial Court of Honor at Forest Lawn.

CALHOUN, ALICE, 65, silent film star, died June 3, 1966 of cancer in Los Angeles. By 1932 when she retired, she had appeared in 52 Vitagraph and Warner Bros. pictures, among which were "The Man Next Door, "Angel Of Crooked Street," "The Man From Brodney," "One Stolen Night," and "The Little Minister." Her husband of 39 years, Max C. Chotiner, a broker, survives.

CAMPBELL, COLIN, 83, veteran actor who began his career in Hollywood in 1916, died March 25, 1966 at the Motion Picture Country Home in Woodland Hills, Calif. He had been active until a year ago when he retired.

CASTLE, DON, 47, former leading man for MGM and Paramount, was found dead in his Hollywood apartment on May 26, 1966 from an overdose of medication. He had recently been in an auto accident and was in great pain. He was associated with International TV Corp., and was associate producer on the "Lassie" TV series. Two daughters survive.

CARETTE, JULIEN, 68, French film character actor, died July 20, 1966 in Paris of burns following an accident. For the past two years he had lived in retirement after being half-paralyzed. He appeared in 115 French films, generally using only his last name.

CHALMERS, THOMAS, 82, opera singer, actor, film director, editor, and writer, died June 12, 1966 at the Laurelton Nursing Home in Greenwich, Conn. Wrote, produced and directed short subjects for Fox Movietone News. Was the father in radio's "Pepper Young's Family" for 18 years, and frequently appeared on TV. Surviving are his wife and daughter.

CHATTON, SYDNEY, 48, film, TV, radio, stage actor, and night club performer died Oct. 6, 1966 of a coronary in Alta Bates Hospital, Berkeley, Calif. At the time of his death he was in charge of film programming for San Francisco's TV station. He is survived by his widow.

CHERKASOV, NIKOLAI, 63, Soviet screen and stage actor, died Sept. 14, 1966. His best known films in the U.S. were "Ivan The Terrible," "Alexander Nevsky," "Don Quixote," "Conquests of Peter The Great," "The First Front" in which he played FDR, and "Rimsky-Korsakov."

CLAYTON, ETHEL, 82, retired film actress, died June 11, 1966 in Oxnard, Calif. Made film debut in 1909. Her credits include "Risky Business," "Sunny Side Up," "The Princess Of Broadway," "The Merry Widower," "Mother Machree," "The Buccaneer," and "Cocoanut Grove." She was divorced from actor Ian Keith.

CLIFT, MONTGOMERY, 45, film and stage actor, died in his NYC home July 23, 1966 from an occlusive coronary artery disease. He had just completed filming "The Defector" in Munich. He was four times Best Actor nominee for Academy awards, and once for Best Supporting Actor. After Broadway success, he went to Hollywood and appeared in "The Search," "Red River," "The Heiress," "Raintree County," "The Young Lions," "Miss Lonelyhearts," "A Place In The Sun," "From Here To Eternity," "The Misfits," "Judgement at Nuremberg," and "Freud." Surviving are his mother, a twin sister, and a brother.

CONNOLLY, MIKE, 52, syndicated columnist for The Hollywood Reporter, died Nov. 18, 1966 after surgery in the Mayo Clinic, Rochester, Minn. He wrote for Daily Variety before joining Hollywood Reporter 15 years ago. He was co-author with Gerold Frank of "I'll Cry Tomorrow," the biography of Lillian Roth that became a movie. Three brothers and a sister survive.

CREHAN, JOSEPH, 82, screen and stage actor, died of a stroke April 15, 1966 in Hollywood. Made film debut in 1934 and appeared in such pictures as "Deadline At Dawn," "Triple Threat," "Red Desert," and "Crazy Legs." Most recently he was in the TV "Bonanza" series and "The Andy Griffith Show." His wife and son survive.

CROUSE, RUSSEL, 73, Pulitzer playwright and producer, died of pneumonia Apr. 3, 1966 in NY's St. Luke's Hospital. In his 32 year collaboration with Howard Lindsay, he co-authored several successful plays that became films, including "Life With Father," "Red, Hot and Blue," "Arsenic and Old Lace," "Call Me Madam," and "The Sound Of Music," their last in 1959. For the screen he co-authored "Mountain Music," "The Big Broadcast," "Artists and Models Abroad," and "The Great Victor Herbert." Surviving are his second wife, a son and daughter.

DAWN, ISABEL, 62, actress and writer, died June 29, 1966 of a pulmonary infection at the Motion Picture Country Home. After Bdwy success, she moved to Hollywood. In addition to appearing in several films, she wrote screenplays for "If I Had A Million," "Girl Of The Golden West," "Shanghai Gesture," "The French Line," "A Man Betrayed," "Behind The News," "Don't Bet On Blondes," "Ice-Capades," "Lady For A Night," "Remember Pearl Harbor," and "Goodnight Sweetheart." Her husband, Ray Herr survives.

DePATIE, EDMOND L., 66, vice-president of Warner Bros. and general manager of its studios, died of a heart attack on Aug. 6, 1966 in Chowchilla, Calif. Surviving are his wife, two sons and a daughter.

Don Castle

Thomas Chalmers

Ethel Clayton

Montgomery Clift

Walt Disney

Eric Fleming

DISNEY, WALT, 65, world famous for his animated cartoons, died Dec. 15, 1966 of cancer in St. Joseph's Hospital in Burbank, Calif. Born in Chicago, reared in Missouri, one of the most creative geniuses in entertainment history, began his multimillion dollar empire in Hollywood in 1928 with Mickey Mouse. Its success provided him with an income to release his imagination to entertain the whole civilized world with such characters as Donald Duck, Snow White and the Seven Dwarfs, Bambi, Dumbo, and many others. In addition to cartoons, he produced feature length animated children's classics such as "Cinderella" and "Sleeping Beauty," animation with live action features, nature films, and full length movies with live actors such as "Treasure Island," "Kidnapped," "Swiss Family Robinson," and "Mary Poppins." He received 29 Academy Awards, four Emmys, Irving Thalberg Award, Presidential Freedom Medal, and the French Legion of Honor. In Anaheim, Calif. he created Disneyland, one of the nation's greatest tourist attractions, and at his death was working on a similar project in Florida, a ski resort in Sequoia Forest, and was leading the development of the California Institute of Arts in Los Angeles. His widow, two daughters, and a brother survive.

DODD, NEAL, 88, Episcopal clergyman, technical advisor on films, and former actor, died May 26, 1966 in Burbank's St. Joseph's Hospital after a lengthy illness. He appeared in over 350 films always as a clergyman, including such films as "Tillie's Punctured Romance," "It Happened One Night," "Anna Christie," "Sorry, Wrong Number," and "Here Comes The Groom." His wife and daughter survive.

DONEHUE, VINCENT J., 50, actor, producer, and screen, TV. and stage director, died Jan. 17, 1966 in Lenox Hill Hospital, NYC of Hodgkin's disease. His best known TV credits were "Peter Pan," "Annie Get Your Gun," and "The Barretts of Wimpole Street." After winning a "Tony" for his Bdwy direction of "Sunrise At Campobello," he directed the film version. and "Lonely Hearts", his only other film. His parents survive. Interment was in his native Whitehall, N. Y.

FARAGOH, FRANCIS E., 71, screen writer, died July 25, 1966 at Kaiser Hospital, Oakland, Calif., of a heart attack following a tracheotomy. After several plays, he went to Hollywood in 1929 and wrote over 20 screenplays, including "Her Private Affair," "Lillies Of The Field," "Back Pay," "The Right Way," "Too Young To Marry," "Little Caesar." "Iron Man" "Frankenstein." "The Last Man," "Undercover Man," "Return Of Peter Grimm," "Becky Sharp." "Easy Come, Easy Go," and "My Friend Flicka." Surviving are his widow, a son and daughter.

FAYE, JULIA, 72, a favorite leading lady for DeMille in his silent pictures, and later a featured player in talkies, died Apr. 6. 1966 of cancer in Hollywood. Among her credits are "Male and Female," "The Ten Commandments." "King of Kings," "Union Pacific." "Til We Meet Again," "Northwest Mounted Police," "Samson and Delilah," and her last "The Last Buccaneer" in 1958.

FELTON, VERNA, 76, film, radio, and TV character actress, died of a stroke in her home on Dec. 14, 1966. She was born in Salinas, Calif., and was its honorary mayor. Her film credits include "New Mexico," "The Gunfighter," "Buccaneer's Girl," "The Lady and The Tramp," "Picnic," and "Little Egypt." She is probably best known for her appearances in the TV series "December Bride" and "Pete and Gladys." A son Lee Millar survives.

FIELDS, JOSEPH, 71, co-author of many Bdwy hits and movies, died March 3, 1966 at his home in Beverly Hills. Most of his writing was done in collaboration with Jerome Chodorov. His film credits include "Annie Oakley," "Louisiana Story," "A Night In Casablanca," "Happy Anniversary," "My Sister Eileen," "Flower Drum Song" and "Tunnel Of Love." Surviving are his widow, and sister Dorothy.

FLEMING, ERIC, 41, stage, film, and TV actor, was drowned Sept. 28, 1966 while filming a scene on the Huallaga River 200 miles from Lima, Peru. His success came as the tall trail boss in the "Rawhide" TV series. He also appeared in the film "Glass Bottom Boat."

FORBES, KATHRYN, 57, author of the best-selling "Mama's Bank Account" from which the hit play and movie "I Remember Mama," and a TV series were made, died May 15, 1966 in Mt. Zion Hospital, San Francisco after a long illness. Two sons survive.

FORD, WALLACE, 68, character actor on Bdwy and in more than 200 films, died June 11, 1966 of a heart attack in the Motion Picture Country House in Woodland Hills, Calif. Born Samuel Jones in Eng. and joined vaudeville troupe at 11. Left Bdwy in 1932 to appear in "Possessed" with Joan Crawford. Among his other movies were "Goodbye Again," "Three-Cornered Moon," "The Lost Patrol," "Men In White," "Spellbound," "Harvey," "The Last Hurrah," "The Informer," and "A Patch Of Blue." He also starred with Henry Fonda in the TV series "The Deputy." A daughter survives.

FORESTER, CECIL SCOTT, 66, famous for his Horatio Hornblower novels which became films, died Apr. 2, 1966 in Fullerton, Calif. after being a semi-invalid for 20 years. He had been paralyzed for 18 months prior to his death. Born in Cairo, he lived in Eng. and France before coming to the US. He wrote more than 40 books among which are "Payment Deferred," "The Good Shepherd," "The Ship," and 10 novels about Hornblower. His second wife survives.

FRAWLEY, WILLIAM, 79, whose career spanned vaudeville, Bdwy, films, and TV, died March 3, 1966 of a heart attack while walking down Hollywood Blvd. After leaving his home in Burlington, Iowa, he became a song and dance man before appearing on Bdwy. Although he made over 100 films, he was probably best known for his regular appearances in the "I Love Lucy" and "My Three Sons" TV shows. Film credits include "The Lemon Drop Kid," "Three Cheers For Love," "The General Dies At Dawn," "High, Wide and Handsome," "Double or Nothing," "St. Louis Blues," "Ambush," "Mother Wore Tights," and "Miracle On 34th Street." Surviving are two brothers and a sister.

GARRISON, MICHAEL, 43, actor and producer, died Aug. 17, 1966 following a skull fracture suffered in a fall in his Bel Air home. Film credits include "Peyton Place," "Long Hot Summer," "The Sound and The Fury," "An Affair To Remember," "The Dark At The Top Of The Stairs," and "The Crowded Sky." He was executive producer of the "Wild Wild West" TV series. Divorced from his wife, a son and mother survive.

GAUNTIER, GENE, pioneer film actress-writer-producer in her 80's, died Dec. 18, 1966 in Cuernavaca, Mex. Born Genevieve Liggett, she began her career in repertory and stock throughout the US. In 1906 organized the Gene Gauntier Feature Players Co. for which she wrote over 300 films, including the first "Ben Hur." She also appeared in many of them. She married director Jack C. Clark and together they made the first US films abroad. During World War I she was a war correspondent, and later became a drama critic and columnist. She retired to Mexico City in 1942. A sister survives.

GERAGHTY, CARMELITA, 65, supporting actress in silent and early talking films, died of a heart attack in the Lombardy Hotel, NYC, on July 7, 1966. After retiring in 1935, she painted professionally. Born in Rushville, Ind., she began her film career in 1925 and appeared in such films as "Passionate Youth," "The Great Gatsby," "The Last Trail," "My Best Girl," "This Thing Called Love," "The Mississippi Gambler," and "Fifty Million Frenchmen." She was the widow of Carey Wilson, an MGM writer and producer. A sister and brother, and step-son survive. Interment was in Los Angeles.

GOLDSTONE, NAT, 62, 20th Century-Fox producer and former talent agent, died of a heart attack in Hollywood on July 24, 1966. During his 35 years as a top agent he handled such talent as Robert Taylor, Ginger Rogers, Robert Young, Rita Hayworth, and Dore Schary. Surviving are his widow, a son and a daughter.

Wallace Ford

Carmelita Geraghty

Hedda Hopper

Buster Keaton

Rex Lease

Herbert Marshall

GRAETZ, PAUL, 66, producer, died Feb. 5, 1966 of a heart attack at his home in Neuilly, France, a suburb of Paris. He was editing his latest film "Is Paris Burning?" He was president of Transcontinental Films. His credits include "Devil In The Flesh," "God Needs Men," "The Doctors," "Monsieur Ripois," "View From The Bridge," and "The Phantom Coach." After acting in Lubitsch's "Passion," he became a producer in Germany, later in France and the U.S. where he became a citizen. Divorced from his wife, a daughter survives. Burial was in Pere Lachaise Cemetery.

GRANT, JAMES EDWARD, 61, writer, and author of more than a score of screenplays, died Feb. 19, 1966 in Burbank after a long illness. He wrote the screenplays for "Sands Of Iwo Jima," "The Alamo," "McLintock," "Whipsaw," "Belle Of The Yukon," "Big Jim McLain," "Hondo," "The Great John L," "Angel and The Bad Man," "Music In My Heart," "The Bullfighter and The Lady," and "We're Going To Be Rich." Surviving are his wife and two sons.

HALE, JONATHAN, 74, character actor, committed suicide Feb. 28, 1966 by shooting himself in his cottage at the Motion Picture Country Home. In over 50 films since 1934, he was best known for his portrayal of Mr. Dithers in the "Blondie" series. Other credits include "Lightning Strikes Twice," "Alice Adams," "Three Live Ghosts," "Call Northside 777," "On The Sunny Side Of The Street," "Duffy Of San Quentin," "The Steel Trap," "Hangmen Also Die," "The Saint," "Charlie Chan," "Night Holds Terror," and "Jaguar" his last in 1958 when he retired. Two sons survive.

HARRIGAN, WILLIAM, 79, stage and screen actor, died Feb. 1, 1966 in St. Luke's Hospital in NYC after abdominal surgery. Acting for more than 60 years, the theatre was his first love, but he appeared in many films including "Cabaret," "Nix On Dames," "Born Reckless," and "The Invisible Man." Interment was in Arlington National Cemetery. His third wife survives.

HARRIS, ELMER B., 88, playwright and film pioneer, died Sept. 6, 1966 in Washington's Doctors Hospital where he had lived since 1960. His best known play was "Johnny Belinda" which became a film. He wrote for Famous Players, Columbia, and MGM. Two sons survive. Interment was in Washington.

HILL, ROBERT F., 79, silent screen writer and director, died March 18, 1966 in Los Angeles after a long illness. Prior to becoming a Universal director in 1923, he wrote screenplays for Goldwyn, among which were "Almost A Husband," "Water, Water Everywhere," and "Jubilo."

HOPKINS, ROBERT EVANS, 80, veteran film writer, died of a heart ailment in Hollywood Dec. 22, 1966. Prior to retirement 14 years ago, he had been at Metro for 30 years and written for such films as the Marie Dressler-Polly Moran comedies, "San Francisco," and "Saratoga." Surviving is his second wife, vaudeville star, Grace Hayes, a sister, and step-son Peter Lind Hayes.

HOPPER, HEDDA, 75, stage and film actress who became a syndicated Hollywood gossip columnist, died of pneumonia at Cedars of Lebanon Hospital in Hollywood on Feb. 1, 1966. After several Bdwy productions, she began her screen career in 1916. In 1936 she became a reporter for papers, radio, and fan magazines. She appeared in 110 films, the last "The Oscar" in 1965. She was born Elda Furry in Hollidaysburg, Pa. where her ashes were interred. A son actor William by her husband DeWolf Hopper survives.

HUME, CYRIL, 66, novelist-poet-screenwriter, died March 26, 1966 at his home in Palos Verdes, Calif. His first novel, "Wife Of The Centaur," was purchased by MGM in 1923, and subsequently he wrote or collaborated on "Tarzan Finds A Son," "The Great Gatsby," "20 Mule Team," "The Bugle Sounds," "Bride Of Vengeance," "Ransom," "Forbidden Planet", and "Bigger Than Life." His fourth wife, two sons and a daughter survive.

JANNINGS, ORIN, 48, playwright and screenwriter, died of a heart attack in Hollywood on Oct. 24 1966. Under contract to several Hollywood studios, his credits include "Force Of Arms," "A Time To Love, A Time To Die," and "The Gene Krupa Story." Surviving are his widow, a son and a daughter.

JIMINEZ, SOLEDAD, 92, pioneer film actress, died of a stroke on Oct. 17, 1966 at the Motion Picture Country House. Appeared in many films including "The Mission Play," "The Cock-Eyed World," "Arizona Kid," "Romance of Rio Grande," "The Texan," "Captain Thunder," "Billy The Kid," "Devil Among Women," "Ten Cents A Dance," "Bordertown," "Rumba," and "In Caliente."

KANE, GAIL, 81, stage and screen star, died Feb. 17, 1966 in Augusta, Maine. After a successful career on Bdwy she went to Hollywood and appeared in more than 35 pictures, including "Nathan Hale" and "White Sister." She retired in 1927. Surviving is one son.

KANE, HELEN, 62, the boop-boop-a-doop singer of stage, screen and TV, died Sept. 26, 1966 in her Jackson Heights, N. Y. apartment of cancer. After a successful career in Bdwy musicals, she appeared in 9 films including "Heads Up," "Pointed Heels," "Nothing But The Truth," "Sweetie", and "Dangerous Nan McGrew." Her voice was used in numerous animated cartoons and for Debbie Reynolds in "Three Little Words." Her first two marriages ended in divorce. Her third husband Daniel Healy, night club MC and singer, survives. Interment was in Veterans Cemetery, Farmingdale, L. I.

KEATON, BUSTER, 70, poker-faced comedian, died of lung cancer Feb. 1, 1966 in his Woodland Hills, Calif., home. Usually wearing a saucer-brimmed porkpie hat, he became one of the three great clowns of silent films. TV in the early fifties, rescued him from obscurity, and he again became a popular comedian. He appeared in more than 30 films including "The General," "The Navigator," "Sherlock, Jr.," "Speak Easily," "Mad, Mad World," "Bedroom, Parlor and Sink," "Beach Blanket Bingo," "Film," "A Funny Thing Happened On The Way To The Forum," and his last "War Italian Style." His biography became "The Keaton Story" in 1956 with Donald O'Connor. His third wife, dancer Eleanor Norris, and two sons survive.

KENT, WILLIS, 87, retired producer, died of a stroke in Hollywood on March 11, 1966. He produced a number of films in the '20's and '30's among which were "Ten Nights In A Barroom," and "Road To Ruin." A daughter survives.

KERN, JAMES V., 57, screen and TV writer-director, died of pneumonia on Nov. 9, 1966 in Encino, Calif. For the past few years he had been responsible for the "My Three Sons," "I Love Lucy," and the Betty White TV series. His films include "Stallion Road," "That's Right, Your're Wrong," "Melancholy Baby," "The Horn Blows At Midnight," and "Doughgirls." A widow and three daughters survive.

KIEPURA, JAN, 62, Polish-born tenor, died of a heart attack at his home in Harrison, N. Y. on Aug. 15, 1966. He appeared on Bdwy, at the Met, and in films. His most popular role was in "The Merry Widow" and he sang it with his wife Marta Eggerth throughout the world. His films include "The City of Song," "Be Mine Tonight," "Give Us This Night," "The Land Of Smiles," "A Song For You," "Farewell To Love," and "My Heart Is Calling." His widow and two sons survive.

LEASE, REX, 65, who starred in many silent action films, was found dead in his Hollywood home of undetermined cause on Jan. 3, 1966. Credits include "A Woman Who Sinned," "Moulders Of Men," "The Law Of The Range," "The Younger Generation," "Sunny Skies," "Hot Curves," "So This Is Mexico," "Why Marry," "Two Sisters," "Is There Justice," and "Custer's Last Stand." Surviving are two sons.

MARSHALL, HERBERT, 75, stage and film actor, died of a heart attack in his Beverly Hills home on Jan. 21, 1966. Born in Eng., a successful Bdwy. career took him to Hollywood where he appeared in such films as "Foreign Correspondent," "The Painted Veil," "The Letter," "The Moon and Sixpence," "The Razor's Edge," "The Enchanted Cottage," "Flight For Freedom," "Blonde Venus," "Trouble In Paradise," "Evenings For Sale," "A Bill Of Divorcement," "The Dark Angel," "Duel In The Sun," "Rip Tide," "Girls Dormitory," "Till We Meet Again," "A Woman Rebels," and his last "The Third Day." His fifth wife and a daughter, actress Sarah Marshall, survive. Burial was in the Chapel of Pines.

Claire McDowell

Eugene O'Brien

Pat O'Malley

Seena Owen

Elizabeth Patterson

Alice Pearce

MATHER, JACK, 58, radio's Cisco Kid, died of a heart attack in Wauconda, Ill., Aug. 16, 1966. His many film roles include "The Bravadoes," "This Earth Is Mine," "Jungle Book," and "Some Like It Hot." He also appeared on TV in "Bonanza," "Dragnet," "Death Valley Days," and "M Squad." His widow and two sons survive.

McDOWELL, CLAIRE, 88, pioneer film actress who began her career in 1910, died after a long illness in Hollywood. She appeared on the stage before making such films as "Big Parade," "Something To Think About," "Ben-Hur," and her last "Two-Fisted Sheriff" in 1937. Two sons survive.

MONTGOMERY, DOUGLASS, 58, retired film and stage actor, died July 23, 1966 in Norwalk, Conn. After several Bdwy successes, he went to Hollywood where he appeared as Kent Douglass in such films as "Waterloo Bridge," and "House Divided," and under his own name in "Little Women," "Music In The Air," "Harmony Lane," "Counsel For Crime," "Life Begins With Love," "The Cat and The Canary," "Way To The Stars," "Woman To Woman," and "Forbidden."

NAGEL, ANNE, 54, retired actress whose career spanned three decades, died of cancer in Hollywood on July 6, 1966. After Bdwy experience, she made her film debut in 1933 in "I Loved You Yesterday," followed by such films as "The Spirit of West Point," "Don't Trust Your Husband," "The Green Hornet Strikes Again," "Women In Bondage," "Murder In The Music Hall," "The Trap." She had been in retirement for several years. Surviving are a brother and niece.

NESTELL, BILL, 71, former western actor who retired 12 years ago, died of a heart attack on Oct. 18, 1966 in Bishop, Calif. Most of his films were made at Republic and Universal. His wife, a son and daughter survive.

NICHOLS, ANNE, 75, author of "Abie's Irish Rose," died of a heart attack Sept. 14, 1966 at the Cliff House Nursing Home in Englewood Cliffs, N. J. Although she wrote over 20 plays, "Abie" was her most successful, and became a film and radio show. A son survives. Interment was in Kensico Cemetery, Valhalla, N. Y.

NOVIS, DONALD, 60, leading lyric tenor of the 1930's died at the Metropolitan Hospital in Norwalk, Calif., on July 23, 1966. After singing in nightclubs and on radio, was cast in such films as "Bulldog Drummond," "Slightly Terrific," "New York Nights," "Monte Carlo," "Irish Fantasy," and "The Singing Boxer." His second wife, singer-actress Dorothy Bradshaw, and two daughters survive.

NUGENT, FRANK S., 57, film writer, and critic died of a heart seizure shortly after being admitted to UCLA Medical Center in Los Angeles. Served as motion picture editor and critic for the NY Times before going to Hollywood to write such screenplays as "Fort Apache," "Three Godfathers," "Wagonmaster," "She Wore A Yellow Ribbon," "The Quiet Man," "Mr. Roberts," "The Searchers," "The Last Hurrah," "Two Rode Together," "The Rising Moon," and "Donovan's Reef." His second wife and an adopted son survive.

O'BRIEN, EUGENE, 85, a "great lover" of the silent screen, died of bronchial pneumonia in Queen of Angels Hospital in Los Angeles on Apr. 29, 1966. He was taken from Bdwy in 1919 and was an immediate success in his first film "The Perfect Lover," followed by such films as "The Voice From The minaret," "Souls For Sale," "Graustark," "Fine Manners," "The Only Woman," "Dangerous Innocence," and "Flamingo Love." He retired in the early 1930's.

O'MALLEY, PAT, 75, silent film star whose career began in vaudeville in 1908, died while at dinner in his Van Nuys, Calif. home on May 21, 1966. His screen career began in 1912 and he appeared in over 400 pictures. Surviving are his widow and three daughters.

OWEN, SEENA, 71, retired silent screen star, died in Hollywood Presbyterian Hospital Aug. 15, 1966. She retired in 1933 after appearing in such films as "The Blue Danube," "The Rush Hour," "Sinners In Love," and "Marriage Playground." A daughter survives.

PAIVA, NESTOR, 61, veteran character actor, died of cancer in Hollywood on Sept. 9, 1966. After appearing on stage and radio, he launched his screen career in 1937 and had roles in over 400 films and TV shows, including "A Medal For Benny," "The Southerner," "Nob Hill," "Joan of Arc," "Humeresque," "Young Man With A Horn," "Phone Call From A Stranger," "Call Me Madam," "New York Confidential," and "Hell On Frisco Bay." Surviving are his widow, a son and daughter.

PASCAL, ERNEST, 70, former president of Screen Writers Guild and a veteran writer, died of a heart attack on Nov. 4, 1966 in Los Angeles. Screen credits include "Lloyds Of London," "Hound Of The Baskervilles," and "Kidnapped." His widow and two daughters survive.

PATTERSON, ELIZABETH, 90, stage, screen, and TV character actress, died in Cood Samaritan Hospital, Los Angeles on Jan. 31, 1966. She had appeared in over 100 films as the mother of almost every Hollywood star. Her pictures include "Kiss The Boys Goodbye," "Her Cardboard Lover," "My Sister Eileen," "Lady On A Train," "Little Women," "Pal Joey," "Sing You Sinners," "Intruder In The Dust." Two sisters survive. Interment was in her native Savannah, Tenn.

PEARCE, ALICE, 47, stage, film, TV, and nightclub comedienne, died of cancer Mar. 3, 1966 in her Hollywood home. She appeared in 10 Bdwy shows, in the "Bewitched" TV series, and in such films as "Kiss Me, Stupid," "Disorderly Orderly," "Bus Riley Is Back In Town," "Dear Heart," "Thrill Of It All," "My Six Loves," "Dear Brigitte," "Tammy and The Doctors," and her last "The Glass Bottom Boat." Her second husband Paul Davis survives.

POMMER, ERIC, 76, German producer, died May 8, 1966 in Hollywood. He was responsible for such classics as "The Blue Angel," "The Cabinet of Dr. Caligari," "Hotel Imperial," "Congress Dances," "Variety," and "Jamaica Inn," "The Beachcomber," "Music In The Air," "They Knew What They Wanted," and "A Love Story," one of his last. He became a U.S. citizen in 1944. A son survives.

RAMBOVA, NATASHA, 69, premiere danseuse, actress, producer, stage designer, and second wife of Rudolph Valentino, died June 5, 1966 in Pasadena, Calif. from dietary complications. She was divorced from Valentino only 6 months before his death. She had lived in Conn. until a few months before her death. Her body was cremated. A half-sister survives.

ROBERTS, WALTER CHARLES, 70, playwright, died Jan. 3, 1966 in his Windsor, N. Y. home. He was story editor of several motion pictures including "The Young Lions." Survivors are a sister and two brothers.

RODRIGUEZ, ESTELITA, 35, actress, known professionally by her first name, died March 12, 1966 in Van Nuys, Calif. Began her career in Cuba at 9, and was later featured in such Hollywood films as "Cuban Fireball," "In Old Amarillo," "Belle Of Old Mexico," "Havana Rose," "Hit Parade of 1951," "Federal Agent At Large," "California Passage" and "The Fabulous Senorita." A daughter, 3 sisters, a brother, and mother survive. Interment was in San Fernando Mission Cemetery.

ROSE, BILLY, 66, producer, composer and lyricist, died Feb. 10, 1966 of Lobar pneumonia in the Eldmire Nursing Home in Montego Bay, Jamaica, W.I. where he was recuperating from heart surgery. Began writing songs and sketches in 1926 and contributed to many Bdwy productions. His songs were used in such films as "The Singing Fool," "Showboat," and "King Of Jazz." His four marriages ended in divorce. Two sisters survive.

Natasha Rambova

Billy Rose

Robert Rossen

Sophie Tucker

June Walker

Clifton Webb

ROSSEN, ROBERT, 57, Academy Award winning writer-director-producer, died in NY's Columbia Presbyterian Medical Center of a coronary occlusion following post-operational complications. In addition to his Oscar-winning "All The Kings Men," he was responsible for "Body and Soul," "The Hustler," "A Walk In The Sun," "The Roaring Twenties," "Edge Of Darkness," "Johnny O'Clock," "They Won't Forget," "The Sea Wolf," "The Strange Love Of Martha Ivers," "The Brave Bulls," "Alexander The Great," and his last film "Lilith." His widow, a son and two daughters survive.

SILVER, ABNER, 67, composer and author, died Nov. 24, 1966, in his apartment in NY's Essex House. Although actively writing songs until his death, he had been suffering from phlebitis for several years. Collaborated with many lyricists and produced many hit songs. His most recent film musicals were for Elvis Presley in "Jail House Rock," "King Creole," and "G.I. Blues." Surviving are two brothers and a sister.

SISTROM, JOSEPH, 53, producer, died in Hollywood Apr. 7, 1966 after a long illness. His films include "The Lone Wolf Spy Hunt," "Sweater Girl," "Wake Island," "Girls Town," "Incendiary Blonde," "The Hitler Gang," and "Atomic City." His widow and two children survive.

STEELE, BOB, 60, retired western film star, died June 25, 1966 in Veterans Hospital, Biloxi, Miss. after a short illness. At the age of 14 he and his twin brother began the Adventures of Bill and Bob series. Subsequently appeared in scores of westerns and in 1942 was the top money-making western star. Recently had appeared in character parts. Among his many credits are "Code Of The Outlaw," "Westward Ho," "Three Mesquiteers," "Santa Fe Scouts," "Cheyenne," "San Antone," "Island Of The Sky," "Drums Across The River," "The Outcast," "The Bounty Killer," "Requiem For A Gunfighter," and "Town Tamer." Interment was in Biloxi.

TAYLOR, DONALD F., 47, writer-producer-director, was found dead Jan. 3, 1966 in his Hollywood home from an overdose of seconal. He was the widower of Marie McDonald who died of barbiturates two months earlier. Among his film credits are "Importance Of Being Earnest," "Point Of No Return," "She Stoops To Conquer," and "Promises, Promises." His mother survives.

TUCKER, SOPHIE, 82, singer and actress whose career spanned 62 years died of lung cancer and kidney failure Feb. 9, 1966 in her NYC home. She had been actively performing until four months before her death. "The Last of The Red Hot Mamas" appeared in several films including "Honky Tonk," "Broadway Melody," "Thoroughbreds Don't Cry," "Atlantic City," "Gay Love," "Sensations of 1945," and "Follow The Boys." A son survives. Burial was in Hartford, Conn.

URECAL, MINERVA, 70, radio, film and TV actress, died Feb. 27, 1966 of a heart attack in Hollywood. Among her picture credits are "Her Husband's Secretary," "Love In A Bungalow," "Life With Love," "Sensation Hunters," "Lost Moment," "Exiled To Shanghai," "Wanderer Of The Wastelands," "Wake Up and Dream," "The Trap," "Lost Moment," and her last "Seven Faces of Dr. Lao." On TV she appeared as Tugboat Annie. Her husband Max Holtzer survives.

WALKER, JUNE, 66, film, stage and TV actress, died Feb. 3, 1966 in the home of her actor son John Kerr in Los Angeles. She had been in ill health for several years. In 1926 she created Lorelei Lee in "Gentlemen Prefer Blondes" on Bdwy. She appeared in many silent pictures for Essanay Films, and subsequently in a variety of talkies, including "War Nurse," "Through Different Eyes," and the most recent being "The Unforgiven," and "A Child Is Waiting."

WATTS, CHARLES, screen, stage, and TV character actor, died of cancer in Nashville, Tenn., Dec. 13, 1966. Had been featured in such films as "An Affair To Remember," "The Big Circus," "Days of Wine and Roses," "Baby The Rain Must Fall," "Giant," and "Wheeler Dealers." During World War II the USO named "Mr. Hollywood" in recognition of his many tours overseas.

WAUGH, EVELYN, 62, author, died Apr. 10, 1966 in his country home near Taunton, Eng. Of his 28 books, "The Loved One" was the only one to be filmed. His second wife, 3 sons and 3 daughters survive.

WEBB, CLIFTON, 72, stage and film actor, died of a heart attack in his Beverly Hills home on Oct. 13, 1966. Although a Bdwy star, he won his greatest fame in such films as "Laura," "The Razor's Edge," "Dark Corner," "Sitting Pretty," "Mr. Belvedere Goes To College," "For Heaven's Sake," "The Silver Whistle," "Cheaper By The Dozen," "Titanic," "The Man Who Never Was," "Boy On A Dolphin," "Three Coins In The Fountain," "The Scoutmaster," "Holiday For Lovers," "Stars and Stripes Forever," and his last "Satan Never Sleeps" in 1961. He was three times nominated for an Academy Award. Entombment was in Hollywood Cemetery.

WELLMAN, PAUL I., 67, author of 27 books that specialized in the American West, and several screenplays, died of cancer in his Los Angeles home. His film credits include "Jubal," "Red Gold," "Diane," "Apache," "The Iron Mistress," and "Jericho." Surviving are his widow and a son.

WHORF, RICHARD, 60, screen, stage, and TV actor-director, died of a heart attack in Santa Monica's St. John's Hospital on Dec. 14, 1966. After successful Bdwy career, appeared in first movie "Blues In The Night" in 1941 followed by "Yankee Doodle Dandy," "Chain Lightning," "The Cross of Lorraine," and "Assignment In Britanny." He directed such films as "Luxury Liner," "Autumn Fever," "Champagne For Caesar," and "Till The Clouds Roll By," and the TV series "My Friend Irma," "The Beverly Hillbillies," "Gunsmoke," "My Three Sons," "The Ann Sothern Show," and "Rawhide." His widow and 3 sons survive.

WOOLF, JAMES, 46, British film producer, died May 29, 1966 of a heart attack in the Beverly Hills Hotel. With his brother he headed Romulus Films and produced such pictures as "The L-Shaped Room," "The Pumpkin Eater," "Moulin Rouge," "The African Queen," "I Am A Camera," "Pandora and The Flying Dutchman," "Of Human Bondage," and "Room At The Top." His brother survives.

WYNN, ED, 79, comedian and star of vaudeville, stage, radio, films, and TV, died of cancer June 19, 1966 in his Beverly Hills apartment. His career spanned 64 years. Acclaimed "The Perfect Fool" from his 1921 show of that name, and Texaco's Fire Chief from his radio series, his films include "The Shaggy Dog," "Marjorie Morningstar," "The Great Man," "The Greatest Story Ever Told," "The Diary Of Anne Frank" for which he was nominated for an Oscar, and "Mary Poppins." He was married and divorced three times. A son by his first marriage, actor Keenan Wynn, survives. After cremation, burial was in Forest Lawn Memorial Park.

YATES, HERBERT J., 85, founder and president of Republic Pictures, died in his Sherman Oaks, Calif. home on Feb. 3, 1966. He produced the singing-cowboy type of film and introduced Gene Autry, Roy Rogers and John Wayne to the public. He retired in 1959. His most critically acclaimed film was "The Quiet Man" in 1952. His second wife, actress-ice skater, Vera Hruba Ralston, was with him when he died. A daughter and two sons also survive.

Richard Whorf

James Woolf

Ed Wynn

244

245